Rebel Economies

Rebel Economies

Warlords, Insurgents, Humanitarians

Edited by
Nicola Di Cosmo, Didier Fassin,
and Clémence Pinaud

LEXINGTON BOOKS
Lanham • Boulder • New York • London

Published by Lexington Books
An imprint of The Rowman & Littlefield Publishing Group, Inc.
4501 Forbes Boulevard, Suite 200, Lanham, Maryland 20706
www.rowman.com

6 Tinworth Street, London SE11 5AL, United Kingdom

British Library Cataloguing in Publication Information Available

Library of Congress Cataloging-in-Publication Data

Names: Di Cosmo, Nicola, 1957- editor. | Fassin, Didier, editor. | Pinaud, Clémence, 1985- editor.
Title: Rebel economies : warlords, insurgents, humanitarians / edited by Nicola Di Cosmo, Didier Fassin, and Clémence Pinaud.
Description: Lanham : Lexington Books, [2021] | Includes bibliographical references.
Identifiers: LCCN 2021010512 (print) | LCCN 2021010513 (ebook) | ISBN 9781793635198 (cloth ; alk. paper) | ISBN 9781793635204 (ebook) ISBN 9781793635211 (pbk ; alk. paper)
Subjects: LCSH: War—Economic aspects. | Regional economics. | Non-state actors (International relations) | War and society.
Classification: LCC HC79.D4 R433 2021 (print) | LCC HC79.D4 (ebook) | DDC 330.9—dc23
LC record available at https://lccn.loc.gov/2021010512
LC ebook record available at https://lccn.loc.gov/2021010513

∞™ The paper used in this publication meets the minimum requirements of American National Standard for Information Sciences—Permanence of Paper for Printed Library Materials, ANSI/NISO Z39.48-1992.

Contents

Acknowledgments

The present volume is the result of a workshop held in Princeton at the Institute for Advanced Study and convened jointly by the School of Historical Studies and the School of Social Science. We want to thank all its participants, including those who are not part of the present volume. We also are grateful to Laura McCune for her kind assistance in the organization of the event and to Munirah Bishop for her remarkable contribution to the preparation of the manuscript.

Introduction

Revisiting Non-States War Economies

Nicola Di Cosmo, Didier Fassin,
and Clémence Pinaud

Non-state war economies are a pervasive phenomenon in today's world. The Islamic State in Syria and Iraq, the Taliban in Afghanistan and Pakistan, Boko Haram in Nigeria and Cameroon, the various branches of al-Qaeda in the Sahelian region, the Sudan People's Liberation Army (SPLA), the Revolutionary Armed Forces of Colombia, and the Tamil Tigers in Sri Lanka are only a sample in a much longer list of non-state forces that have been the protagonists of recent conflicts, all of which involved complex economic dimensions. Contrary to conventional wars among opposing states—the two world wars being typical examples—these conflicts mobilize instead armed groups, often the expression of distinct ethnic and political entities, that rebel against states, fight against each other, or combat invading powers. Whatever the means or goals of their fight, they require human, material, technological, and financial resources. In other words, such wars rely on an economy. This is certainly the case also for conflicts between states, but while states legally levy taxes and have national budgets, non-state actors must create their own economy. The various forms of these economies are the object of the present volume.

Often non-state entities are regarded as either the peculiar product of so-called failed states or the breakup of former nation-states within a given geopolitical context and are analyzed from the viewpoint of local politics or regional affairs. While these are valuable perspectives, they tend to limit the phenomenon to a specific range of actors, be it the expression of religious fundamentalism, ethnic strife, or national and liberation struggles. Thus, they erase those commonalities that, in our view, make non-state war economies a specific and pervasive phenomenon, often transcending not just cultural and political boundaries but also historical ones, whereby morphological differences are in fact essential to the identification of similarities. Thus, to investigate non-state war economies as a unified, congruent phenomenon—yet extremely varied in its manifestations—we expand the disciplinary palette and present in this book economic, historical, anthropological, sociological, and political approaches, so as to explore, in the past and present, and across three continents, the nexuses between economy, war, social transformation, and state-building.

The principal goal of the book is twofold. First, it aims to rethink much of the debate around non-state war economies by critically evaluating the contributions that past studies have made. Second, it proposes to expand the conversation by consciously treating non-state war economies as a far broader and more conspicuous aspect of both economy and war than the focus on present-day insurgent, rebel, and generally anti-state warfare (often reduced to social, political, and religious elements) tends to privilege.

The migration of concepts such as the theory of the generative function of war in state-building by Charles Tilly (a historian) or the theory of the "stationary bandit" in war taxation from Mancur Olson (an economist) into the analyses of political scientists is an example of concepts that have influenced the thinking of a variety of analysts without the benefit of a proper cross-disciplinary evaluation of their applicability. By presenting not just different concepts and approaches but different ways to conceptualize and problematize the issues related to non-war economies, the chapters included in this volume serve the additional purpose of reflecting on the genesis of current theories while expanding their empirical range and setting side by side historical and contemporary case studies.

This is not just a different approach but a fundamental departure from how current debates on non-state war economies, which have informed research orientations over several decades, typically frame the question. In the 1990s, the academic scene was divided between those who believed that "greed" motivated people to take up arms, and those who argued that neither the pursuit of gain nor other economic opportunities could explain why insurgents fight states, and focused instead on "grievances." This scientific dispute had important political implications.

The "greed" camp, led by Paul Collier, who was director of the World Bank's Development Research Group, was influenced by neoliberal approaches to war and state-building (Collier, Hoeffler, and Sambanis 2005; Collier 2008, 2009). Its main premise, that the rebels had no legitimate political demands but were solely motivated by gain, implied that the state had to be protected and strengthened, thus delegitimizing political protests (Keen 2012a). This approach privileged "motive" over means, and while it also served to find out the means by which greedy rebels accessed wealth through war, its main line of argument was not about the construction of a war economy by non-state entities (regardless of motive) but about the goal itself of the armed struggle. This approach and its attending interpretations supported the view that "weak" states needed to be assisted economically and politically and legitimized foreign military intervention. State-building processes were mostly technical and justified by the purported goal of promoting global stability through peace (Duffield 2001: 12). The "false grievances" of enemies of the state (such as armed insurgents) were to be ignored.

This school of thought was countered by researchers who were critical of poorly-designed quantitative methods that informed these studies (Keen 2012a: 761–62). Their approach was based on fieldwork in war-torn areas, which produced compelling narratives through investigative analysis of the local conditions. While these studies established the close relationship between armed rebellions and political grievances, they also subordinated the question of a non-state war economy to social and political instances that intersect but do not explain economic processes.

Whereas, in the academic sphere, the inquiry into the complexities of the relationship between war and economy, as well as the causes of war and its effects, moved the debate onto a level more sophisticated than the simplistic "grievance versus greed" dichotomy, greed advocates continued to prevail in policy circles, remaining alive and well in the World Bank and the agencies of the United Nations, even though there existed some agreement that grievances, too, should be considered reasons for conflicts (Keen 2012a: 765). The representation of illegitimate rebels in search of material gain and personal enrichment continued to obscure or even erase the political aspects of conflicts, thereby favoring the argument that states, and the elites that controlled them, were to be supported as a matter of legal and moral right. While eventually the "grievances" camp mostly won in the intellectual arena, the economic questions did not rise to the level of an independent object of investigation as the "greed" side reduced it to a rational actor approach with little interest in the specific contexts and complex logics, and this is, in a nutshell, our specific contribution to the debate, in addition to an expansion of the landscape of manifestations of the phenomenon into past instances and across the planet.

The changing nature of both agents and economies requires to step back from such stark and reductionist dichotomies as well as from the "now and there" and seek instead parameters that go beyond specific theaters and limited variables, typically informed by international economic policy and foreign affairs debates. As relevant as these debates are, academic involvement is vitally important not just to take a critical stance from the more politically laden positions but also to lead the way toward a more theoretically and empirically rich discussion, which is transformative of these debates and opens new avenues to analysis and interpretation. Especially crucial in this respect is a confrontation between different academic fields. This is where we would like to position this volume.

While every collection of chapters as interdisciplinary as this one lends itself to a degree of subjectivity in its organization, we have opted for grouping the chapters into three parts on the basis of their coherence and affinity with respect to the overarching themes of the book. The volume begins with theoretical and empirical frameworks and definitions that critically appraise the notion of a "non-state war economy" from a variety of standpoints, while reviewing the evolution of the debate over the past several decades. The second section extends the chronological range of the investigation to historical cases, which contribute to our understanding of non-state war economy by examining the economic logic of nomadic conquerors, mercenary armies, and warlordism, and investigating, within different time frames and scales, the links between state and non-state war economies and their connections to state formation, more specifically in China and Italy. Finally, the third section includes three cases that, with distinct configurations, illustrate contemporary realities of war economies, focusing on war-generated social changes in South Sudan, the Iraq-Syrian oil fields exploited by the Islamic State, and the economic intervention in Afghanistan. These studies tackle critical aspects of war economics, such as the role of natural resources, the resort to humanitarian action, and the making of social differentiation in warfare, explaining in the process the complex relationship between war, social dynamics, and economic goals. By privileging methodological clusters rather that other types of connections based on regional, chronological or other features, the volume, taken as a whole, puts front and center the study of "non-state war economy" as a conscious analytical effort to expand traditional boundaries (in every discipline involved) and show the benefits of adopting a more expansive (not just comparative) and more critical (not merely descriptive) approach.

In other words, we aim to intervene in the current debate by extending the range of questions inherent to the study of the relationship between resources and conflicts and by offering broader perspectives, inclusive of both contemporary and historical cases. At the same time, conscious of extant differences and opposing interpretations at the intellectual level and their reverberations at the policy level, our contributions open new avenues of research, especially in terms of intellectual frameworks and fundamental questions. What all authors have in common is a reflection on these socioeconomic structures that cause war, sustain it, and create long-lasting political and social crises that can reignite it as well as on the multiple economies generated by warfare. In this sense, they consider wars to be economically destructive and productive. Moreover, exploring war economies controlled by non-state actors inevitably results in questioning the origin and perimeter of the state, the definition and delimitation of war and peace, and the continuation of war economies beyond the official peace.

In this spirit, we focus more on similarities than differences between state and non-state war economies. Adopting a long temporal framework and diverse geographical contexts, we show that the distinction between state and non-state actors, and between state and non-state war economies, is in large part elusive. The methods of wealth accumulation and their social impact, once seen across time and in multiple cultural contexts, bear surprising resemblances. War economies in Asian nomadic steppe empires and in rebel South Sudan similarly consist of large-scale raids, racketeering money, international trade, and tax collection, which contribute to developing the premises of a state bureaucracy. Thus, the focus on the actors' motivations is partly displaced by putting greater emphasis on the economic requirements of state-building and on the effects of such requirements on the creation or transformation of social and political structures. Both Nicola Di Cosmo and Zachariah Mampilly show the political and symbolic functions of wartime taxation, and challenge Mancur Olson's view that taxation is mostly an economic tool allowing for the transition of "roving bandits" into "stationary" ones. In the same vein, studying the role played by oil in the conflict involving the Islamic State in Iraq and Syria, Philippe Le Billon establishes that it is valued for all parties involved and that it provides minimal public services to the population, thus avoiding the simplification of mere greed.

While such discussions have somewhat abated in the last ten years, and the number of books published on the topic of war economies has declined, progress has been made on a few fronts. The most important contributions, of late, can be found in studies such as David Keen's *Useful Enemies*, which looks at the multiple benefits that some political actors obtain from waging indefinite wars that are not meant to be won (Keen 2012b). Another notable contribution has been Philippe Le Billon's *Wars of Plunder*, which examines differences among various resource sectors related to war, and shows how they were related to conflict (Le Billon 2012). In *Inequality, Grievances and Civil War*, Lars-Erik Cederman, Kristian Skrede Gleditsch, and Halvard Buhaug reopened the debate by quantifying grievances related to horizontal inequalities, that is, disparities between groups, in the emergence of conflicts. Relying on the same quantitative methods adopted by "greed" champions, they reached diametrically different conclusions (Cederman, Skrede Gleditsch, and Buhaug 2013). More recently, Gilles Carbonnier, in *Humanitarian Economics*, extended his predecessors' work on the relationship between humanitarian aid and war economies, arguing for a new field of inquiry that explores the linkages between humanitarian action and war economies (Carbonnier 2015).

Non-state armed actors and their social impact through the war economy also share many commonalities over time. For instance, Clémence Pinaud's South Sudanese warlords resemble those of Edward McCord's nineteenth-century China, who deploy the same techniques of tax evasion as William Caferro's businessmen of war and mercenaries from Renaissance Italy. In these cases, much like in contemporary Mozambique analyzed by Christopher Cramer, control over war economy is what drives social and cultural transformations. In particular, it generates social differentiation, consolidating warriors' ascendency and cultural innovations, with displays of militarized distinction. Thus, the multidisciplinary approach of this volume illuminates the numerous facets and ways in which non-state war economies are actively and directly implicated in the making of new polities and societies, from steppe empires to guerilla proto-states.

Such transformations also involve a moral dimension, of which humanitarian actors are emblematic. They have become part and parcel of contemporary war economies, as Gilles Carbonnier demonstrates through various examples, from the ransoming and kidnapping of humanitarian staff to the effects of economic sanctions on countries at war. Yet, morality and politics are often inseparable, and Jonathan Benthall analyzes the ties between charities and diplomatic, financial and military support for the mujahideen of 1980s and 1990s Afghanistan. This dual dimension goes beyond the sole humanitarian world, and includes the construction of the image of wars as just or unjust and the differentiation of groups with a legitimate, that is, soldiers, or illegitimate, that is, civilians, reason to kill, which leads Didier Fassin to plead for a better connection between the political economy and the moral economy of warfare.

In an initial attempt to reflect on the conceptual framework of the volume, Didier Fassin problematizes the three terms that inform the object of our investigation. First, while wars can be declared by the various belligerents, more often than not, their very status is controversial. It may be acknowledged by one side only, as was the case for the Algerian War of Independence, which was not recognized as such by the French government despite its more than 300,000 deaths. At times, the boundary between war and peace may become blurred, as is the case in the Palestinian Territories, whose inhabitants do not speak of their situation in terms of war and peace but of unending occupation of their land, which has caused the exodus of five million refugees. Who is entitled to define a situation of conflict as a war? What is a war, such as that on terror, which has not for enemy a state or a group but an abstract reality like the war on terror? What are the consequences of labeling a given conflict in terms of the differentiation between soldiers and civilians? These questions have important concrete implications. Second, the term *non-state* meets several obstacles as one tries to apply it to political entities, which is partly exemplified in Le Billon's taxonomy, inclusive of "proto-state" and "near-states" entities. Typically seen as non-state agents, for instance, the self-styled Islamic State presents certain characteristics of statehood, whereas the militant group Hezbollah is a political party whose members sit in the Lebanese parliament and government. Moreover, non-state agents often have ties to their national state or foreign states, which support them with funds and weapons. Even their connection with warfare can be relatively loose as some are more involved in banditry or mafias than armed insurgency. Moreover, besides warlords, rebels and revolutionaries of various kinds, contemporary battlefields have seen the participation of new actors, in particular humanitarian organizations. Third, the notion of economy is subject to multiple interpretations, from the calculation of the economic impact of war to the game theory construction of war waging. Broadening its meaning can be useful to connect the political economy of war, that is, the production, circulation, and appropriation of goods and services, notably through taxing and looting, and the moral economy of war, that is, the production and circulation of values and affects, which determine what is good and bad, fair and unfair, while mobilizing indignation or compassion, hatred or disgust. War involves not only rationalities but also norms and emotions.

In line with this critical perspective, Christopher Cramer proposes to review the main trends in the field of war economics by examining numerous cases across the planet. He explores the intellectual history of economists' approaches to war economies, from liberal interpretations of war to neoclassical economic domination. The liberal interpretations of war regard warfare as destructive, and therefore negative from an economic viewpoint. War has a cost, which can be measured, and therefore waging a war can be modelled, according to rational choice theory. This approach considers the costs of recruitment rebel soldiers and the opportunity costs of the rebellion itself, and infers that the lower they are, the more likely war will be. However, this approach, long supported by the World Bank, ignores the fact that ideas, social bonds, and national identities play a major role in conflicts. Economic interests can provide incentives, but ideological elements, whether religious or political, are often even more prominent. War is not only about greed, it is also a matter of grievances. Yet, beyond their differences, all these neoclassical theories hold that warfare is detrimental to the economy and that, in the context of the Global South, it is contrary to development. Alternative perspectives argue that wars are not simply destructive; they are also transformative. In Afghanistan, the war against the Soviet Union has led to strengthening peripheral territories of the country and to shifting the traditional economy of wheat cultivation and livestock exportation to a more profitable economy of poppy cultivation and opium exportation. Interestingly, war economics has recently moved beyond the economies of war strictly speaking, focusing on conflict prevention and post-conflict reconstruction, thus pushing the temporality of warfare to the phases preceding and following the actual conflict. It has also expanded spatially, either regionally or globally. The civil wars in Colombia and Syria are incomprehensible unless we take into account, respectively, the trafficking of cocaine in the United States and the massive displacement of the Syrian population to Turkey, Lebanon, Jordan, and Europe. Finally, it is remarkable that higher-income countries' war economies increasingly resemble lower-income countries' non-state war economies.

As Zachariah Mampilly observes, the most significant element of non-state war economies is taxation. Because the collection of revenues is supposed to be the exclusive prerogative of the state, when a non-state group begins to tax the citizens living on territories nominally under a state's sovereignty, such an action is regarded by most analysts as both illegal and illegitimate, that is, mere extortion. Rebels practicing this form of racketeering are criminals seeking profit rather than pursuing the objectives of liberation that they proclaim. Those who defend this viewpoint are influenced by Mancur Olson's views but disregard the fact that contemporary African and Latin American national contexts are completely different from those pertaining to the formation of European states. Against such anachronistic approaches, it is necessary to account for practices of taxation from the agents' perspective, rooted in a specific reality. Thus, the Colombian guerrilla cannot be reduced to a form of banditry. Its Marxist-Leninist ideology implied a political project with a form of governance combining social control over, and public services for, the population of the areas where they claimed authority. More generally, in contexts of civil war, taxation may achieve several goals. It manifests an aspiration to sovereignty; it tests the legitimacy of the rebels and the loyalty of the population; it establishes the foundations of a state bureaucracy by building the accounting and levying apparatus; and, finally, it generates revenues that can be used to consolidate the insurgency. Rebel taxation is thus about much more than generating revenue. It is a highly symbolic and political technology of governance, which exceeds its economic benefits.

One aspect that has long been neglected in non-state war economies is the presence, in the context of contemporary wars, of agents that are not waging war. This is the case of the humanitarian agencies discussed by Gilles Carbonnier. They have been extremely successful at fundraising, reaching a global budget that, according to official data, has grown by a factor of twenty-two in the past quarter century, if one combines public and private sources. Relief organizations intervene either on the ground, after agreements have been reached with the various military parties, as in the Democratic Republic of Congo, or, if security cannot be guaranteed, by remote control, that is, from a site distant from the theater of war, as in Syria. In some cases, the presence of humanitarian agencies requires paying taxes to factions that are supposed to guarantee their protection; this is what happens with the Taliban in Afghanistan and Al-Shabaab in Somalia. In other cases, humanitarian workers have been taken hostage by local groups, for instance, in Chechnya. This practice has proven particularly effective not only for the abductors, who request high ransoms to free captives, but also for the insurance companies which have developed a lucrative business by proposing the reimbursement, in case of kidnapping, of the ransom as well as the fees for the intermediaries. Beyond the growing concerns regarding the security of their personnel, relief organizations are confronted with complex situations in which their resources, including food and drugs, can be appropriated by the most powerful local agents. This is particularly the case when international sanctions are imposed on a country, with the aid agencies being caught between a rock and a hard place since both donors and local actors vie to control the aid distribution, often to the detriment of those in need. The emergence of humanitarian assistance in today's war economies thus poses unprecedented problems and adds a new dimension to the actions of warring parties.

Moving to a historical perspective, Nicola Di Cosmo examines the links between state and non-state war economies, and their connections to state formation. The Eurasian nomadic empires that developed over a period of 2,000 years are a case in point. Indeed, steppe nomads, in some instances, transcended their territorial and organizational limits to create empires, some ephemeral, others long-lasting. Tracing the history of these empires from the Xiongnu, which appeared at the end of the third century BCE, to the Qing dynasty founded by the Manchus (1644–1911), it is possible to bring out, beyond the multiple differences between them, a series of common elements that define the economic requirements for the constitution of new and expansive polities through warfare. Due to the limitations of their pastoral economy and ecology, steppe nomads required external resources to support the political and military requirements of large political formations: such resources could only be acquired through war. To raise an army and to ensure the loyalty of the elite, which were two essential conditions to remain in power and maintain the state's stability, the steppe ruler needed to wage wars. Against the threat of centrifugal forces exerted by tribal leaders and members of the aristocracy, the economy of war and the means of revenue extraction associated with it were indispensable to the survival of a unified and centralized political system. The political economy of steppe empires involved four strategies. Raiding and pillaging carried out by huge armies allowed for a redistribution of the spoils among the aristocracy as well as the soldiers. Tribute extorted in exchange for peace through treaties had the advantage over looting of being more sustainable in the long run. Trade became increasingly important and lucrative as the silk road and long-distance trade developed, facilitating the development of market towns, merchant networks, and the beginnings of transnational commerce to which nomads also contributed by providing military protection. Finally, taxation of conquered populations was probably the most effective since it did not deplete the local economies and relied on a bureaucracy and other civil institutions that contributed to the formation and consolidation of state structures. Nomadic empires thus confirm Charles Tilly's famous adage about European history according to which war made the state and the state made war, but they push it into an extreme, in the form of a vicious circle in which only by making war can states secure their existence.

On a different temporal and spatial scale, William Caferro explores non-state wars in Italian cities of the Renaissance. The conflicts between these small entities are especially revealing because they call into question the very definition of non-state wars. On the one hand, powerful Italian cities such as Venice or Genoa can be assimilated to states, since their military included local soldiers and foreign mercenaries. On the other hand, the permanent situation of conflict between and within Italian cities blurred the line between war and peace and even rendered the notion of warfare an inappropriate descriptor. Moreover, understanding the economic dimension of war-ridden northern Italy requires that the broader social context of the fourteenth and fifteenth centuries be taken into account. This is a time characterized by recurrent plague epidemics and famines that imposed a heavy burden on the demography and finances of the competing states. In this context, the phenomenon of mercenary armies hired by the various cities is economically and socially significant because it made war a major drain on resources as well as a significant element of social change as people were forced to move frequently. Raids on villages and sacks of cities by armed parties caused substantial displacements of populations, including the skilled workers necessary to the flourishing of the local industries, who were fleeing not only the scourges of plague and war but also the swelling taxes imposed by governments to pay mercenary armies. Considering the cost of maintaining armies to protect the cities, leagues were often formed to join their military efforts, such as one that saw the union of Florence, Verona, Milan, Mantua, Ferrara, and Naples in the fourteenth century. Rather than creating new states, wars had the effect of consolidating alliances between cities incapable of paying by themselves for the military protection they needed. The effects of having foreign soldiers, mainly from Germany and England, in the employment of Italian cities, especially in the fourteenth century, had significant economic implications. One of the most relevant was the transfer of wealth from Italy to northern countries, as the proceeds of military wages and other forms of income were invested, via the developed Italian banking system, to the places of origin of the military commanders. This led to the depletion of local economies. Only in the fifteenth century did armies begin to be mostly composed of native soldiers, who spent the money earned in conspicuous consumption, a feature of the Italian Renaissance. In sum, the connection between non-state wars and the formation of states in northern Italy is far from a linear one, since conflicts often contributed to economic exhaustion and political weakening. Moreover, the lines between state and non-state war economies were blurred as states had to raise financial resources through public fiscal extraction to fund non-state military actors. Fiscal and social consequences, compounded with political ones, made war and its economy a central transformative element in late medieval and early modern Italy.

Returning to China, but this time in the much more condensed period of the early twentieth century, Edward McCord analyses how the phenomenon of warlordism in China displayed special characteristics, in that it was connected closely with the preexisting state apparatus, which allowed military leaders to raise taxes and maintain a bureaucracy. Moreover, with the development of Chinese nationalism, regional military commanders did not aspire to build independent states but kept a formal allegiance to a unified and sovereign China. Rather, their power was derived from official functions of governorship in the name of the central state, whose fiscal and military functions they appropriated. The relationship between politics and militarization is remarkable, since the rise of warlordism resulted from a dual phenomenon of politicization of the military, as young officers became involved in the debates of their time, and of militarization of politics, as the political arena was dominated by opposing regional armies. The stability of the system depended upon two types of constraints: the loyalty of the officers and their men, and the warlords' own allegiance to the two nominal central governments, whether located in Beijing or Canton. It was also predicated on the financial capacity to support and even expand modern professional armies. Levying land taxes had long been the most effective way of supplying the necessary funds, but the increasing budgetary demands led to the diversification and proliferation of taxes increasingly drawn from the urban population, which made the occupation of cities especially profitable. There were, however, limits to how many taxes could be extracted, and other sources of revenue were used, including loans from foreign banks and manipulation of currency. Such a multiplicity of interests and financial dealings made the quality of the warlords' economic power not just regional but nodal. Whereas the personal wealth accumulated by many warlords can be assimilated to a form of predation, some of them also used these resources to develop welfare programs and modernization projects in the regions they controlled. But the general economic outcome of warlordism in these decades seems to be largely negative with the destruction of properties, the loss of lives, the interruption of agricultural cycles, and the impoverishment due to rapacious taxation. Beyond the economic consequences, an assessment of warlordism in modern China must take into account the political transformations that it produced, and in particular the emergence of a revolutionary movement mainly opposed to warlordism. Most significantly, the case of warlordism in China blurs the lines between state and non-state military actors, and, within the particular context of nationalist China, the behavior of various warlords does not conform to a single pattern.

Opening the section on contemporary wars, Jonathan Benthall examines the increasingly important economic role of charities, starting with the war fought from 1979 to 1989 between the Democratic Republic of Afghanistan supported by the Soviet Union and Afghan mujahideen backed by Pakistan, Saudi Arabia, and the United States, a war that caused half a million deaths. The anti-Soviet alliance proved decisive not only to bolster the resistance of the mujahideen, and defeat the loyalist and Soviet troops, but also to generate the Islamic fundamentalist groups, including the Taliban. This war was also a foundational and formative experience for the recently created Doctors Without Borders. Contravening the humanitarian principle of neutrality, the organization sided with the mujahideen, and its director even visited the United States to plead for its military support. In fact, humanitarian and military efforts went hand-in-hand, since both Christian and Muslim charities were mobilized to assist the mujahideen and benefited from tax exemption in the United States for their war effort. While the Soviet Union denounced this practice as one that supported international terrorism, it was only after the 9/11 attacks that the White House decided to blacklist and criminalize a number of Islamic charities which, ironically, had been used earlier to achieve military objectives in Afghanistan. Any support to these organizations, henceforth classified as terrorist by Western powers, was condemned and prosecuted even if it concerned a branch exclusively involved in medical aid or welfare programs such as the social services wing of Hamas. The history of the relationships of religious and secular charities with the United States and its allies in the Middle East thus reveals the ambiguities and even contradictions in the involvement of these non-state actors that mix a discourse of neutrality with a practice of partisanship, and are alternatively encouraged and sanctioned by Western powers. Whereas charities are definitely engaged in relief efforts to assist conflict victims, it would be naïve not to see the more complex and perplexing picture of their engagement in warfare and of their relationship with states.

It is also a change in perspective in the way a non-state actor is represented in the international public sphere that draws the attention of Clémence Pinaud as she considers how the image of the SPLA changed over time, depending on international politics. Until December 2013 and the new civil war, this organization was perceived as a political movement with legitimate grievances because it suited the foreign policy goals of Western countries and particularly the United States. Western powers supported the rebels against the Sudanese government accused of ties with the Muslim Brotherhood and al-Qaeda. Cleverly orchestrated by its leader, the portrayal of the SPLA allowed international advocates to turn a blind eye to the predatory violence against local populations it claimed to liberate in the South. In fact, the organization of the war economy in SPLA-controlled areas, which depended on the building of a predatory state supported by the international community, induced transformations of the Sudanese society. Wartime predation initiated a process of new social class formation characterized by extractive and sexual violence. This process was controlled by the military aristocracy as a dominant class rather than a nobility. War-torn South Sudan shared many characteristics with the feudal societies described by Marc Bloch, characterized by economic exploitation and relationships of vassalage. The military aristocrats established long-term social, political, and military dominance through the reinvestment of their wealth into large-scale polygamy. They also created a lower stratum through gifts of women and bridewealth, thus developing networks of courtiers. To consolidate their dominant-class ascendency, they defended their interests by controlling markets and yielding as much surplus value as possible. Their strategies in defending their class interests and in consolidating their status resulted in a form of wealth hyper-concentration, which contributed to shape a patrimonial capitalist system, compounded by their dominant position on the marriage market. In using marriage as a tool of social differentiation and class consolidation, the military aristocracy devised extreme inequalities. In this case, if wars make states, war economies also make social classes and highly unequal societies, in which women are commodified.

Just as interpreting non-state wars in terms of grievances is reductive, Philippe Le Billon argues that the invocation of greed often appears to be a simplification. While archeologists and evolutionary biologists relate early warfare to the control of subsistence resources, political science and economics often consider that, in the absence of foreign support and ideological motivation after the end of the Cold War, states and non-states of the Global South have made the competition for the exploitation of natural resources one of the main causes of contemporary wars. But the very idea of resource-based wars brings with it the automatic delegitimation of the rebels as political actors and their criminalization, thus drawing attention away from the political roots of the conflict. Recent reassessments of these wars have emphasized a series of factors that need to be considered for a more nuanced analysis. Among these, the following are especially relevant. To begin with, the resources at stake are extremely diverse, from gemstones to wildlife products, and often circulate between states and non-states agents by means of corruption or co-optation.

Moreover, a wide range of actors are involved, including civilians, and these resources provide means of survival to certain populations. Various resources can affect the shape and duration of warfare, and the stakes they represent exist in both war and peace. To comprehend the nature of so-called resource wars, the case of the Islamic State is of particular interest as it reveals how the usual representation of its actions utterly simplifies what is in fact a complex picture. For instance, while oil was a substantial source of revenue during the four years when the Islamic State controlled a significant part of the Syrian and Iraqi territories, it is difficult to deny that its rationale was ideological and its project political, as specified in the very words of its name. In the short term, oil production certainly contributed to the consolidation of the Islamic State not only from a financial perspective but also for what it meant by way of negotiations with local actors, maintenance of the infrastructure, and distribution of the proceeds of sales. The links between oil and warfare were, in this case, multiple. More than access to the resource per se as a mere source of enrichment for the rebels—as some have argued—the takeover of oil fields mainly served to ensure the functioning and the expansion of the Caliphate. Yet, the Islamic proto-state faced many challenges in the exploitation of the oil fields due to the bombings by Western powers, the lack of technical experts, the pressures exerted on intermediaries, and, at some point, the sharp decline of the international price. Within a few years, from being an asset, oil became a liability.

As in the previous case studies developed in the book, both historical and contemporary, only a thorough empirical examination of a given conflict and its specific context can make non-state war economies more intelligible beyond simple dichotomic explanations and mere ideological judgments.

REFERENCES

Carbonnier, Gilles. 2015. *Humanitarian Economics: War, Disaster and the Global Aid Market*. Oxford: Oxford University Press.

Cederman, Lars-Erik, Kristian Skrede Gleditsch, and Halvard Buhaug. 2013. *Inequality, Grievances, and Civil War*. Cambridge, UK: Cambridge University Press.

Collier, Paul. 2008. *The Bottom Billion: Why the Poorest Countries Are Failing and What Can Be Done About It*. Oxford: Oxford University Press.

———. 2009. *Wars, Guns, and Votes: Democracy in Dangerous Places*. New York: Harper Collins.

Collier, Paul, Anke Hoeffler, and Nicholas Sambanis. 2005. "The Collier-Hoeffler Model of Civil War Onset and the Case Study Project Research Design." In *Understanding Civil War: Evidence and Analysis*, pp. 1–33. Edited by Paul Collier and Nicholas Sabanis. Vol. 1—Africa. Washington, DC: World Bank.

Duffield, Mark R. 2001. *Global Governance and the New Wars: The Merging of Development and Security*. London and New York: Zed Books.

Keen, David. 2012a. "Greed and Grievance in Civil War." *International Affairs* 88 (4): 757–77.

———. 2012b. *Useful Enemies: When Waging Wars Is More Important Than Winning Them*. New Haven and London: Yale University Press.

Le Billon, Philippe. 2012. *Wars of Plunder: Conflicts, Profits and the Politics of Resources*. London: Hurst & Company.

Tilly, Charles. 1985. "War Making and State Making as Organized Crime." In *Bringing the State Back In*, pp. 169–91. Edited by Peter B. Evans, Dietrich Rueschemeyer, and Theda Skocpol. Cambridge, UK: Cambridge University Press.

Part I

FRAMEWORKS

Chapter 1

What Are Non-State War Economies?

Prefatory Remarks

Didier Fassin

"War made the state, and the state made war," Charles Tilly (1975: 42) famously wrote, his statement having become the motto of the so-called bellicist theory of state-making. But more than the obvious military connection between war and the state—the state needs an army to wage a war, and this army reciprocally allows the state to consolidate its existence against its enemies in wartime—the economic dimension was for him crucial to the relationship between the two entities. "Taxes, conscription, requisitions, and more," which aimed at building strong armed forces, ultimately served to "deliver resources to the government for other purposes," therefore becoming tools for the strengthening of political institutions. One could therefore go as far as saying that, in Tilly's view of the formation of European polities—and only those polities, as he straightforwardly argued that "Europe will not occur again"—this predatory economy represents the link between war and the state. It does so in two symmetrical ways. On the one hand, the state extorts levies from its population to wage wars. On the other hand, it legitimizes itself by assuring the protection of its population against potential internal or external enemies. While this theory has been quite influential in political history and political science, it is in fact part of a broader approach to state-making and war making in these disciplines, which has been systematized via statistical data and enriched to take into account national identification (Wimmer 2013). In this approach, war is a conflict between states and states are the products of wars.

This traditional state-centered understanding of wars is reflected in the elaboration of the important Correlates of War Project, which consists in collecting for statistical purposes exhaustive information about warfare over the past two centuries, using for definition conflicts between participants with armed forces having caused more than 1,000 battle-related fatalities among combatants, this figure having later been specified as a yearly minimum. For those who imagined the project in 1963, the "primary interest was in developing a typology" that was "based on war participants," and therefore "on states, which by definition had to have the means of exerting their independence and playing a role in international relations" (Sarkees 2007). It took the authors of the project more than thirty years to begin revising their typology so as to include non-states as agents involved in conflicts both national and international. Such a late integration shows how much the ideas of war and state are inseparable not only for common sense but also in the academia. Until recently, non-state wars seemed to be, for many, unidentified political objects.

The awareness of the existence of non-state wars and of the urgency to study them is often said to be related to the 9/11 events, as if the attacks on New York's Twin Towers and the call for the war on terror had generated awareness about the fact that militant groups could be part of armed conflicts. This certainly betrayed a dominant presentist and Western-centered view that was ignorant of the reality of non-state wars in the past and present. Indeed, historians have for a long time written about warlords in various parts of the world, notably China, anthropologists have dedicated studies to contemporary ethnic wars also across the planet, especially on the African continent, and the parallels between the Chinese past and the African present have even appeared to be heuristic as in the Chadian case (Charlton and May 1989). The observers' blindness was even more troubling—and yet less surprising—when one considers that the majority of the victims of militias, insurgents, radical factions and criminal gangs live in the so-called Global South. Indeed, more than to the states' security, which is generally invoked as being at stake, it is to the security of local communities that these various groups pose a threat: they are those who pay the highest price (Engelhart 2016: 171). Typically, the Islamic State has been responsible for far more casualties in the Middle East, particularly among the Yazidi population, than in Europe and North America, via its attacks. Among the first twenty-five countries appearing on the global terrorism index, only one is situated in the Western world, the others being in Asia and Africa (Statista 2020). Thus, in 2017, it is Afghanistan and Iraq that have suffered the most fatalities from these attacks, followed by Nigeria and Somalia. In sum, the late consciousness of the significance of non-state armed groups in contemporary warfare came with the perception of the threat posed by terrorism to the West, although these regions were far less affected than the rest of the world.

In this post-9/11 context, the economic dimension of these conflicts resurfaced. But it mainly did so in a specific way. Early reports mostly assessed the consequences of the new risk on insurance coverage and premiums, transportation and trade costs, and security spending, with relatively optimistic predictions in terms of financial stability and economic growth (Lenain, Bonturi and Koen 2002). Again, the viewpoint was that of the state, more specifically those of Western countries. Yet, when considering the economic impact of terrorism in terms of direct and indirect costs due to deaths and injuries as well as property destruction, the ten countries that suffer most economic losses in proportion of their GDP are in the Middle East and Africa (Institute for Economics and Peace 2017). Besides, such analyses, like most of those conducted in recent years, were essentially limited to what was categorized as terrorist attacks. However, in Iraq, which is the country most affected by such acts, the number of fatalities they caused between 2000 and 2016 amounted to 9,765, while, according to the conservative assessment of the Iraq Family Health Survey Study Group (2008), the number of violent deaths related to the war conducted by the United States and its allies against local belligerents is estimated at a minimum of 151,000 for the sole period from March 2003 through June 2006. Terrorism, even in the Global South, is only a small part of the death toll of, and price paid by, populations where non-state wars occur. Finally, it should be added that analyzing the economy of conflicts only in terms of impact and costs is legitimate but restrictive. If wars have consequences, they also have causes. And these causes are in part economic. By focusing on the economic effects of war, one misses the crucial point of the economic logics of the production and perpetuation of warfare, in particular, albeit not only, the economic logics of the agents involved, whether they have to do with the conquest of territories, the access to natural resources, the appropriation and distribution of riches, the levying of taxes and raising of an army.

Thus, with few notable exceptions, non-state war economies have not received the attention they deserve and, when they have, it has been through presentist and Western-centered lenses, more concerned with terrorism in the North than conflicts in the South and with consequences than causes. Examining afresh non-state war economies therefore provides an opportunity to open less often addressed issues. But do we even have a clear idea of what is meant by non-state war economies, and are there not a series of questions to answer in the first place? Are we sure that there is a consensual definition of war? Are we certain of how to characterize a non-state actor involved in a conflict? Are we confident in our understanding of what the boundary of the economic domain is? In this chapter, I want to reflect critically on the three elements that compose the object of our collective inquiry in order to enlighten and perhaps complicate its contents and contours. To address the theoretical questions each of them pose, I will limit my empirical cases to contemporary situations.

WAR

Prima facie, what a war is seems to pose little problem; Famously, Carl von Clausewitz (1976: 75) presented it as “an act of force to compel our enemy to do our will." Dictionaries define it as a state of armed conflict between countries or between groups within a country. In certain cases, things are clear: there is a declaration of war. For instance, the Congress of the United States has approved eleven resolutions declaring war with various countries, from Great Britain in 1812 to Axis-allied Bulgaria, Hungary, and Rumania in 1942. But since then, none of the military interventions of the United States in Korea, Lebanon, Vietnam, Iraq, Afghanistan, or Libya, among others, have been preceded by a declaration of war. Most significantly, there is no official war between the United States and Yemen, where 329 strikes have been responsible for more than 1,000 deaths since 2002, or Pakistan, where 430 strikes have killed more than 2,500 people since 2004. So, how do we know that a given armed conflict is a war—and who decides?

For more than four decades, the Algerian War of Independence was officially referred to in France as *les événements d'Algérie*, the events of Algeria, since the official position of the French government when it started was to deem Algeria a part of France and therefore the rebellion of the Algerians a mere internal public disorder (République française 1962). Only in 1999 did the French president Jacques Chirac acknowledge that the conflict between France and the National Liberation Front, which had caused the death of 23,000 French and more than 300,000 Algerians, was indeed a war. In contrast, on the other side, the official designation was "Algerian Revolution." It should, however, be noted that for ordinary people things were much more straightforward: in France, people spoke of *la guerre d'Algérie*, the Algerian war, while in Algeria, they simply talked about *la guerre*, the war. Thus, for the colonial state, the deadly war was downgraded to mere unrest and treated as a policing issue, whereas for the non-state belligerent it was elevated to the status of an act of emancipation of an oppressed people. On both sides, the language of war was considered to be irrelevant—except for distant spectators and local victims.

Three days after the November 13, 2015, attacks in which 130 people were killed in Paris and for which the Islamic State claimed responsibility, the French president François Hollande convened the French parliament and solemnly started his speech with the sentence: "France is at war" (Sénat 2015). The nine perpetrators, who were almost all French and Belgian citizens trained in Syria, were depicted as "a jihadist army." For the head of state, this declaration of war justified the heavy bombing, the night before, of the Syrian city of Raqqa, the stronghold of the Islamic State, and the objective of the "destruction" of the Salafi militant group. Yet, contrary to what these statements implied, Operation Chammal mobilizing French troops as part the international coalition against the Islamic State had begun one year earlier. But there was no question of war then; the term used was *frappes aériennes*, airstrikes. French people did not think of their country as being at war. The perception was undoubtedly different for people living under the bombs in Syria. The attacks in Paris could thus be described by the French government as the triggering factor of what became officially designated as a war of self-defense, whereas the Islamic State presented their attacks in Paris as a retaliation for Operation Chammal which had already caused numerous casualties in their ranks. Thus, for France, choosing the right moment to declare the war served to overlook the previous military involvement and justify the amplification of the airstrikes as a just response, while for the Islamic State, speaking of reprisal for bombings which had killed militants as well as civilians permitted to authenticate the ongoing warfare and legitimize the attacks in Paris. On both sides, the language of war was strategic—but for symmetrical reasons.

From this parallel between a war that is not named as such by the belligerents and a war that is acknowledged as such by them yet at different moments, what lessons can we draw? Is a war only a war when it has been recognized as such—and by whom? What interest does one have in declaring a war—or instead in denying it? Whereas the question of whether there was a time when the definition and delimitation of war was undisputed remains open—one could think of wars between states starting with a proclamation and ending with an armistice or a surrender—it is clear that it is not the case anymore. Think of Palestine where Palestinians do not see their condition as one of warfare, although it is punctuated with Palestinian uprisings and Israeli deadly military interventions, but as one of unending occupation which started with the Nakba in 1948; "Occupied Palestinian Territories" is in fact the official expression used by many international organizations, as the conflict has caused the death of more than 10,000 people and the exile of almost 5 million refugees among the Palestinians. Think also of Colombia, where Colombians have experienced one of the longest situations of warfare of the twentieth century involving the national army, paramilitary groups, and several guerrilla organizations; the term *La Violencia* initially used in 1948 has been the common way of referring to the conflict, as it is estimated that more than 200,000 people have died and more than 5 million have been internally displaced. In the Palestinian case, the enemy is the occupier, like Germany was for France during the Second World War. In the Colombian case, the enemy is within, like in the United States at the time of the Civil War. But in both cases, despite the militarization of the conflict and the number of casualties, the everlasting context of threat and violence makes the unnamed warfare the rule, and the elusive peace the exception. For those living in these contexts, the boundary between war and peace is obscured. In the Occupied Palestinian Territories still today, people know that they can be shot, arrested or dispossessed of their land almost at any moment. In large areas of Colombia until recently, people knew that they could be kidnapped, killed, or chased from their home at almost any time; and in fact, even the signing of the peace agreement has not changed that situation for many. For Palestinians living in Occupied Territories that are constantly reduced by settlers' colonization and for Colombians living in unsafe zones where paramilitaries and militants still operate, war is a form of life. It is part of their ordinary existence. A sort of silent warfare seems normalized to the point that it is no more recognized as such. In fact, it is probable that it has long been the case in many parts of the world, when insecurity was the norm, when the state was almost inexistent, and when non-state armed agents were the main players.

The relatively indistinct character of many contemporary wars—whether they are not named or acknowledged as such, whether they are not well defined or clearly delimited in time or space—is indeed in part the consequence of the involvement of non-state agents. Declaring the "war on terror," as George W. Bush did in September 2001, was more a rhetorical gesture than a diplomatic statement. The enemy was not clearly designated, even if in the context of the 9/11 attacks, al-Qaeda was the main target. In fact, his successor in the White House, Barack Obama, stated in May 2013 that the United States should not be involved in a "boundless global war on terror" but instead in "targeted efforts to dismantle specific networks of violent extremists," thus renouncing the lexicon of both war and terror (Obama 2013). In the meantime, however, the United States had declared two wars which presented most characteristics of usual conflicts between states—against Afghanistan in 2001 and Iraq in 2003, bombing and invading both countries. Thus, while it is true that non-state wars often involve specific forms of warfare, such as guerilla combat or suicide bombing, they have not abandoned traditional forms, with their battlefields, fronts and seizing of cities, the main difference residing then in the contrast between the sophistication of the states' military equipment and the often limited and aging weaponry of the non-state actors. The support of international powers on both sides tends nevertheless to reduce the gap between them as does the dissemination of weaponry in the aftermath of the fall of a regime, like in Libya in 2011 when al-Qaeda in the Islamic Maghreb took hold of Muammar Gaddafi's armament, or as a result of the debacle of a national army, as was the case in 2014 when the Iraqi army was defeated by the Islamic State in Mosul. For these various reasons, the specificity of wars involving non-state actors should therefore not be overstated.

There is, however, a singularity of this form of warfare: the confusion between civilians and combatants, or better said, the blurring of the line between the two. On the one hand, under occupation, civilians can become militants to defend their country, while militants can hide in plain-clothes to perpetrate an attack. The distinction between the two can even become meaningless as the passage from one status to the other may be unpredictable and reversible, often the consequence of particular circumstances. On the other hand, in such scenario, the occupying army becomes suspicious of the entire local population, distrust and doubt causing the killing of individuals without any evidence of their involvement in an armed group. Indeed, faced with the potential risk for their life of an error of judgment, soldiers consider them combatants until proven civilians. This confusion has produced both a considerable number of unjustified deaths and a series of heated controversies about the counting of casualties in Afghanistan and even more Iraq. Indeed, under the law of war, specified in modern times as International Humanitarian Law, the distinction between civilians and combatants is crucial. In drone attacks conducted by the United States against the Taliban, the killing of civilians who happened to be close to the supposed combatant being targeted is deemed the inevitable cost of a necessary operation. But in the bombing by Israel of Gazan civilian edifices such as schools, the argument is reversed as the combatants are accused of using the population as human shields. In these cases, a justification for the killing of civilians still seems needed for the states fighting non-state actors so as to legitimize their action. However, in most cases, non-state actors do not even feel bound by international laws, and the Shining Path in Peru, the Lord's Resistance Army in Uganda, and the Islamic State in Syria do not bother with the weak distinction between civilians and combatants: they indiscriminately massacre the peasants from villages suspected of collaboration with the enemy. In fact, the armies of the respective states often do not act otherwise—which certainly calls for a closer examination of the differences and relationships between state and non-state.

NON-STATE

The negative designation of entities as what they are not is always problematic. First, it supposes that what they are not is itself indisputably defined and delimited—in that case, the state, about which so many theories, debates, and disputes have been generated. Second, it implies that there is some empirical homogeneity or at least theoretical coherence in gathering them under the same label—yet, militant groups, nongovernmental organizations, and multinational corporations have little in common (National Intelligence Council 2007). So, what are non-state actors, and in which way do they intervene in warfare?

While this is not the place to ask what a state is, it may still be relevant to observe via concrete cases how perplexing the description of an actor as non-state can be. Let us consider three emblematic cases in the Middle East. The Islamic State is a self-denominated state created in 2014 but deemed by the other nations of the planet a non-state actor, alternatively designated as a militant group, a terrorist organization, and a crime syndicate. Albeit not recognized as a state, it presents—or at least has presented during a certain period of time—various signs supposed to be characteristic of statehood, such as sovereignty over a territory, levying of taxes, policing of its population, and provision of social and health services, among others. The Palestinian Authority, by contrast, is since the 1995 Oslo Accords the legal government of the Occupied Territories, but it has no effective sovereignty over its territory—although the state of Palestine is recognized by a majority of the members of the United Nations. This government is the emanation of the Palestine Liberation Organization, which is a liberation movement long considered to be a terrorist organization by Israel and the United States as well as a confederation of political parties in exile historically dominated by the Fatah. Finally, the Hezbollah is a political party and militant group that was formed by the reunion of Shi'a militias in 1982 to fight the Israeli occupation of South Lebanon. Regarded as a resistance movement in part of the Arab world and as a terrorist organization in most Western countries, it has representatives elected in the Lebanese parliament and ministers in the government. In a nutshell, these non-state actors, which are viewed as liberation or resistance movements by some and terrorist or criminal groups by others, can be self-designated as states (Islamic State), appear as the backbone of a quasi-state (Palestine Liberation Organization) or participate in the institutions of a fully instituted state (Hezbollah). Considering their functional and structural role in their respective state, it is easy to see that the label "non-state actor" is profoundly deceptive for these three entities. In fact, all have been making states by making war, each in their own way, and all are crucial to the existence and viability of these states.

The Middle East is certainly no exception in this respect. In South Africa, the Umkhonto weSizwe, the armed branch of the African National Congress cofounded by Nelson Mandela fought against the apartheid regime by resorting to guerrilla warfare, bombing, and sabotage; it was declared a terrorist organization by the South African government as well as the United States; and it eventually gave the country the first three presidents of its democratic era after 1994. In Uruguay, the Movimiento de Liberación Nacional-Tupamaros, a political organization which turned into a guerrilla group, robbing banks to distribute their booty to the poor, and kidnapping of high-profile politicians, was severely repressed under the dictatorship; it joined the political coalition Frente Ámplio after the return of the democracy in 1984, one of its members later becoming president. In northern Syria, the Democratic Union Party, narrowly connected with the Kurdistan Worker's Party of Turkey which is designated as a terrorist organization by most Western countries but not by the United Nations, has created in 2012 an autonomous region that it administrates as a quasi-state. These various examples show how the boundary between non-state actors and states is tenuous and porous as militant organizations once called terrorist may form the basis of, or provide significant contributions to, the state.

But there is another way in which opposing states and non-state actors can be misleading. Although a common representation shows them at war against each other—the state against the guerrilla or terrorist groups—the relations and complicities between them are much more complex. Examples abound, with the support and financing of the premises of al-Qaeda by Saudi Arabia, of Hezbollah by Iran, and of the Taliban by the United Arab Emirates and probably at some point by the United States themselves. Such connections form part of the complex geopolitics involving, in each conflict, great powers as well as regional governments, and they contribute to fueling conspiracy theories as was the case in the aftermath of 9/11. Most of the time, the labyrinthine circuits involved in these transactions remain hidden. In some cases, the support to combatants is overtly discussed. In 2011 and 2012, during the early years of the Syrian civil war, several Western countries, including France, were willing to provide weapons to rebel groups that fought against the Assad regime, although they were concerned that this armament could fall into the hands of what might turn out to be terrorist organizations. In other cases, states even use militias for their own bellicose purpose. From 2003 to 2006, the Sudanese government armed the Janjaweed groups to combat the secessionist insurgency of the Sudan Liberation Army in Darfur, these dreaded warriors causing the deaths of tens of thousands of civilians.

These forms of passage and links between states and non-states actors suggest that, paradoxically, to understand non-state actors, one has to bring the state back in (Evans, Rueschemeyer, and Skocpol 1985). When studying non-state wars, one should not forget that the states are never far away as major players.

Until now, these entities have implicitly been presented as combatant organizations involved in conflicts to liberate their country from an oppressor or an occupier, to disseminate their religion or their ideology, or to expand their territory. Whatever one thinks of the goal they pursue, such representations tend to ennoble their action as if it were purely politically motivated. But the boundary between militancy and banditry is often porous. Not only are looting, trafficking, and racketeering frequent means to support the war effort of these organizations, but they can also be ends as such. The most obvious cases are the Italian mafia, the Colombian drug cartels and the Chadian highway robbers, who have various types of connections with local authorities but do not have a political agenda beyond the support of politicians whom they can corrupt. But other configurations offer less clear-cuts. The civil war in the Central African Republic is an illustration of the confusion between warfare and brigandry. The mostly Christian anti-Balaka militias were initially local vigilante groups created to protect villages from highwaymen, poachers, and cattle-raiders, but were later used by the putschist president François Bozizé to combat the predominantly Muslim Séléka rebels. In an endless conflict transformed into a series of religious pogroms, both groups, often joined by opportunists and mercenaries, committed exactions and massacres while practicing extortion and looting.

But non-state actors involved in warfare also belong to an entirely different world: that of humanitarianism (Carbonnier 2016; Fassin 2012). Whereas the creation of the International Committee of the Red Cross dates back to the second half of the nineteenth century, with the Red Crescent Societies being added to the movement after the First World War, humanitarianism has had a rapid expansion at the end of the twentieth century, initially with the birth of nongovernmental organizations such as Doctors Without Borders in 1971 and later with the adoption of its language and project by states and international agencies culminating in the Responsibility to Protect doctrine voted for by the United Nations in 2005. Today, the presence of humanitarian workers in contexts of warfare is inescapable with their medical teams, their aid convoys, their food programs, their logisticians and their epidemiologists, their tents and their camps. The humanitarian marketplace of philanthropic donations by individuals and corporations and public subsidies from states and international agencies today represents one-eighth of the global development assistance. Again, while many organizations have indisputably strict assistance-oriented activities, the boundaries delimiting the humanitarian world are not always evident. On the one hand, certain charities collaborate with the intelligence services of their country's government. The Humanitarian International Services Group, which was celebrated by the president of the United States, George W. Bush, for its work with disaster victims, was thus heavily funded by the Pentagon through a highly classified program (Cole 2015). It was used by the Defense Department in an espionage operation in North Korea, where its Christian evangelical founder was able to introduce various military equipment and radio beacons. On the other hand, certain militant organizations develop important aid activities for their population. Hamas, the Palestinian resistance organization listed as terrorist by most Western countries and some of their Arab allies, has had affiliations—varying at times between definite and moot—with welfare and health programs that have contributed to humanitarian relief in the Occupied Territories (Benthall 2016). These programs have been deprived of international funding via charity trusts and individual donations since such support is criminalized.

Non-state actors are therefore not only diverse in their relation to warfare (from combatants to bandits, from resistance fighters to humanitarian workers, and one should add political movements such as the neoconservatives in the United States, religious groups be they evangelical, Jewish or Muslim, multinational corporations whether they are involved in the extraction of natural resources or the sale of weaponry, and even medias with the extreme case of Radio Mille-Collines in Rwanda) but also multifaceted in their projects and actions (the line between these apparently exclusive or contradictory categories being partially blurred and their connections not easily penetrable). These multiple actors and their respective activities form part of an economy that mobilizes all sorts of items.

ECONOMY

The economics of warfare is a field of research in its own right, but one not entirely pacified. Debates regard the question of what is to be analyzed as well as, more broadly, what economics is about. Some are interested in the consequences of wars; others in their causes. Some proceed by accounting methods; others provide theoretical models. Some use rational choice theory and propose a political psychology; others rely on history and develop a political economy. So, what do economists have to say about war economies?

A first approach, especially relevant to governments and international agencies, concerns consequences in terms of the impact and the cost of war (Edwards 2010 and Watson Institute 2019). It is fundamentally an accounting approach. It implies complex decisions about what to include: destructions of properties and shortfalls in revenue, military expenses and veteran benefits, productivity loss due to deaths and medical provisions for the injured, and so on. Whereas it may seem a pure arithmetic exercise, it involves philosophical questions with financial repercussions, such as that of the value of life (Fassin 2018). However, many of these analyses are asymmetrical, being essentially attentive to the Western side of impact and cost. While evaluations of the economic consequences for the United States of the wars in Afghanistan and Iraq are thoroughly well assessed, little is known about these consequences for the latter two countries. An indication of this asymmetry is that the number of dead soldiers is known down to the unit level for the U.S. army, but the number of casualties among combatants and civilians in Afghanistan and Iraq is estimated with a margin of error of several hundreds of thousands depending on the sources. However imperfect it is, the accounting approach is always implicitly characterized by its negative perspective: it explores the ravages of war. Yet, not only has war politically positive consequences such as state-building, as evoked earlier, but it also has economically positive effects, notably on the military-industrial complex, which benefits from it directly, through the expansion of the national defense budget—that of the United States represents more than one-third of the total worldwide—and indirectly, via the thriving of arms trade—the United States has more than one-third of the global sales of weaponry (Sipri 2017). Needless to say, the terms *negative* and *positive* do not presuppose a judgment regarding the evil or good dimension of war. They simply indicate a factual analysis of what is lost and gained, the argument being that it is not possible to understand the logics of wars if one does not take into account their economic benefits for certain social agents.

A second approach, which has undergone a spectacular development in past decades, is that of rational choice theory (Fearon 1995). It focuses on the causes of war and bases its analysis on the supposed psychology of actors. Game theory is its privileged method as it reveals the presumed reasoning behind the preferences expressed through the decision to wage war. Fundamentally, the point is to understand why there is war when it has such negative consequences. To do so, these economists or political scientists imagine scenarios in which two actors assess the potential costs and potential payoffs of a military contest as well as their probability to win it, compared to alternative options, such as negotiating with the adversary. Resulting calculations are meant to represent, or at least simulate, the way of thinking of agents, either states or non-state actors. And indeed, to give an appearance of realism to these analyses, actual cases are provided to illustrate how politicians purportedly evaluate risks and benefits before deciding to engage in a conflict, for instance, German leaders when they declared war in 1914, or Saddam Hussein when he resolved to invade Kuwait in 1990. These examples rely on the hypothetical understanding of the psychology of these characters and via the bold projection of their mode of reasoning—without any empirical evidence of neither one of them. Besides, they convey the idea that the decision is a pure exercise in rationality without any role of the social and political forces at work—as if methodological individualism could replace the thorough analysis of the historical context and of the tortuous logics at stakes. However, this simple one-on-one game eludes the complex power game involving an intricate network of national and international actors. Aware of the issue, some economists have introduced so-called costs of coordination, regarded as transactions costs, in their mathematical models. Thus, to predict whether a rebel group will decide to embark in civil war, they calculate what they designate as rebel utility, based on the size of the population, the costs of coordination, the per capita income, the taxable capacity of the economy, the expected duration of warfare, the probability of rebel victory, the gain conditional upon victory, and even the discount rate (Collier and Hoeffler 1998). Analyzing on this basis why the African continent had more civil wars than the rest of the world since 1960, these economists only take into account these internal variables, while overlooking the weight of colonial history, which precisely ended at that time, and the role of the great powers, which were then involved in the Cold War.

A third approach is that of political economy. It corrects the limitations of the accounting model by analyzing both positive and negative dimensions of war, and it addresses the flaws of rational choice theory model by substituting history for mathematics (Cramer 2002; Le Billon 2004). It inscribes military conflicts, whether between states or with militant groups, in their context, both national and international, even sometimes local, identifying the interests of the social agents at play, whether armed or not. They often use the wealth of archives and sometimes the refinement of ethnography to recount complex narratives that are not reducible to a series of variables to be included into a linear equation. Monographs thus allow for a thickening of specific conjunctures instead of providing the thin generalizations relying on questionable statistics. They show that, in Colombia, the war has been perpetuated for decades because military, paramilitary, and narco-traffickers built alliances based on shared economic interests that also benefited the upper class, while guerrilla groups often received the support of local peasant communities, which they protected from the aggressive practices of rich landowners and to which they provided minimal welfare services in the stead of the absent state. Similarly, they demonstrate that, in Afghanistan, in the context of the end of the Cold War, the withdrawal of the Soviet army has led to the drying out of its subsidies to the regime in power as well as the end of the support of the United States to the rebels, thus generating needs for new economic resources that were filled by poppy cultivation and opium exportation, while less lucrative wheat cultivation and livestock exportation waned. And they establish that in South Sudan, the civil war has been fueled by a system of predation that facilitated the formation of a military elite which could affirm its power through clientelism and nepotism as well as forms of distinction via the display of signs of wealth, including large-scale polygamy (Richani 1997; Goodhand 2002; Pinaud 2014). Each of these cases reveals the uniqueness of the historical contexts and cultural backgrounds, and therefore the limits of mere accounting and mathematical models.

However different these various approaches are, they have in common to approach economy as the production, circulation, appropriation, consumption, and destruction of goods and services, whether natural resources, taxation money, compensation benefits, military industry, health care, or international subsidies—with certain similarities as well as major differences between countries or between state and non-state actors. This corresponds to the classic understanding of what economy is about, with the singularity that it is applied in the present case to war, and more specifically to atypical sorts of war. But economy can be viewed otherwise. Instead of goods and services, one can consider values and affects that agents have regarding the conflict, the protagonists and their actions, the treatment of material commodities and the population involved, and so on. If some wars can be deemed just and others unjust—and not everyone agrees, of course, on the criteria to establish such distinction—it means that a certain moral dimension is engaged in warfare (Walzer 2015). Morality should be understood here as combining a moral sense and moral sentiments, in other words, norms about what is good or bad, fair and unfair, as well as a range of emotions, from indignation to compassion, from fervor to dismay. It is of major import to apprehend this dual dimension of war—normative and emotional—since this endeavor often renders intelligible ways of acting which would otherwise remain incomprehensible or would merely be seen as irrational. For instance, insurgents discredited as criminal groups may rebel against the injustice and autocracy of the regime in place, and the levying of taxes depicted as financial extortion can also be deemed a source of revenue to provide services to the population, as was the case for the Liberation Tigers of Tamil Eelam in Sri Lanka (Mampilly 2011). Such reading does not mean the legitimation of the agents' moral justifications, and analysts should avoid adding their own moral judgment to that of the protagonists. Thus, seeing warfare as a marketplace of loyalties does not imply an approval of the alliances made between African warlords, but the recognition that they obey a certain moral logic (De Waal 2009). But in a more obvious way, the moral world of contemporary war also includes, as mentioned earlier, the expanding domain of humanitarianism, which brings together, in often conflictive ways, states, international agencies, and nongovernmental organizations. One can therefore speak of the moral economy of warfare to designate the production, circulation, and appropriation of values and affects related to war and its actors (Fassin 2009). It is essential to integrate it in the inquiry into non-state war economies, which are not only about goods and services, and could not be understood without taking into account norms and emotions.

CONCLUSION

The critical approach to the three terms that compose the object of our collective endeavor is neither a rhetorical exercise nor a relativist stance. It does not suggest that wars are an elusive reality because their definition and delimitation are problematic, that the existence of authentic non-state actors is deceptive because they have obscure connections with states, and that the economy of non-state wars is too complex to be seized because they involve not only material but also moral dimensions. It simply invites us not to take for granted these seemingly so self-evident words and the facts that they are supposed to represent.

Such complexification has for consequence that the study of non-state war economies gains from being a multidisciplinary endeavor, associating historians, anthropologists, and sociologists as well as political scientists and legal scholars with economists. Paraphrasing Georges Clémenceau, the French prime minister during the First World War, we could say that non-state war economies are too serious a matter to entrust to economists.

REFERENCES

Benthall, Jonathan. 2016. *Islamic Charities and Islamic Humanism in Troubled Times.* Manchester: Manchester University Press.

Carbonnier, Gilles. 2016. *Humanitarian Economics: War, Disaster, and the Global Aid Market.* Oxford: Oxford University Press.

Charlton, Roger, and Roy May. 1989. "Warlords and Militarism in Chad." *Review of African Political Economy*, no. 45/46: 12–25.

Clausewitz, Carl von. 1976. *On War.* Translated by Michael Howard and Peter Paret. Princeton: Princeton University Press. 1st German edition 1832.

Cole, Matthew. 2015. "The Pentagon's Missionary Spies." *The Intercept.* 12/4/2020. https://theintercept.com/2015/10/26/pentagon-missionary-spies-christian-ngo-front-for-north-korea-espionage/.

Collier, Paul, and Anke Hoeffler. 1998. "On Economic Causes of Civil War." *Oxford Economic Papers* 50, no. 4 (October): 563–73.

Cramer, Christopher. 2002. "*Homo Economicus* Goes to War: Methodological Individualism, Rational Choice and the Political Economy of War." *World Development* 30, no. 11 (November): 1845–64.

De Waal, Alex. 2009. "Mission Without End? Peacekeeping in the African Political Marketplace." *International Affairs* 85, no. 1 (January): 99–113.

Edwards, Ryan. 2010. *A Review of War Costs in Iraq and Afghanistan.* Cambridge, MA: National Bureau of Economic Research, Working Paper 16163.

Englehart, Neil. 2016. "Non-State Armed Groups as a Threat to Global Security: What Threat, Whose Security?" *Journal of Global Security Studies* 1, no. 2 (May): 171–83.

Evans, Peter, Dietrich Rueschemeyer, and Theda Skocpol, eds. 1985. *Bringing the State Back In.* Cambridge: Cambridge University Press.

Fassin, Didier. 2009. "Moral Economies Revisited." *Annales: Histoire, Sciences Sociales* 64, no. 6: 1237–68.

Fassin, Didier. 2012. *Humanitarian Reason: A Moral History of the Present.* Berkeley: University of California Press. 1st French edition 2010.

Fassin, Didier. 2018. *Life: A Critical User's Manual.* Cambridge: Polity Press. 1st German edition 2017.

Fearon, James. 1995. "Rationalist Explanations for War." *International Organization* 49, no. 3 (Summer): 379–414.

Goodhand, Jonathan. 2000. "From Holy War to Opium War? A Case Study of the Opium Economy in Northeastern Afghanistan." *Disasters* 24, no. 2 (June): 87–102.

Institute for Economics and Peace. 2017. *Global Terrorism Index: Measuring and Understanding the Impact of Terrorism.* Sydney: IEP.

Iraq Family Health Study Group. 2008. "Violence-Related Mortality in Iraq from 2002 to 2006." *The New England Journal of Medicine* 358, no. 5: 484–93.

Le Billon, Philippe. 2004. "The Geopolitical Economy of 'Resources Wars'." *Geopolitics* 9, no. 1: 1–28.

Lenain, Patrick, Marcos Bonturi, and Vincent Koen. 2002. *The Economic Consequences of Terrorism.* Economic Department Working Paper 334. Paris: OECD.

Mampilly, Zachariah. 2011. *Rebel Rulers: Insurgent Governance and Civilian Life During War.* New York: Cornell University Press.

National Intelligence Council. 2007. "Nonstate Actors: Impact of International Relations and Implications for the United States." 12/4/2020. https://www.dni.gov/files/documents/nonstate_actors_2007.pdf.

Obama, Barack. 2013. "Remarks by the President at the National Defense University." *The White House.* 12/4/2020. https://obamawhitehouse.archives.gov/the-press-office/2013/05/23/remarks-president-national-defense-university.

Pinaud, Clémence. 2014. "South Sudan: Civil War, Predation and the Making of a Military Aristocracy." *African Affairs* 113, no. 451 (April): 192–211.

République française. 1962. "Les accords d'Évian du 18 mars 1962." *Université Laval.* 12/4/2020. http://www.axl.cefan.ulaval.ca/afrique/algerie-accords_d'Evian.htm.

Richani, Nazih. 1997. "The Political Economy of Violence: The War-System in Colombia." *Journal of Interamerican Studies and World Affairs* 39, no. 2 (Summer): 37–81.

Sarkees, Meredith Reid. 2007. "The COW Typology of War." *The Correlates of War Project.* 12/4/2020. http://www.correlatesofwar.org/data-sets/COW-war/the-cow-typology-of-war-defining-and-categorizing-wars/view.

Sénat. 2015. "Les messages du Président de la République au Parlement. " *République française.* 12/4/2020. https://www.senat.fr/evenement/archives/D46/hollande.html.

Sipri. 2017. "Trends in International Arms Transfers, 2017." *Stockholm International Peace Research Institute.* 12/4/2020. https://www.sipri.org/publications/2018/sipri-fact-sheets/trends-international-arms-transfers-2017.

Statista. 2020. "Global Terrorism Index 2019: 50 Countries." *Statista.* 12/4/2020. https://www.statista.com/statistics/271514/global-terrorism-index/.

Tilly, Charles. 1975. "Reflections on the History of European State-Making." In *The Formation of National States in Western Europe*, edited by Charles Tilly, 3–83. Princeton: Princeton University Press.

Walzer, Michael. 2015. *Just and Unjust Wars: A Moral Argument with Historical Illustrations.* New York: Basic Books. 1st English edition 1977.

Watson Institute. 2019. "Costs of War." *Brown University.* 12/4/2020. https://watson.brown.edu/costsofwar/.

Wimmer, Andreas. 2013. *Waves of War: Nationalism, State Formation, and Ethnic Exclusion in the Modern World.* Cambridge: Cambridge University Press.

Chapter 2

War Economies and War Economics

Christopher Cramer

What we think a war economy is, where it comes from, what its longer-term implications are—these depend on the kind of economic analysis applied. There is a spectrum of perspectives on war economies. From one end, a clear view reveals a panorama of utter devastation. From the other, change and regeneration out of the charred stumps of violent conflict come into view as well.

The differences between these perspectives are of more than intellectual interest. They matter not only for how most accurately we understand the features and dynamics of war economies, historically and nowadays, but also for the policies advocated to prevent violent conflicts and for those promoted to stabilize postwar economies and to encourage longer-term postwar recovery, reconstruction, and development.

In this chapter, I trace the key differences between these economic perspectives on war economies and highlight their significance. I also try to put these views within some historical context, showing how the fortunes of different ideas have shifted over time. Perhaps the neatest example of this is how economic historians have thought about the American Civil War. A long and complex debate has veered between the view of the Beards (Beard and Beard 1927) and later summarized by Hacker (1940: 373) that the war's "striking achievement was the triumph of industrial capitalism," to the view that late nineteenth-century U.S. economic expansion evolved *despite* the civil war, or even that, in Cochran's (1961) view, the war positively slowed industrial expansion.[1]

The angle of the latter view is that of neoclassical economics. It took shape long ago in what came to be called the liberal interpretation of war. That interpretation, one that claims that all war is negative in all its effects, continues to generate a rich form of analysis of the *costs of war* (and other forms of violence). But it is also linked (especially since the Cold War) to rational choice, neoclassical economic *explanations* of war. The first view—at its extremes a Heraclitan argument that "war is the father of everything"—encompasses a range of approaches: those that argue that war may create conditions that underpin longer-term economic development and structural change; and those that focus more on the technical and distributional implications of how resources are mobilized to sustain war—they range from the Marxist to the Keynesian. In between the two sharp angles, the light thrown on war economies leads to combinations of assumptions and analyses.

Along another axis, there are different shifts in perspective on war economies. For some, the most appropriate or even only relevant view is that of the local dimensions—the interaction of economic actors within the most immediate locus of violent conflict, in South Sudan or Syria, in eastern DRC or in Colombia. But for others, this is only a part of the picture, whose whole frame includes a broader, global set of interactions, including the ramifications of global trade in commodities and international financial flows. From one viewpoint, the appropriate unit of analysis is the nation (failed) state. Methodological nationalism like this is underpinned by large datasets like the Correlates of War or the Uppsala Conflict Data Programme (UCDP). These enable statistical analyses of patterns of war onset, longevity and so on. But from a radically different stance, playing havoc with the coding rules of large-N datasets, it has been argued that we all live, in the early twenty-first century, in a single, global civil war, in which war has been raised to an ontological level. A global civil war means a global war economy.[2]

Below I summarize the liberal interpretation of war. I trace development from its original version, which focused on the *effects* of war and war economies, to its kindred, the application of rational choice neoclassical economic analysis to assessing the features of war economies and the economic *causes* of war. Next, I look at analyses that claim to offer a more complex and mixed analysis of war economies. If the neoclassical economics of war emphasizes incentives faced by individuals, other economic approaches emphasize relations between groups and they focus more on institutional change and the distributional consequences of different policies to mobilize for and reproduce war. I draw briefly on case study material from Mozambique, Afghanistan, and El Salvador.

As well as drawing out the main features of different approaches to war economics, this chapter hopes to show the continued relevance of war economies and war economics in three areas. The literature on conflict prevention depends on ways of thinking about war economies. Mostly, this literature has been shaped by cost of war economics. It has been poor at accommodating more heterodox and interdisciplinary political economy. Postwar reconstruction—and war to peace transition—literature has also increasingly recognized the relevance of war economies and war economics after and beyond wars themselves. The varied ways in which societies and governments (with and without international support) have paid for peace, produced peace, and worked for peace are still under-researched. And war economies, and war economics, are also central to understanding the global interdependencies between societies that are fuelled by and regulated by violence.

The chapter separates out strands of economic thinking about war and war economies, but should not be taken to imply that all economists neatly fit just one of these types. Just as war economies typically involve combinations of the factors highlighted by different economists, so economists working within particular traditions are not always bound by a single idea or line of analysis.

THE UNDOING PROJECT:[3] THE LIBERAL INTERPRETATION OF WAR

Perhaps the longest-running economic analysis of wars has held that, and quantified the extent to which, war is always negative in all its consequences. What Milward (1984) called the classical liberal interpretation of war led to the concentration of economists' efforts on enumerating the costs of war. Such an approach had—still has—several uses. It helps in assessing the likely cost of reconstruction after a war. It helps in showing how the economic cost of war rises far above the relatively straightforward costing of direct war damage (to bridges, roads, health posts, ports, roads, schools, housing stock). It helps in building arguments against war and in favor of conflict prevention (since it may readily be argued that the cost of prevention is very low compared to the likely direct and indirect cost of any war).[4]

From assessments of the cost of the First World War, through Goldin and Lewis (1975, 1978) estimating the cost of the American Civil War and a number of exercises to pin down the cost of U.S. intervention in wars in Central America and southern Africa during the Cold War (Greene 1994; Stewart 1993), to the Bilmes and Stiglitz (2008) estimate of a $3 trillion (and rising) war waged by the United States in Iraq and Afghanistan, cost of war exercises have formalized and extended Samuel Johnson's argument in 1749 that "Reason frowns on War's unequal Game/Where wasted Nations raise a single Name/And mortgag'd States their Grandsires Wreaths regret/From Age to Age in everlasting Debt."[5]

War has often spurred shifts within economics. In trying to sum up aggregate estimates of the cost of the First World War, for example, economists tried to weigh the comparative cost to the United Kingdom and to other countries, including Germany. One basis for doing this might involve weighing up the difference in lost economic contribution for a British versus a German casualty and this led economists to develop the notion of human capital. A dead American soldier "was a much greater loss to the economy than a dead Serbian solder, since not only was he a piece of human capital who had been much more expensive to educate and train to the moment of his death, but his subsequent productive capacity, had he not died, would have been much greater" (Milward 1984: 12/13).

It is precisely where wars, by this kind of measure, are "cheap" that some economists came to think the statistical probability of "civil wars" is highest. Reason, here, would lead richer countries, in particular richer individuals, to realize the high opportunity cost of war and to choose to avoid war. And reason, the pursuit of individual self-interest and utility maximization through rational choice, may in low-income countries crack a smile on war's game. This was a big shift and one that came for a while to have a substantial influence on thinking in aid agencies and international financial institutions about civil war or internal wars in developing countries after the end of the Cold War. Rather than just assessing the effects or cost of war, this approach looked closer at the agency of destruction: a war economy was to be seen through the micro-economics of individual material choices to indulge in violence and to loot. The next step was to see a war economy as a set of "revealed preferences" that indicated the source, origin, and opportunity for or indeed cause of wars.

This was also another way in which war pushed the boundaries of economics. One of the leading economists shaping this "economic perspective" on war (and later on terrorism) was Jack Hirshleifer. An unapologetic (and witty) advocate of "economics imperialism," the view that rational choice economic theory is a superior social science that can explain all social phenomena, Hirshleifer developed his wider ideas through modelling conflict. He argued (Hirshleifer 1994) that economists had gone soft, focusing exclusively on "the way of Coase" (where economic agents would not willingly pass up opportunities to cooperate and to manage transaction costs) and forgetting the "way of Macchiavelli" (where actors would not willingly pass up the chance to exploit and extort one another). Reintroducing "the dark side of the force" by applying economic analysis to war and other conflicts would make economics whole. Landing on the unexplored terrain of conflict, economists would discover backward tribes (anthropologists, sociologists, etc.) and would need to educate them. They would find some of these folks rather bright but in such cases they inchoate economists.

And one of the key things involved in doing economics is applying the concept of opportunity cost. This led Hirshliefer to argue that effectively the poor have a comparative advantage in violence. With little invested in their "human capital," they would have few economic opportunities and little prospect of earning significant returns on their meagre outlays on education and health. So the prospect of earning a buck on the back of a rebellion or counterinsurgency recruitment drive may be appealing, even rational. It took others to try to put some empirical flesh on the theoretical bones of this approach. One of the more influential for a while was Collier, whose string of models (1999, 2000, 2004, 2009, etc.), combined with a post as head of the World Bank's research department, helped make the idea widely known. And at its most basic, the idea was that individual greed was a better predictor of civil war than social grievance. Grievances are real and widespread, but they do not clear the market because of the presence of collective action problems. Only where recruitment costs for rebellion are low, and the opportunity costs of violence low, perhaps where the attraction of lootable resources and goods is also strong, will people overcome the fear of free riders and other constraints on collective action, and take up arms.

This Yahoo theory of war (Cramer 2006) spawned a debate and a substantial critical literature.[6] Much of the criticism came from precisely the backward tribes Hirshleifer predicted economists would need to educate, and they proved more resilient and sophisticated, dare one say civilized, than anticipated (Wood 2003; Gutiérrez-Sanin 2009; Nathan 2003). But the criticism also came from political economists (Cramer 2002, 2006). Horror of horrors, mainstream economists eventually ripped into at least the cruder versions of this approach. Part of the Deaton report, an assessment of research carried out at the World Bank between 1999 and 2005, focused on the work on conflict and rated it very poorly (Acemoglu 2005): the work regressed endogenous variables on endogenous variables, failed in Acemoglu's view to incorporate any theoretical advances in economics during the previous twenty-five years, and came to conclusions unsupported by the evidence presented.

Some highlighted the failure of neoclassical economic approaches to take seriously enough the "noneconomic," for example, the possibility that people may engage in collective violent action despite its likely high costs and often low returns, despite evidence that many people joining insurgencies were previously employed and even at above average wages, and that they may do so driven by socially shaped norms and values. One unusual piece of research with much wider plausibility showed how elites (not the poor) participated directly in and led civil war violence in Colombia (Gutiérrez-Sanin 2017). Others challenged the theoretical grounds and the evidence used or argued, as did Acemoglu, that often these models performed poorly empirically. The World Bank, which had celebrated these crude neoclassical models in its "Breaking the Conflict Trap" (Collier 2003) report, increasingly distanced itself from such an approach. In the *World Development Report 2012* (on violence) and that of 2017 (on governance), flagship Bank reports revived the significance of social and political grievances in the causation of conflict.

And the 2018 *Pathways to Peace* (UN/World Bank 2018: 109) emphatically notes that many of "today's conflicts relate to group-based grievances," drawing on literature including Cederman et al. (2013) and Stewart (2011) as well as drawing on a wider disciplinary base.

If homo economicus was badly wounded in these intellectual skirmishes, the creature survived and came to be rehabilitated, no longer quite the clunky avatar of 1990s economics imperialism but an upgraded version. The new model "representative agent" was sent out to account for terrorism, and it seemed to correct for a number of bugs. In many versions of the "economic perspective" on terrorism, homo economicus was now a more social creature, took norms and even religious values seriously, maximized utility through social bonds, and was overall a more rounded psychological being.[7] On the one hand, the economic approach to terrorism represented a more advanced economics that acknowledged some criticisms and adapted to take account of insights from other sciences (a more even relationship than for Hirshleifer's economics conquistadores) while remaining fundamentally a neoclassical economic approach; on the other hand, at best, the analysis was no longer strictly speaking economics." At worst, critics suggested the model still could not fully account for terrorist activity as it remained too attached to its fundamental assumptions (Cramer 2010).

The economic explanation of civil wars took inspiration from the same classical liberal interpretation of war that has underpinned cost of war exercises. It also drew on the equally old ideas of the liberal theory of peace. The World Bank's (2003) statement that "war is development in reverse," that "war retards development and development retards war," captured perfectly the stew of ideas that lay behind the "invention of peace" (Howard 2000). A war economy, this view suggested, was an unravelling, an undoing of "development." First, the violence of war causes destruction of physical capital stock and human capital losses. Second, it erodes the efficiency of public spending (rerouting spending to violence rather than production), weakens property rights, and raises transaction and contract enforcement costs (Collier 1999). Third, people respond to a worsening economic environment by dis-saving, and they engage in portfolio substitution—above all, there is flight of capital and labor out of the country: an "exodus of factor endowments" (Collier 1999: 170). Feeding expected changes in factor endowments into a standard Cobb-Douglas function, the go-to (but contested) basis for neoclassical economic growth and productivity analysis, leads to an expectation of weaker returns.

Brück's (1997) analysis of the Mozambican war economy constructs a neoclassical growth model in which, among other assumptions, there are perfectly competitive markets and war acts as an exogenous shock, and then maps the model onto an economy for which war economy effects are captured through a range of proxies, "due to the deficiencies of the data in Mozambique" (Brück 1997: 35). One may be skeptical about an analysis combining an unrealistic (if mathematically tractable) model with very poor evidence. But the analysis tried to draw on what data it could and generated some interesting impressions. One of these, to which we return later, is the idea of a retreat into subsistence. Many people were forced into "extreme forms of self-reliance"; subsistence agriculture was an "enforced alternative for previously fortunate producers of cash crops, a deliberate choice of survival activity for some peasants, and an unattainable means of survival" for others (Brück 1997: 38). The outcome of a war shock may in rural areas involve an unravelling of Adam Smith's evolution of the extent of the market and the division of labor. "The war induced isolation of households in rural Mozambique implied that most households were nearly self-sufficient in most commodities" (Brück 2004: 7).

This kind of analysis then easily supports the idea that a postwar economy is rendered by war a "blank slate" institutional vacuum.[8] That has in the past been convenient as a launch for arguments in favor of radical and rapid economic reform in the wake of peace settlements, to take advantage of a presumed "institutional vacuum" (see below).

TRANSFORMERS: WAR ECONOMIES AND SOCIOECONOMIC CHANGE

For neoclassical economics, war economies typically depart from optimal (competitive market) conditions: war " distorts" prices, raises barriers to entry, stretches risks and returns, and interrupts the flow of information. Since economic development from this perspective involves moving closer to perfectly competitive market conditions (with full and evenly available information) by "getting prices right," naturally, war economies are anti-developmental, development in reverse. If some individuals do well out of war, they are profiteers—especially traders who take advantage of shortages and interrupted (high-risk) supply routes and raise their profit margins. A profiteer is a special class of rentier, capturing the profits over and above what would be possible in a (hypothetical) perfectly competitive market.

A different approach eschews methodological individualism and rational choice economics. A richer political economy may be less amenable to formal modelling, but it is also less beholden to restrictive assumptions and misleadingly limited axioms of behavior. What is common to many other approaches is the observation of war economies as transformative, not merely destructive.

These other approaches may more clearly distinguish, for example, between the combat, shadow, and coping or survival economies and the way that interaction among these dimensions of a wartime economy may change "actually existing development, leading to the transformation of social and economic relations" (Goodhand 2004: 155). Goodhand's analysis draws on field research in Afghanistan. He argues that wars have always been the "defining moments of change" in the protracted, ongoing, and unsettled relationship between the central state, such as it has been, and peripheries. Afghan wars have also tended to "empower borderlands," reproducing over time a fraught and contested process of state formation, interrupted. The combat economy includes the activities around the production and reproduction of violent conflict: both destructive activity and active mobilization of resources. But there are also entrepreneurs who are not immediately part of the combat economy but who trade (literally) on the limited reach of state regulation and the market conditions created by armed conflict. Then there is the coping and surviving economy where people either just about hold onto their asset base and income levels or survive but only be depleting their assets (e.g., by distress sales of land or livestock). The distinctions between the parts of Goodhand's war economy are in reality blurred and the combat economy is likely only to be reproducible so long as the other dimensions do not break down.

In Afghanistan, opium has become a significant part of these overlapping dimensions of the war economy. Rather than reading back from a resource with high rents derived from illegality and deriving a revealed preference that somehow explains the cause of war, close observers of Afghanistan emphasize how conflict encouraged the narco-economy. Indeed, the opium economy has at various times helped underpin political stability in Afghanistan, whereas eradication programs have done more to fuel conflict (Goodhand 2008; Mansfield 2016). Opium production under wartime conditions is a good illustration of how war economies involve socioeconomic change as much as simple destruction and loss. For the cultivation (and processing, trade, and logistics) of opium, poppy has accelerated socioeconomic differentiation in rural areas, as some lease out land to opium producers and accumulate on the back of initial land and capital assets, while others are pushed further into debt and/or wage employment.

As with the opium economy and other parts of the Afghan war economy, a kind of "indigenous capitalism" evolved in the "central margins" of the eastern DRC war economy (Raeymaekers 2014). It evolved over a long time before the wars of the 1990s and 2000s, during Mobutu's rule of Zaire, but took new shape during war—though arguably the distinction between "war" economy and the economy of Mobutu's Zaire is a very weak one. In eastern Congo, during the 1990s, new forms of governance evolved: Peace—of sorts—did not unravel wartime accumulation patterns and networks but led to their integration into formal domains of state power.

Wood's (2003) fieldwork in El Salvador also led to an emphasis on transformation, but at the same time stressed the variations in the forms this took across different rural research sites. In many parts of El Salvador, this involved a reconfiguration of land ownership—through wartime occupation of estates by *campesinos*—and production. But it also involved completely new forms of participation in political life that had been impossible before. "Thus de facto agrarian property rights, land use and civil society had been transformed in some areas. Yet in other areas, continuity rather than change was the dominant pattern" (Wood 2003: 52).

And research on Mozambique's war economy also shows that there was far more to it than a retreat into subsistence, development in reverse, or the creation of a vacuum. Indeed, the evidence suggests that war accelerated socioeconomic differentiation and created new patterns of accumulation, the very features that historically have been central to capitalist development. "Far from retreating into a subsistence economy, therefore, the war and crisis heightened the need for the poorer peasantry to sell their labour to obtain cash to buy food and other rural wage goods" (Wuyts 2003: 147). And a range of actors—state farms, the odd multinational hanging onto land through war, and emerging private landholders (wartime accumulators)—mobilized resources to meet demand. As one researcher put it: "the war resolved their labour recruitment problems" (O'Laughlin 1996: 32). The dynamics of war, proletarianization, and accumulation in Mozambique, as in Afghanistan, the eastern DRC, and elsewhere, had a regional dimension. Many rural Mozambicans fled from violence across the border into South Africa, among them many women who, as illegal immigrants, ended up a conveniently docile source of wage labor in large, high-value agricultural exporting firms in the northeast of South Africa.[9]

And as in rural Mozambique, so in Nepal, the transformations of a war economy had significant gendered effects.[10] Menon and Rodgers (2015) found that war increased the likelihood that Nepalese women would enter wage labor markets. Here, the destructive side of war—the "weakening of social fabric" as households struggled to survive—and the structurally transformative, women's entry into wage employment are very clearly and directly bound together.[11]

There is no linear, law-like trajectory of outcomes from war economies. The combination of shifting and varied reallocation of violence rights, the varying ability of particular organizations to effectively mobilize resources to war ends (and even a varying interest in doing so), the varied interactions between prewar patterns of development and accumulation and wartime possibilities, the interactions between utter destruction, organizational change, technical and institutional change, and new or accelerated trajectories of accumulation: all these and other variables influence outcomes. The binary opposition between war as state-making (Tilly 1992) and war as utterly destructive is too stark.[12] In between is a realm of unclear outcomes. There is no knowing what the political and economic consequences of the huge Syrian, regional and global trade in the illicit drug captagon will be, for example, though one analysis suggests the dynamics are both destructive and at the same time reproductive of the organization of power and political economy in Syria (Dent 2017).

If war economies in developing countries do not follow uniform trajectories, the same is true of war economies in advanced capitalist economies with strong states. In the Second World War, very different societies—the United Kingdom and the United States, Germany, the Soviet Union—converged on forms of *économie mobilisée* with a large role for planning. But they did so to varying degrees of commitment and with large variations in effectiveness. During the war, for example, the prevailing idea in the United Kingdom was that the German state was running a "total war" economy. It turned out, when the Allies later carried out detailed research into why Germany had lost the war, that the German war economy fell far short of its "war potential": "the picture of the German war effort which dominated Allied imagination was very largely a false one" (Kaldor 1945–46: 33). Everything was on paper controlled, but in reality controls were clumsy; there were too many conflicts between parts of government, few clear distinctions between responsibilities of different agencies, and a strong tendency for the politicization of policy by the Nazi party.

Meanwhile, war often also plays havoc with commitments to liberal ideology—as it does with other ideologies. So in the Second World War, the Soviet Union withdrew from purist commitment to central planning and in some cases actively encouraged free markets, while in the United Kingdom there was a shift toward centralized control of food production and trade.

It is misleading to claim that wars between advanced countries may lead to some forms of economic development but that wars within developing countries only lead to development in reverse. It may also be misleading to imagine that "state" war economies are categorically different from "non-state" war economies. This means there is a connection between, for example, the transformations through war economies in El Salvador or Mozambique and the shifts in business practice through war economies in, for instance, the United Kingdom during the First and Second World Wars. There are compelling reasons to believe that the United Kingdom adopted a far more "corporatist" embrace of big business and a closer link between the state and capitalist firms through the experiences of war in the twentieth century.[13] But there were deeper shifts in British political economy through war too. For example, although Churchill had been reluctant early on in the Second World War to interfere with people's freedoms, the government quickly realized it had to—both to preserve the war effort and to ensure the legitimacy of that war effort, through a (relatively) egalitarian food rationing system (Collingham 2012). "No one would want to sing the praises of war" (Cairncross 1995). "But it has its uses . . . Above all, it [the Second World War in the United Kingdom] demonstrated to the satisfaction of everyone, except possibly Professor von Hayek, that in some circumstances market forces simply will not do the trick or will not do it fast enough, and have to give way, as they do in the individual enterprise, to managerial direction and coordination" (Cairncross 1995: 36). The transformations within low-income developing economy civil war economies are different. But across the range, war can clearly wreak deep structural changes. These changes may unfold within the formal, state mobilization of economies for war (in Ethiopia or apartheid South Africa, for example) and within the "non-state" war economies of parts of Afghanistan or El Salvador.

WAR ECONOMIES BEYOND WARS: CONFLICT PREVENTION, POST-CONFLICT RECONSTRUCTION, AND GLOBAL POLITICAL ECONOMIES OF VIOLENCE

The study of war economies extends in three main directions beyond the economies of specific countries at war. War economics has been drafted into thinking about conflict prevention. How we understand war economies affects planning for postwar reconstruction and development. And the closer we look at war economies, the more difficult it is to restrict the analysis to the parameters of discrete nation-states. The differences between analytical approaches to war economies play out unevenly across these three fields. Neoclassical economic, and broadly liberal interpretation of war, perspectives have held sway over the conflict prevention literature and have tended to have a stronger influence on the policy world concerned with postconflict transitions, though the broader research literature on these transitions is more varied and pluralist. By contrast, the more non-mainstream perspectives have tended to lead the literature on, first, the regional dimensions of violent conflicts and, then, the broader global political economy of violence.

Conflict Prevention

Brück et al. (2012: 252) are quite wrong to claim that the "estimation of the economic costs of conflict is a relatively new field of research." This approach is more than a century in the making and has been an important, for a long time perhaps the main, way of thinking about the economics of wartime. But war costing has evolved. It has become increasingly refined and sensitive to a greater range of direct and indirect, at times difficult to measure, costs. One example is Plümper and Neumayer's (2006) estimate that the greater cost of war is borne by women, based on the way that the gender gap in life expectancy shrinks or is reversed during and after many "civil" wars.

Estimating the economic costs of violent conflict has long been central to anti-war arguments. During the latter part of the Cold War, cost of war exercises formed an important part of a growing criticism of international stoking of violent conflict in lower-income countries (Green 1994; Fitzgerald 1987; Hanlon 1986). More recently, war costing has become a key component of arguments in favor of greater resource allocation to conflict prevention. The conflict prevention literature almost entirely ignores the "transformative" political economy of conflict.

A succession of attempts have been made since the end of the Cold War to shore up the case for conflict prevention on specifically economic grounds. They argue that spending money to prevent large-scale violence is an economy; it is far cheaper than the huge costs of warfare. The back of the envelope idea that an ounce of prevention is worth a pound of cure evolved into the more precise (though it was false precision) idea that each pound (sterling) spent on prevention by the U.K. government would save £4 on the costs of conflict resolution and peacebuilding that would be incurred by having to intervene in distant wars (Chalmers 2007). The "Spending to Save" methodology combined a model of the probability of violent conflict with a somewhat sketchy idea of the possible costs of wars and intervening in them. The predictive conflict model was based on the Collier approach to the causes of (or correlates of) civil war that, as discussed above, has come to be rejected by many people. The analysis largely dismissed the counterfactual problem—if money is spent on conflict prevention and there is no war, how can we be sure that the prevention is why there was no war?—that has dogged the conflict prevention literature (Brown and Rosecrance 1999; Cramer 2010).[14] Neither the counterfactual problem nor the fundamental methodological difficulties have prevented the case being made in largely the same way over time. The most recent illustration is the joint UN and World Bank "Pathways to Peace" report, for whose authors the Carnegie Commission report (1997), Brown and Rosecrance (1999), the U.K. "Spending to Save" report (Chalmers 2007) and others provides "evidence that the prevention of violent conflict is associated with enormous returns in terms of cost avoidance" (UN/World Bank 2018: 2).

The methodological problems of cost of war estimates are legion and have been elaborated since the early twentieth century. They typically require heroic leaps to overcome the debilitating lack of reliable data. Distributional arguments typically make sweeping generalizations (retreat into subsistence, etc.). Counterfactual projections are made about the trajectory of political economies had they not experienced violent conflict. These and other problems apply in different ways to whatever approach is taken to assessing the costs of war. There is, as Hillier (2007) noted, "no standardised methodology to calculate the cost of conflict." The more sophisticated approaches acknowledge the implications of the profound uncertainty affecting all methods: "When we take into account the fundamental uncertainty associated with models of growth, we are unable to draw clear conclusions" (Imai and Weinstein 2000: 20).

These cost of war and cost-effectiveness of conflict prevention exercises all indulge in a very poor form of cost-benefit analysis. They completely ignore the possibility of what Gutiérrez-Sanin (2009) calls "anti-intuitive externalities." "The theoretical possibility that the benefits of war may outweigh the costs must still inform our analysis of the costs of violence" (Gutiérrez-Sanin 2009: 22). To do that would involve drawing on the large recent research literature on the complex political economies of war across a range of countries. Neither Pathways to Peace, nor the earlier big conflict prevention reports, pays adequate attention to this literature.

Post-Conflict Reconstruction

For the UN and World Bank jointly to point out that "economic development alone is not a guarantee of peace" (UN/World Bank 2018: 1), that (p. 8) group-based "grievances . . . are an important precursor to collective mobilization to violence," and that these grievances, "arising from inequality, exclusion and feelings of injustice" (p. 109) need to be tackled head-on represents an important shift. Elsewhere, an evaluation of World Bank operations in situations affected by violence captured the growing awareness in the "development community" that violent conflict is not simply a feature and function of low-income status, since organized violence incidence in middle-income countries has come to exceed that in low-income countries (World Bank 2016). Economic growth and development may not only have weak prophylactic powers against violence, but also it is difficult to avoid the idea that some forms of development may be active ingredients in the causal swirl generating violent conflict. The idea that war retards development and that development retards war had become a rhetorical commonplace in the 2000s. The rhetoric has a puncture now, but the idea is not yet quite reduced to the historical curiosity that Albert Hirschman thought it was when he wrote *The Passions and the Interests*.

For the underlying idea that capitalist development is a powerful force for enduring peace has continued to be hugely influential in global policy interventions during war to peace transitions. The influence crystallized into the "liberal peace thesis." Again drawing on very old ideas (Howard 2000) and reviving them in very new ways, this thesis pulls together an array of intellectual ideas, political interests, and development agency practices with the common threads suggesting that democracy (political liberalization), security sector reform (liberal governance, accountability, and transparency), and economic liberalization (privatization, market deregulation, trade and financial market liberalization) would each and jointly underpin lasting peace. From this perspective, Collier et al. (2008) could argue that a rapid rate of economic growth (presumed to follow from a package of "good policy") was the single most important variable affecting the statistical likelihood of a return to war within a few years of the signing of a peace agreement. The statistical claim was supported by a hunch that growth would "work" through the employment mechanism, raising the costs of recruitment for potential rebels. War economics influenced post-conflict reconstruction thinking in two main ways. First, the cost of war approach formed a basis for assessing the reconstruction bill and identifying postwar needs. Second, the neoclassical economics of war economies stressed the damage and undoing done by war and highlighted the role in this of exaggerated market imperfections. War had made prices even more "wrong" than they are typically reckoned to be in low-income economies. Hence the case for a particularly determined effort to free up markets in the interests of rapid movement toward "getting prices right." As Collier and Pradhan (1994: 133) put it: "The period of transition to peace is a particularly suitable time for radical policy reform."

From this perspective, a huge number of interventions were launched and programs of policy advice promoted, all encouraging market liberalization in the cause of growth and peace. At their most gung-ho, these drew on arguments that conflict produced a blank slate on which it would be easier to sketch out radical market reforms because of an "institutional vacuum" (Haughton 1998).

But the broader political economy of war began to filter into development agencies. So too did a creeping awareness of the limitations of all-out economic liberalization as a base for economic development, let alone lasting peace. "Since economic growth and large-scale aid are not necessary preconditions for post-war peace, aid strategies that prioritize economic growth in the post-war decade may well be inappropriate if the primary objective is to stabilize and sustain the peace" (Suhrke and Buckmaster 2005: 22). Meanwhile, there was a broader shift away from the extremes of the Washington Consensus.[15] In its place came a greater commitment to the quest for "inclusive" postwar development rather than the "narrow" development encouraged before (Addison et al. 2001; Stewart 2005).

At the fringes of international financial institution and development agency thinking, there was also some greater attention to the work on war to peace transitions and the way that the characteristics of war economies carry over into peace economies (Cramer 2005; Goodhand 2004). Criminalized war economies often become criminalized peace economies. Pugh (2005) details this for Bosnia. SIGAR (2016) highlights the astonishing corrupt capture of U.S. reconstruction efforts in Afghanistan. The difficulty is that donors have not yet found effective and coherent ways of reconciling peace and patronage (Smoke and Talercio 2007).

Linking the concerns of recent work on the political economy of war to peace transitions to the developments within economics during wartime in advanced industrialized societies, it is possible to take inspiration from Keynes. Keynes (1940) and Kaldor (see King 2007), among others, understood the U.K. war economy during the Second World War as a challenge to do more than merely find the simplest way to finance the war effort. First, partly for reasons of political legitimacy, it was important to find a distributionally progressive way to pay for the war. Second, they both understood that the productive energies of mobilizing for war might be turned to create longer-term economic advantages. Keynes (1940: iii) sought to "snatch from the exigency of war positive social improvements." For example, forced savings imposed on wartime factory workers might generate social welfare payments after the war. There have been other ways too, in which wartime labor has been repaid with peace dividends that have helped to assuage postwar political instability, for example, through the U.S. GI Bill. Of course, contexts differ, but this experience of advanced capitalist war economies (and war economics) may be relevant to the analysis of and policy thinking about war, and war to peace transitions, in lower-income war-affected economies.

Drawing on this intellectual and policy history, there is a triple policy problem for postwar reconstruction and development: how to pay for the peace (which, at the same time, is a question of who ends up paying for peace, how the cost of peace is distributed); how to produce peace; and how to work for peace.[16] The question is how to encourage production that helps pay for peace, by generating foreign exchange and tax revenues; and how to encourage production that draws in labor to higher productivity and better-remunerated work. These are not technical but deeply political challenges. For example, policy officials would want to attract savings accumulated during war into investment in activities that generate employment, foreign exchange, and fiscal contributions. That is likely to involve doing deals to manage the politics of a postwar centralization and reallocation of violence rights while asserting some authority over property rights and income streams. Boyce and O'Donnell (2007) are among the very few who have addressed some of these issues directly, emphasizing the importance of fiscal settlements in war to peace transitions and mindful of the carry-over of war economies into peacetime. Such an approach also raises the question of how to find ways to mobilize resources—for reconstruction and development—from the gains of global war "profiteers."

Beyond Methodological Nationalism: Inside Out and Outside In

Different approaches to the economics of war economies converge on the realization that war economy dynamics cannot be contained within nation-state borders. Borders and borderlands, indeed, are often exactly where the political economies of war unfold in most intriguing ways (Goodhand 2005). The "relatively invisible . . . ultra-mobile" (Collier 1994) forms in which wartime accumulators may prefer to hold wealth are commonly spirited across borders: war wealth then either pays for imported means of violence and other goods needed to reproduce war or it is stored overseas. One of the first signs of recognition in the post–Cold War economy economics was the emergence of the idea of "regional conflict complexes." This then broadened to the international market and institutional features of "conflict commodities." In an analysis based on a decade or more of humanitarian practice and academic research in DRC, Seymour (forthcoming) argues that we "can no longer deny our interconnection to lives lived and violence experienced in the DRC" because of the violent regulation of production of so many materials used in everyday consumption—cobalt, columbine tantalite, and more.

Analysis of the cross-border idiosyncrasies of war economies and the spillovers—of refugees, goods, capital, arms, and violence—may be seen as the "inside out" perspective on the regionalization and broader internationalization of war economies. A different perspective is more "outside in" and focuses on the global political economy of war, conflict management, and security. The concerns here range from the implications of global efforts to arrogate violence rights to a specific set of actors, to the huge array of interests thriving on global military expenditure. Global interests and institutions are not so much noises off as a fundamental element of the reproduction of war economies. Dent (2017), for example, suggests that Swiss banking regulations allow for a globalized set of transactions facilitating the circulation of capital and reproduction of power in Syria, partly through the financing of (and investments out of profits from) the captagon trade. Another "outside in" example might be the intersection of the U.S. opioid epidemic, North American porous borders, the Global War on Terror, and the Afghan opium trade. In a presentation in London, the Special Inspector General for Afghan Reconstruction (SIGAR), John Sopko, spoke of how an estimated 1–2 percent of opium consumed in the United States comes directly from Afghanistan; but an estimated 80 percent of opium entering Canada comes from Afghanistan, and there is a "pretty porous border" between Canada and the United States.[17]

It may deprive the field of analytical traction to think of the United States/Canada border as a war economy borderland (an extension of the porous borders immediately surrounding Afghanistan) or to reach for ideas like that of a "global civil war." But it is important to identify the global ramifications (inside out) of violent conflicts concentrated in Afghanistan, Colombia, the DRC, or Syria and the international political and material interests in advanced economies (outside in) that both reproduce and regulate violent conflict around the world. War economies are globalized. And "violent conflict is an integral part of the world economic structure" (UN/World Bank 2018: 33). Work at this level nicely brings together some of the strands that at times seem set against one another in war economics. Thus, some of the formal analysis of neoclassical war economics can help identify some of the features of markets and commodities that tend to characterize war economies and their regional and international spillovers. Cost of war exercises increasingly look not just at the costs within a specific country and during the obvious coding-rule parameters of "civil war onset" and formal victory or peace settlement but also at regional costs, longer-term costs to health and education and economic development, and at international costs of intervention, conflict resolution, and peacebuilding. And the more extended versions of cost of war accounting start to merge also with the perspectives of political economy to identify not only the costs but also the transformative dimensions of conflicts, the ways that war economies can shift the structure and relations of production and material interests.

War economies can reorder as well as undo societies, political orders, and dynamics of economic change. A globalized war economy also breaks down in yet another way the distinction between rich and poor country war economy analysis (and that between state and non-state war economies). A sharp example is Bilmes's (2017) idea of the U.S. "credit card wars."[18] This analysis goes far beyond the sheer immensity of U.S. war expenditure. It has echoes of earlier anxieties about a "permanent war economy" (Melman 1985) and Eisenhower's fears of the power of the military-industrial complex. Bilmes points out that all previous U.S. wars, before 9/11 and the Global War on Terror, were financed through the budget and so involved trade-offs and committee scrutiny, as well as being at least in part funded by hikes in taxes on the wealthy. But since 9/11, the United States has fought long and hugely expensive wars globally through supplementary appropriations and through debt, while taxes on the wealthy have been reduced. Fewer and fewer Americans are actually fighting in these wars. So they are politically easy to fight: few are fighting and nobody is paying, for now. These wars fought on tick recall Keynes's (1940) criticism of the "false remedies" of paying for war by inflation or debt. Wars fought by few and on the never-never are also unaccountable. In these ways, they come to resemble more and more the features of war economies in lower-income countries. And they resemble the features of non-state war economies as much as state-mobilized war economies.

CONCLUSION

There are varieties of war economy and of war economics. War economies range from those dominated by an effective state that mobilizes resources to the war end and is strengthened by war, to those that are desperate improvisations by non-state (or delicate state) organizations, many of which are further weakened by violent conflict. This may suggest a sharp distinction between the war economy of an advanced capitalist economy (like the United States or United Kingdom in the twentieth-century world wars) and that of a low-income country (like Mozambique in the Cold War or Afghanistan in the twenty-first century). But this chapter has argued that the distinction is overdrawn and misleading. There are features that both types (archetypes even) of war economy have in common. A contest over violence rights comes to regulate markets and reorient incentives in ways that depart dramatically from the benchmarks of perfect competition conditions often dominating the minds of orthodox economists. War rents play significant roles in both, and may have longer-term consequences for patterns of accumulation. Transparency and accountability go missing in action. Most importantly, war can reorder societies, polities, and economies in lasting ways. Finally, in contemporary wars, one of the things that draws low- and middle-income war economies closer to the economies of advanced economies (with their own violence economies and interests) is the interaction between them that war produces: "violence without borders has emerged" (UN and World Bank 2018: 49).

The development of war economics also may be accelerated by paying closer attention than is normal to the differences—in assumption, method, and typical argument—between contrasting economic perspectives. I have highlighted three main approaches. Most of the time, these three varieties of war economics ignore one another. There is surely greater scope to put them in dialogue directly with each other, even to combine some of their elements, just as war economics also needs—as in this volume—to be put in dialogue with (rather than dominate) other disciplines.

NOTES

1. For an overview of the historiography of the economics of the American Civil War, see Ransom (2001).

2. The genealogy of the term *global civil war* includes the work of Carl Schmitt, as well as more recent elaborations by Agamben (2005) and Hardt and Negri (2004). Duffield (2008) sees global civil war in terms of a conflict between the insured and the uninsured, manifest in struggles around the efficacy of "containment," restricting the flow of the uninsured to the domain of the insured.

3. With due apologies to Michael Lewis (2016).

4. Chalmers (2007). For a critique of the methodology of cost of war exercises see Cramer (2010).

5. Quoted in Milward (1984: 10).

6. In Gulliver's Travels (Swift 1995), the Houyhnhnms explain to Gulliver that the fiercest fights between the hirsute creatures that the reader realizes are all too human take place when they squabble over bright shiny stones in the ground.

7. See Frey (2004); Llusa and Tavares (2007); Wintrobe (2003, 2006).

8. See Cramer (2006: 255–56).

9. See also Nordstrom (2010).

10. On the intersections of gender, war economies, and class formation in Sudan see Pinaud (2016).

11. Meanwhile, Pivovarova and Swee (2015) found that despite "the widely held view that war is detrimental to human capital formation," the data show no effect of war intensity on schooling attainment.

12. A more nuanced analysis disaggregating the pathways through which war may affect economic change, institutional change, and "ideas of the state," applied to the civil war in Yemen in the 1960s, is Rogers (2018).

13. See Coleman (2006) on ICI.

14. Let alone the possibility that preventive interventions might aggravate conflict dynamics.

15. The Washington Consensus captured the essence of the heyday of International Financial Institution policy pressure on developing countries to privatize, deregulate, and liberalize their domestic markets and their trade with the rest of the world.

16. This would be an alternative to the "triple transition" (political liberalization, market liberalization, and security sector governance reforms) summarized in Ottaway (2002).

17. John F. Sopko, during presentation "Afghanistan Reconstruction: Lessons from the USA," Chatham House, London, December 6, 2017 (https:chathamhouse.org/events/all/members-event/afghanistan-reconstruction-lessons-us-experience).

18. Bilmes (2017).

REFERENCES

Acemoglu, Daron. 1998. "Evaluation of World Bank Research." Angus Deaton (Chair), Abhijit Banerjee, Nora Lustig, and Ken Rogoff, An Evaluation of World Bank Research 2005.

Addison, Tony, and S. Mansoob Murshed. 2001. "From Conflict to Reconstruction: Reviving the Social Contract." WIDER Discussion Papers//World Institute for Development Economics (UNU-WIDER).

Agamben, Giorgio. 2005. *State of Exception*. Vol. 2. University of Chicago Press.

Azam, Jean-Paul, Paul Collier, David Bevan, Stefan Dercon, Jan Gunning, and Sanjay Pradhan. 1995. "Some Economic Consequences of the Transition from Civil War to Peace." World Bank Policy Research Working Paper No. 1392. Washington: World Bank.

Beard, Charles A., Mary R. Beard, and Vernon Louis Parrington. 1927. "The Rise of American Civilization." *International Journal of Ethics* 38 (1): 112–15.

Bilmes, Linda J. 2017. "The Credit-Card Wars: Post-9/11War Funding Policy in Historical Perspective." Statement in Congressional Briefing, "The $5.6 Trillion Price Tag of the Post-9/11 Wars and How We Will Pay for It," hosted by Senator Jack Reed, November 8th. Watson Institute International and Public Affairs, Brown University. https://watson.brown.edu/costsofwar/files/cow/imce/papers/2017/Linda%20J%20Bilmes%20_Credit%20Card%20Wars%20FINAL.pdf.

Bilmes, Linda J., and Joseph E. Stiglitz. 2008. *The Three Trillion Dollar War: The True Cost of the Iraq Conflict*. WW Norton & Company.

Boyce, James K., and Madalene O'Donnell. 2007. *Peace and the Public Purse: Economic Policies for Postwar Statebuilding*. Lynne Rienner Publishers, Incorporated.

Brown, Michael E., and Richard N. Rosecrance. 1999. "The Case for Conflict Prevention." In *The Costs of Conflict: Prevention and Cure in the Global Arena*, edited by Rosecrance, R.E., Brown, M.E., Talentino, A.K., Blakley, M., de Nevers, R., and Thayer, B. Lanham, ML: Rowman & Littlefield, 221–32.

Brück, Tilman. 1997. "Macroeconomic Effects of the War in Mozambique." SSRN Scholarly Paper ID 259490. Rochester, NY: Social Science Research Network. https://papers.ssrn.com/abstract=259490.

———. 2004. "The Welfare Effects of Farm Household Activity Choices in Post-War Mozambique." Working Paper 413. DIW Discussion Papers. https://www.econstor.eu/handle/10419/18109.

———. n.d. "Macroeconomic Effects of the War in Mozambique." Working Paper 11. QEH Working Paper Series. Oxford: QEH.

Brück, Tilman, Olaf J. De Groot, and Carlos Bozzoli. 2012. "How Many Bucks in a Bang: On the Estimation of the Economic Costs of Conflict." In *The Oxford Handbook of the Economics of Peace and Conflict*, edited by Garfinkel, M.R. and Skaperdas, S. Oxford: OUP.

Cairncross, Alec. 1995. "Economists in Wartime." *Contemporary European History* 4 (01): 19–36. https://doi.org/10.1017/S0960777300003246.

Cederman, Lars-Erik, Kristian Skrede Gleditsch, and Halvard Buhaug. 2013. *Inequality, Grievances, and Civil War*. Cambridge University Press.

Chalmers, Malcolm. 2007. "Spending to Save? The Cost-Effectiveness of Conflict Prevention." *Defence and Peace Economics* 18 (1): 1–23.

Cochran, Thomas C. 1961. "Did the Civil War Retard Industrialization?" *The Mississippi Valley Historical Review* 48 (2): 197–210.

Coleman, Kim. 2006. *IG Farben and ICI, 1925–53: Strategies for Growth and Survival*. Houndmills, Basingstoke, Hampshire; New York, NY: Palgrave Macmillan.

Collier, Paul. 1999a. "Doing Well Out of War." In *Conference on Economic Agendas in Civil Wars*, London, 26:27.

———. 2003. *Breaking the Conflict Trap: Civil War and Development Policy*. World Bank Publications.

Collier, Paul, and Anke Hoeffler. 2000. "Greed and Grievance in Civil War, World Bank Policy Research Working Paper 2355." World Bank. http://www. Worldbank. Org/Research/PDF.

———. 2004. "Greed and Grievance in Civil War." *Oxford Economic Papers* 56 (4): 563–95.

Collier, Paul, Anke Hoeffler, and Dominic Rohner. 2009. "Beyond Greed and Grievance: Feasibility and Civil War." *Oxford Economic Papers* 61 (1): 1–27.

Collier, Paul, Anke Hoeffler, and Måns Söderbom. 2008. "Post-Conflict Risks." *Journal of Peace Research* 45 (4): 461–78.

Collier, Paul, and Sanjay Pradhan. 1994. "Economic Aspects of the Ugandan Transition to Peace." *Some Economic Consequences of Transition from Civil War to Peace*.

Collingham, Lizzie. 2012. *Taste of War: World War II and the Battle for Food*. Penguin.

Cramer, Christopher. 2006. *Civil War Is Not a Stupid Thing: Accounting for Violence in Developing Countries*. London: Hurst & Co.

———. 2009. "Trajectories of Accumulation through War and Peace." *The Dilemmas of Statebuilding: Confronting the Contradictions of Postwar Peace Operations*, 129–48.

———. 2010a. "Methodological Challenges of Assessing Cost-Effectiveness of Conflict Prevention." Working Paper 1. What Price Peace? London: SOAS, University of London.

———. 2010b. "Racionalidad Económica y Terrorismo: Una Fórmula Explosiva." *Análisis Político* 23 (70): 3–24.

Duffield, Mark. 2008a. "Global Civil War: The Non-Insured, International Containment and Post-Interventionary Society." *Journal of Refugee Studies* 21 (2): 145–65.

———. 2008b. "Global Civil War: The Non-Insured, International Containment and Post-Interventionary Society." *Journal of Refugee Studies* 21 (2): 145–65. https://doi.org/10.1093/jrs/fem049.

Fitzgerald, Edmund Valpy Knox. 1987. "An Evaluation of the Economic Costs to Nicaragua of US Aggression: 1980–1984." *The Political Economy of Revolutionary Nicaragua*, 195–213.

Frey, Bruno S. 2004. *Dealing with Terrorism: Stick or Carrot?* Edward Elgar Publishing.

Goldin, Claudia D., and Frank D. Lewis. 1975. "The Economic Cost of the American Civil War: Estimates and Implications." *The Journal of Economic History* 35 (2): 299–326.

———. 1978. "The Post-Bellum Recovery of the South and the Cost of the Civil War: Comment." *The Journal of Economic History* 38 (2): 487–92.

Goodhand, Jonathan. 2004. "From War Economy to Peace Economy? Reconstruction and State Building in Afghanistan." *Journal of International Affairs*, 155–74.

———. 2005. "Frontiers and Wars: The Opium Economy in Afghanistan." *Journal of Agrarian Change* 5 (2): 191–216.

———. 2008. "Corrupting or Consolidating the Peace? The Drugs Economy and Post-Conflict Peacebuilding in Afghanistan." *International Peacekeeping* 15 (June): 405–23. https://doi.org/10.1080/13533310802058984.

Green, Reginald H. 1994. "The Course of the Four Horsemen: The Costs of War and Its Aftermath in Sub-Saharan Africa." In *War and Hunger*, edited by Macrae, J., Zwi, A., Duffield, M., and Slim, H. London: Zed Books, 37–49.

Gutiérrez Sanín, Francisco. 2009. "Stupid and Expensive?: A Critique of the Costs-of-Violence Literature." Crisis States Research Centre Working Paper Series 2, 48, Crisis States Research Centre, London: LSE.

Gutiérrez-Sanín, Francisco, and Jenniffer Vargas. 2017. "Agrarian Elite Participation in Colombia's Civil War." *Journal of Agrarian Change* 17 (4): 739–48.

Hacker, Louis Morton. 1940. *Triumph of American Capitalism*. New York and London: Columbia University Press.

Hanlon, Joseph. 1986. *Beggar Your Neighbours: Apartheid Power in Southern Africa*. Vol. 356. Indiana University Press.

Hardt, Michael, and Antonio Negri. 2004. *Multitude*. Vol. 13. New York: Penguin.

Haughton, Jonathan. 1998. "The Reconstruction of War-Torn Economies." Harvard Institute for International Development (June).

Hillier, Debbie. 2007. *Africa's Missing Billions: International Arms Flows and the Cost of Conflict*. Oxfam Briefing Paper, London: Oxfam.

Hirshleifer, Jack. 1994. "The Dark Side of the Force: Western Economic Association International 1993 Presidential Address." *Economic Inquiry* 32 (1): 1–10.

Howard, Michael. 2000. *The Invention of Peace: Reflections on War and International Order*. Yale University Press.

Imai, Kosuke, and Jeremy M. Weinstein. 2000. *Measuring the Economic Impact of Civil War*. Citeseer.

Kaldor, Nicholas. 1945. "The German War Economy." *The Review of Economic Studies* 13 (1): 33–52.

Keynes, John Maynard. 1940. *How to Pay for the War: A Radical Plan for the Chancellor of the Exchequer*. Harcourt, Brace.

King, J.E. 2007. "Kaldor's War." Discussion Paper 25/07. Department of Economics Discussion Papers. Melbourne: Monash University.

Lewis, Michael. 2016. *The Undoing Project: A Friendship That Changed Our Minds*. WW Norton & Company.

Llusa, Fernanda, and José Tavares. 2007. "The Economics of Terrorism: A Synopsis." *The Economics of Peace and Security Journal* 2 (1): 62–64.

Lowenstein Dent, Anita. 2017. "New Wars, Old Games: The Political Economy of Captagon in the Syrian Conflict." Unpublished MSc dissertation. London: SOAS, University of London.

Mansfield, David. 2016. *A State Built on Sand: How Opium Undermined Afghanistan*. Oxford University Press.

Melman, Seymour. 1985. *The Permanent War Economy: American Capitalism in Decline*. Touchstone.

Menon, Nidhiya, and Yana Van der Meulen Rodgers. 2015. "War and Women's Work: Evidence from the Conflict in Nepal." *Journal of Conflict Resolution* 59 (1): 51–73.

Milward, Alan Steele. 1984. *The Economic Effects of the Two World Wars on Britain*. London: Macmillan.

Nathan, Laurie. 2003. "The Frightful Inadequacy of Most of the Statistics: A Critique of Collier and Hoeffler on Causes of Civil War." *Track Two: Constructive Approaches to Community and Political Conflict* 12 (5): 5–36.

Nordstrom, Carolyn. 2010. "Women, Economy, War." *International Review of the Red Cross* 92 (877): 161–76.

O'Laughlin, Bridget. 1996. "Through a Divided Glass: Dualism, Class and the Agrarian Question in Mozambique." *The Journal of Peasant Studies* 23 (4): 1–39.

Ottaway, Marina. 2002. "Rebuilding State Institutions in Collapsed States." *Development and Change* 33 (5): 1001–23.

Pinaud, Clémence. 2016. "Military Kinship, Inc.: Patronage, Inter-Ethnic Marriages and Social Classes in South Sudan." *Review of African Political Economy* 43 (148): 243–59.

Pivovarova, Margarita, and Eik Leong Swee. 2015. "Quantifying the Microeconomic Effects of War Using Panel Data: Evidence From Nepal." *World Development* 66 (February): 308–21. https://doi.org/10.1016/j.worlddev.2014.08.026.

Plümper, Thomas, and Eric Neumayer. 2006. "The Unequal Burden of War: The Effect of Armed Conflict on the Gender Gap in Life Expectancy." *International Organization* 60 (3): 723–54.

Pugh, Michael. 2005. "Transformation in the Political Economy of Bosnia since Dayton." *International Peacekeeping* 12 (3): 448–62.

Raeymaekers, Timothy. 2014. *Violent Capitalism and Hybrid Identity in the Eastern Congo: Power to the Margins*. New York, NY: Cambridge University Press.

Ransom, Roger L. 2001. "The Economics of the Civil War." *EH. Net Encyclopedia* 24. http://web.mnstate.edu/stutes/Econ411/Readings/civil.htm.

Robinson, Joan. 1977. "The Guidelines of Orthodox Economics." *Journal of Contemporary Asia* 7 (1): 22–26. https://doi.org/10.1080/00472337785390031.

Rogers, Joshua. 2018. "Violence and the (Trans)formation of the State in the Yemen Arab Republic 1962–1970." PhD Thesis, London: SOAS, University of London.

Seymour, Claudia. forthcoming. *Unending Violence: War, Survival and the Myth of International Protection in the DRC*. University of California Press.

SIGAR. 2016. *Corruption in Conflict: Lessons from US Experience in Afghanistan*. Washington DC: Special Inspector General for Afghan Reconstruction.

Smoke, Paul, and Robert Taliercio. 2007. "Aid, Public Finance, and Accountability: Cambodian Dilemmas." In *Peace and the Public Purse*, edited by Boyce, J. and O'Donnell, M., 55–84. Boulder, CO: Lynne Rienner.

Stewart, Frances. 1993. "War and Underdevelopment: Can Economic Analysis Help Reduce the Costs?" *Journal of International Development* 5 (4): 357–80.

———. 2005. "Horizontal Inequalities: A Neglected Dimension of Development." In *WIDER Perspectives on Global Development*, 101–35. Basingstoke and New York: Palgrave Macmillan.

———. 2011. "Horizontal Inequalities as a Cause of Conflict: A Review of CRISE Findings." World Development Report Background Paper, Washington, DC: World Bank.

Suhrke, Astri, and Julia Buckmaster. 2005. "Post-War Aid: Patterns and Purposes." *Development in Practice* 15 (6): 737–46.

———. 2006. "Aid, Growth and Peace: A Comparative Analysis." *Conflict, Security & Development* 6 (3): 337–63.

Swift, Jonathan. 1995. "Gulliver's Travels." In *Gulliver's Travels*, 27–266. New York: Palgrave Macmillan.

Tilly, Charles. 1992. *Coercion, Capital, and European States, AD 990–1990*. Oxford Blackwell.

United Nations and World Bank. 2018. "Pathways for Peace: Inclusive Approaches for Preventing Violent Conflict." Conference edition. Washington DC: UN and World Bank.

Wintrobe, Ronald. 2003. *Can Suicide Bombers Be Rational*. University of Western Ontario, 5.

Wood, Elisabeth Jean. 2003. *Insurgent Collective Action and Civil War in El Salvador*. Cambridge Studies in Comparative Politics. New York: Cambridge University Press.

World Bank. 2011. *World Development Report 2011: Conflict, Security, and Development*. Taylor & Francis.

———. 2016. *World Bank Engagement in Situations of Fragility, Conflict and Violence*. Washington, DC: World Bank.

———. 2017. *World Development Report 2017: Governance and the Law*. Washington, DC: World Bank.

Wuyts, Marc. 2003. "The Agrarian Question in Mozambique's Transition and Reconstruction." In *From Conflict to Recovery in Africa*, edited by Addison, T., 141–54. Oxford: OUP.

Chapter 3

War Economies and Humanitarian Action

Gilles Carbonnier

Since the end of the Cold War, the international humanitarian market has boomed from $1.2 billion in 1990 to $27.3 billion in 2016 (Development Initiatives 2017).[1] The number and variety of donors have multiplied, with Gulf States and Turkey as major players while over a quarter of total funding accrues from private sources (individuals, foundations, corporations, etc.). The number and variety of aid suppliers have skyrocketed as well.

Despite all this hype humanitarianism, as translated into operational reality in armed conflict, is in crisis. The number and intensity of war crimes have risen, as illustrated by indiscriminate attacks on civilians as well as the deliberate targeting of medical personnel and facilities in Afghanistan, Iraq, Syria, and Yemen. Humanitarian organizations often do not have direct access where it matters most, that is, in the midst of war, leaving millions of people largely unassisted and unprotected, as recently witnessed in rebel-held enclaves in Aleppo and Eastern Ghouta in Syria or in Mosul in neighboring Iraq. At times, aid becomes yet another resource fuelling war economies. Worse, humanitarian workers themselves have become a valuable resource in a vibrant kidnap-and-ransom market. No doubt, humanitarian action is part and parcel of contemporary war economies.

Economic analysis can greatly help better understand the complex dynamics at play and devise innovative responses. Since the mid-1990s, an increasing number of economists turned to the study of armed conflict, looking in particular at war costs and benefits, rebel finance including drugs trade, diaspora remittances, and the economic agendas pursued by warlords and transnational criminal organizations. The economic profession (re)discovered that combatants can make more than a "decent" living by looting, kidnapping, racketeering, exploiting, enslaving, and taxing. It has turned to the whole spectrum from the micro-determinants of rebellion and suicide bombing to the role of aid and natural resources in armed conflict, or the study of vulnerability and coping mechanisms in protracted conflicts. Such analysis helps to uncover how humanitarian assistance risks becoming—inadvertently or not—a resource-fuelling conflict, and how to better deal with that risk. Drawing on rational choice and emphasizing costs and benefits, or interests and leverage points, economic analysis provides relevant insights for humanitarian negotiations with warring parties, for example, when it comes to influence combatant behavior toward greater compliance with International Humanitarian Law (IHL).

When analyzing the behavior and decisions of armed groups, it has become critical to consider issues such as territorial control, conflict finance, including access to valuable resources and trading routes, as well as mobilization and opportunity costs. Analyzing economic agendas in war shows that the boundaries between organized political and criminal groups are increasingly blurred. This, in turn, provides a wealth of insights not only on the functions of—and rationale for—violence but also on the potential incentives, levers, and entry points in humanitarian negotiations. It further contributes to identifying aid diversion and security risks and redesigning aid delivery modes and supply chains accordingly.

Against this background, this chapter introduces humanitarian economics as an emerging field of study and practice that deals with the economic dimensions and the political economy dynamics of armed conflict and humanitarian action. Humanitarian economics offers a largely untapped potential to connect conflict economics with humanitarian dilemmas and outcomes.[2] The next section illustrates this by focusing on selected interactions between war economies and humanitarian action, be it in relation to conflict finance, to kidnap and ransom and the treatment of prisoners, or in the case of economic sanctions.

WAR ECONOMIES AND HUMANITARIAN ACTION

War economies feature as a key topic under humanitarian economics, a field of study that deals with the economics and political economy of armed conflict and humanitarian action. Foreign aid is not treated as an exogenous reaction to adverse shocks. Instead, humanitarian economics considers aid as part and parcel of contemporary war economies. While it draws on different subfields such as development economics and war economics, humanitarian economics presents a set of distinctive features. From a normative viewpoint, it is driven by a deep concern for humanitarian outcomes, which influences the research agenda and ethics.

In common parlance, the notion of a war economy often equates with the generation, mobilization, and allocation of resources to sustain a war effort.

Yet, this is artificially dissociated from economic activities undertaken by civilians who attempt to survive in the midst of wars and by relief agencies striving to assist them. This is a category of prime interest to humanitarian agencies: survival activities are undertaken by people seeking to preserve their livelihoods.

This is the case of countless informal miners digging for gold and coltan in eastern DRC, or of farmers growing poppies in Afghanistan, where the opium economy generates not only huge profits, but also employment and income for tens of thousands of rural Afghans. As such, poppy production or informal and artisanal mining represent vital income sources for vulnerable households in Afghanistan and the DRC. Cracking down on these activities might push them into destitution, thus creating greater needs for external assistance. The contribution of Congolese miners or Afghan farmers to the war economy may be voluntary or coerced. In return, they usually benefit from an income and some degree of protection granted by those who thrive on their work. Virtually all profits accrue to armed groups, transnational criminal organizations, government officials, and others who have a vested interest in the perpetuation of wars that instil a climate of impunity propitious to illegal activities. But these miners and farmers also face a greater risk of attack by opponents who wish to curtail the funding sources of the enemy or win an elusive war on drugs. Such issues should be taken into account when designing humanitarian operations aimed at protecting civilians.

Humanitarian action may be primarily geared toward supporting coping mechanisms and survival strategies, or substituting for them when they fail. Yet, part of the resources brought to the field may end up benefiting warring parties, including human resources, as the kidnap-and-ransom industry illustrates. Thus, war economy comprises four categories that overlap and interact with each other: (i) conflict finance, or activities to fund and sustain the war effort; (ii) survival activities associated with coping mechanisms and strategies to avoid destitution; (iii) criminal and informal activities that flourish under a general climate of impunity generated by the war; and (iv) international trade and financial relations connecting the above three categories to the global marketplace. While humanitarian actors tend to be narrowly interested in the second category, that is, to what extent and how do civilians survive in the midst of war, the other categories should also be factored into the analysis. This is paramount not only because the three other war economy categories have a direct bearing on the needs for humanitarian assistance and protection, but even more because bringing humanitarian assistance in a war economy will have an impact not only on the vulnerable striving to make a living, but also on the political and military actors involved in the other categories of activities typically embedded in war economies.

Against this background, abrupt commodity price shocks on world markets can have a dire impact on specific conflict zones. The link between the Dot-Com Bubble, the boom and bust of coltan prices, and the attendant risk of a cholera outbreak in Kisangani provides a telling case in point. Since the mid-1990s, the DRC has been a significant producer of columbo-tantalite, a metallic ore known as coltan. The price of this mineral mined in the eastern DRC followed a trajectory similar to that of the NASDAQ Composite index of high-tech firms in New York. During the NASDAQ bubble at the turn of the millennium, coltan price multiplied tenfold from $30 per pound in 1999 to $300 per pound by the end of 2000. A swift tenfold coltan price crash followed in 2001 as the NASDAQ bubble burst.

The coltan fever took place in the midst of the Second Congo War (1998–2003) where nine African countries sent troops to the DRC or supported different Congolese armed factions. As coltan prices skyrocketed, many farmers in North Kivu moved into mining. As demand from mining areas increased while agricultural production declined, food prices reached new heights and food security deteriorated in the region (Jackson 2003: 16). The commercialization of coltan became a highly lucrative venture for armed groups who fought over the control of mining sites and trading routes. These included militias backed by neighboring Rwanda and Uganda, such as Bemba's Mouvement pour la Liberation du Congo (MLC) and the Rassemblement Congolais pour la Démocratie (RCD). The latter attempted to concentrate all coltan purchases under the Société Minière des Grands Lacs (SOMIGL) while processing and commercialization were allegedly in Rwandan hands. The 2001 coltan price drop put stress on RCD's finances and the armed groups turned to alternative funding sources with hardly any concern for the humanitarian consequences.

At the same time, the UN Security Council mandated a "panel of experts" to examine how mining in particular contributed to funding various armed groups that committed war crimes in the region. In its final report to the UN Security Council of October 2002, the panel of experts noted:

> Another strategy for raising revenue is to use RCD-Goma's public sector façade to requisition funds from public enterprises. On 21 November 2001 [just when coltan prices crashed], the Secretary General of RCD-Goma requisitioned by decree all revenues generated by public utilities and parastatals. On the following day the Secretary General annulled all existing collective agreements for workers in those enterprises. The decrees were applicable to all public enterprises, including the water utility, the airport authorities, the electricity utility . . . . Within a month, the water utility lacked sufficient funds to purchase water purification chemicals in Kisangani and Bukavu and power stations stopped functioning for lack of necessary repairs. The International Committee of the Red Cross [ICRC]

> has stepped in to provide 60 tons of chemicals for water purification and has financed costly repairs at Tshopo power station to avert a discontinuation of water supply in Kisangani and avert a cholera outbreak. (UNSC 2002)

As militias preyed on public utilities to make up for the losses ensuing from the collapse of global coltan prices, a humanitarian organization managed to keep Kisangani's water treatment plant operational. If the ICRC had not stepped in, much of the city's 600,000 inhabitants would likely have lost access to safe drinking water, increasing the risk of renewed cholera outbreaks. The question is the role of humanitarians to step in and provide the chemicals together with the repair and maintenance services to avert a cholera crisis, or whether their role should not be restricted to insist that the looting of public utilities does not materialize in the first place.

CONFLICT FINANCE AND HUMANITARIAN NEGOTIATIONS

For aid practitioners, it is generally easier to deal with highly structured armed groups involved in conventional warfare than with loose networks of fragmented groups involved in hit-and-run and criminal operations. The way armed groups finance themselves or seek to extract profits from war has a bearing not only on how the conflict evolves, but also on how warring parties behave vis-à-vis local communities and relief organizations. Why would a warring party change its behavior or grant unimpeded access in response to humanitarian organizations' requests? Why, for instance, do some non-state armed groups agree to sign the Deeds of Commitment of the nonprofit organization Geneva Call whereby they commit to avoiding the use of anti-personnel mines, sexual violence, or violence against children?

An armed group's inclination to grant access to humanitarian agencies or to uphold IHL norms often depends on a cost-benefit calculus involving military, economic, and political considerations. Valuating techniques associated with calculating the costs of war, and in particular the costs of lives lost and impaired, raise tough ethical issues and methodological questions when it comes to establishing the value of a statistical life (VSL)[3] for people bereft of solvent demand. Existing VSL valuation techniques provide an estimation of nearly zero the killing of thousands of civilians and combatants in poorer countries, while the life of a single U.S. or NATO soldier is routinely valued well above a million USD. In the long run, greater financial inclusion and insurance penetration may alter this equation.

There are obviously many variables beyond economic ones that explain the behavior of combatants, such as an armed group's identity, ideology, political agenda, positioning, and communication. Advances in behavioral economics provide powerful insights on the role of shifting social norms and preestablished mental models with important insights for international assistance program, as illustrated through practical examples drawn from development cooperation in the World Bank's *World Development Report 2015* entitled *Mind, Society, and Behavior* (World Bank 2014). There remains much to gain from deeper scrutiny into the changing role of social norms and mental models in the context of armed conflict (Carbonnier 2015).

That said, looking more narrowly at the economic agendas of armed groups helps grasp the cost-benefit constraints of warring parties that have to generate sufficient resources to cover the costs of mobilizing and maintaining their fighting capacity in relation to the relative strength of the enemy (see, e.g., Wennmann 2009). Non-state armed groups typically receive funding from voluntary or coerced contributions from diasporas and domestic constituents—depending on the extent of territorial control—and from foreign allies. An armed group will adapt its behavior with regard to its current financial situation and future funding prospects. To the extent that external funding is sufficient, the armed group does not need to extract more resources locally. This can have a direct impact on the capacity of humanitarian actors to influence the behavior of combatants toward greater respect of IHL, as some scholars find that armed groups that do not depend on the backing of the local population tend to turn more indiscriminately violent (see, e.g., Weinstein 2006; Khalivas 2006).

In other words, humanitarian negotiators may have little leverage on an armed group that is financially self-sufficient, unless a powerful external sponsor agrees to push for behavioral change, for example, by threatening to cut down its support in the case of renewed mass atrocities. When an armed group gets poorer or fears for its future financial viability, it may be more prone to engage humanitarian organizations in order to gain broader support and legitimacy vis-à-vis local communities and external backers. Conversely, however, as it becomes cash strapped, an armed group may turn against civilians and relief organizations to extract resources required for its military and political survival. The history of the Liberation Tigers of Tamil Eelam (LTTE) illustrates how the situation can rapidly evolve in this regard. Once Indian support waned after the 1991 assassination of Rajiv Gandhi by a Tamil suicide bomber, the LTTE relied increasingly on taxes levied among diaspora communities and in LTTE-controlled territory. Diaspora networks such as the Sri Lankan Tamil emigrants are usually too dispersed, divided, and weak to be mobilized by humanitarian organizations hoping to wield influence on rebels.

More generally, as an armed group gains effective control over a territory and its population, it may shift from ad hoc predatory attacks involving looting and kidnapping to more permanent methods of extraction combined with a greater role in the local economy and stronger trade and financial relations. Full territorial control often leads to an armed group exercising de facto governmental functions, which include permanent taxation and the provision of security and quasi-public services (Olson 1993). If the rebels originate from that territory, they may display a greater interest in basic service delivery to the communities with whom they are closely related, and may enjoy greater political support from the host population. Strangers may have more incentives to exert violence as a way to spread fear among the population while striking selective deals with local criminal groups and political leaders.

In many instances, war offers vast opportunities for illegal economic activities carried out in impunity. The Fuerzas Armadas Revolucionarias de Colombia (FARC) developed ties with coca producers in the areas under their control as early as the 1980s but did not take an active role in the narcotics business (beyond taxing it) until the 1990s, when some elements of the armed group engaged in production and trade. Together with kidnap-and-ransom activities developed at a quasi-industrial scale, it managed to secure a comfortable annual income in the 2000s. The FARC has been considered to be largely self-sufficient financially, which meant that humanitarian organizations had less leverage through third parties, but also that the FARC had an interest in mustering support from host communities through a combination of welfare provision and restraint in the exercise of violence, which aligned well with the objectives and services provided by humanitarian organizations. In Afghanistan, warring parties thrive notably on the drugs business as well as on the foreign aid enterprise. For example, the Taliban have been known to levy a 10 percent tax on poppy production, as well as taxes on drug traffickers and protection rackets or "protection services" more or less forcibly sold to international organizations and their Afghan partners (UNODC 2013).

"Taxing" humanitarian operations is a well-documented source of conflict finance. In Afghanistan, the Taliban have often resorted to a protection racket, that is, selling "protection services" more or less forcibly to international organizations and their Afghan partners (UNODC 2013). In Somalia during the 2011–2012 famine, Al-Shabaab, a Somali rebel group with alleged ties to al-Qaeda, appointed local humanitarian coordination officers whose task was to regulate and monitor the activities of aid agencies. This included taxation: the group argued that being the de facto government in the areas of operations of humanitarian agencies, it was responsible for the security of aid workers. This, in turn, required financial support from the humanitarians who "required protection." Initial registration fees could be as high as $10,000, followed by taxes on individual projects and on staff income (Jackson and Aynte 2013).[4] In this context, it is critical for humanitarian agencies to weigh the effective humanitarian outcomes that can be attributed to their operations against the risk of fuelling the conflict via aid taxation and diversion. Besides, they should consider how a protection racket and extortion affect civilian welfare among host communities. While ad hoc extraction—for instance, in the form of forced labor—primarily has a negative impact on households, more regular and institutionalized extraction seemed to have improved the welfare of "tax payers" in some cases but not in Somalia, where multiple forms of taxation imposed by Al-Shabaab has weakened traditional redistribution channels and solidarity networks (Maxwell and Majid 2014). This, in turn, erodes the coping mechanisms of affected communities and enhances their vulnerability, which may in turn call for increased humanitarian assistance.

PRISONERS OF WAR AND KIDNAPPING FOR RANSOM

Protecting detainees in war is one of the long-standing objectives pursued by IHL. Since ancient times, preserving the life and dignity of prisoners of war has been addressed by various normative frameworks. The age of chivalry in medieval Europe has been hailed as a time when the lot of the vanquished improved. Social scientists have highlighted the role of knightly values that glorified acts of mercy in war, with an emphasis on warriors' concern for reputation and inner emotions of pride, guilt, and shame. Economists have emphasized the changing costs and benefits of keeping prisoners alive: granting captors property rights over their prisoners raised the incentive to keep them alive, at least those prisoners expected to be ransomed for a good price. A monarch with limited resources to pay for the war had an interest in granting each soldier the rights to their own spoils of war. Battles pitting man against man made it possible to clearly identify who was made prisoner by whom and to assign property rights accordingly. Under these circumstances,

> [A soldier] acts rationally when he decides either to kill or to spare a defeated enemy. If he kills him he eliminates any risk of the defeated soldier striking back. The advantage of sparing a defeated enemy, on the other hand, is the monetary benefit of selling him at a price determined by the prisoner himself, his family, or whoever else is interested in his release . . . . The (net) value of a defeated enemy thus depends on a number of empirically observable factors influencing benefits and costs, given the particular form of property rights. (Frey and Buhofer 1988: 21)

During the Hundred Years' War, Henry V departed from the prevailing normative system of chivalry that favored sparing the vanquished. The English king, victorious over the French in Agincourt in 1415, ordered the execution of all the prisoners including "the flower of French nobility and chivalry" (Meron 1999). The English knights refused to execute the order not only because they repudiated such an unchivalrous task, but also to preserve the benefit of later ransoming "their" prisoners. King Henry V hence then ordered his archers to do the dirty work. The massacre was later explained, if not justified, on grounds of necessity: the sheer number of French prisoners made it too costly to keep them alive in the event of another French assault. Guarding the prisoners to prevent them from taking up arms would have diverted English forces away from combat.

The rise of nation-states, forced conscription, and new military technology altered incentives to take part in war. The adoption of the first Geneva Convention in 1864 coincided with the final transfer of property rights over prisoners from individual combatants to states. Aware of the budgetary constraints to pay for modern warfare, Henry Dunant, the founding father of the Red Cross and promoter of the Convention, drew attention to the benefits of effective sanitary services for the wounded in his *Memory of Solferino*: "by reducing the number of cripples, a saving would be effected in the expenses of a Government which has to provide pensions for disabled soldiers" (Dunant 1862/1959: 122). Since then, however, millions of detainees have continued to suffer from massive, repeated violations of basic rules and principles of IHL. This hints to the fact that it is far from easy to transit from material incentives to legal norms and, up to this day, cost-benefit analysis can help understand and influence armed groups' behavior. As recently witnessed in Afghanistan, Syria, and elsewhere, humanitarian actors can alter the captors' cost-benefit calculus in favor of sparing the prisoners by contributing to the orderly transfer of the vanquished away from the war zone.

Kidnapping has become one of the biggest threats to humanitarian workers: the number of aid workers kidnapped (and not killed thereafter) multiplied by eighteen in just a decade (Humanitarian Outcomes 2014). This involves a fluid mix of economically and politically motivated kidnappings. Syria is a case in point. By December 2014, the Islamic State (IS) was believed to hold at least twenty-two foreign nationals captive in Aleppo in northern Syria. Negotiations were especially difficult because they involved a diverse range of home states and employers, each following different principles, policies, and practices. IS had kidnapped some of the hostages directly, while it had bought or acquired others by force from other warring groups. The group had both political and financial demands, such as releasing prisoners in France and the United Kingdom and ransom payments. In Somalia, too, aid workers and business employees kidnapped by Al-Shabaab affiliates have been sold to other groups, including organized criminal groups.

Kidnap and ransom (K&R) is a low-cost tactic that can yield substantial financial return, in particular in the case of expatriates whose value tends to be much higher than national aid workers. The latter may thus face a greater probability of being killed rather than kidnapped (Fassin 2012). Negotiated release may imply the direct or indirect payment of a ransom by the employer, the family, or the home government of the victim. If no ransoms were paid and no concessions granted, the market would dry up. Yet, given the human and political costs, most policymakers in democracies are not ready to implement such a policy. The United States and the United Kingdom may be exceptions, but also enjoy a greater capacity to set up covert rescue operations. In a mediatized case, a Swiss court ordered Doctors Without Borders (MSF) to reimburse part of the ransom paid by the Dutch government for the release of an MSF employee, setting a worrying precedent for humanitarian organizations.[5] Besides, it is not easy for a state to prevent a family or a private company from paying a ransom for the release of a loved one or an employee, which may be all the more tempting when costs are covered by an ad hoc insurance policy. A whole industry has developed with specialized consultancy firms providing comprehensive service packages that range from risk monitoring to managing K&R crises, including handling relations between the hostage's family, the kidnappers, and potential intermediaries. The insurance industry has also become an important actor on the market, whereby insurance companies do not directly pay ransoms but typically reimburse the insured party for any ransom paid, as well as all the other related expenses, including fees paid to consultancy firms contracted to help manage the crisis.

K&R insurance is a surrealistic business filled with contradictions. First, an insured employee should not be informed about the insurance policy because of a moral hazard. The insured could arguably behave in a riskier manner once aware of the coverage. Worse, the insured could co-organize his or her own kidnapping in order to get a share of the ransom when reimbursed by the insurance. Second, kidnappers typically ask that no one be informed of the kidnapping except the employer or the family members to be extorted. Hence, informing the insurance company about the incident can put the hostage's life in danger. But the insurance company can turn down later reimbursement requests if it was not informed about the kidnapping event in a timely fashion. Third, selling K&R insurance goes against the stated policy of the United States and many other Western countries and international organizations not to pay ransom fees to any designated terrorist organization.

This booming K&R market has dramatic consequences for those humanitarian organizations, which has no alternative beyond ceaselessly striving to open up and preserve a space for strictly impartial, neutral, and independent humanitarian action with field access tolerated by all warring groups, including those designated as terrorists. Beyond long-lasting trauma on the victims and their families, kidnapping incidents also gravely affect the operational capacity of relief organizations. Cases of kidnappings have repeatedly led humanitarian agencies to withdraw from a region or a whole country altogether. More importantly, perhaps, it is not only the resources brought in war zones by humanitarian organizations that may end up fuelling war economies but it is also the humanitarian workers themselves that are regarded as a valuable, tradable asset.

ECONOMIC SANCTIONS

Relief organizations increasingly operate in contexts where part of the territory is under the control of groups and individuals designated as terrorist by the United Nations and major aid donors such as the United States and the EU. Economic sanctions against designated terrorist organizations can have dire humanitarian consequences for the population under the control of those organizations. Sanctions can further entail criminogenic effects in that criminal networks flourish by investing in the lucrative business of circumventing the sanctions and other measures designed to counter the financing of terrorism.

Imposing sanctions has been considered as an alternative to going to war, or as an option among a range of actions that can be taken against armed groups and belligerent countries. Sanctions aim to signal the disapproval of the countries imposing the sanctions, to push for behavioral change, or simply to constrain and limit the target's agency. Evidence on the effectiveness of targeted sanctions highlights that sanction regimes have been successful in coercing change in a very limited number of cases (about 10 percent). They have been slightly more successful in signaling discontent and constraining behavior with a success rate of 27 percent (Biersteker, Eckert, and Tourinho 2015). The impact of sanctions is particularly weak when it comes to autocracies with limited trade and financial relations with sender countries anyway.

Just like foreign aid, sanctions are fungible. The sanctioned elite can transfer the burden onto weaker segments of society, for example, by reducing social expenditures or preying on civilians to compensate for losses. Except for very specific sanctions such as individual travel bans and asset freezes, the eventual cost of targeted sanctions can be transferred onto the vulnerable. The negative humanitarian impact of sanctions has been emphasized in several studies, most notably in the case of the UN sanctions imposed on Iraq from 1990 to 2003. The impact on public health has been found to be negative and substantial. Since the end of the 1990s, humanitarian exemptions have become standard practice in UN Security Council resolutions imposing sanctions. Despite such exemptions, which allow trade in essential goods and services, the long-term impact of sanctions on the health of the target country's population has often been significant. Financial sanctions, in particular, disrupt the inflow of remittances and cash assistance, which is compounded by the withdrawal of development assistance and the gradual deterioration of healthcare education and knowledge as a consequence of long-term sanctions.

On the other hand, economic sanctions tend to have strong criminalizing effects, boosting the economic and political power of sanctions busters who circumvent trade and financial bans, as illustrated by the much-publicized UN oil-for-food scandal in the case of Iraq. The U.S. Congress estimated that Iraqis with close ties to Saddam Hussein's regime earned more than $10 billion illegally from smuggling oil and extorting kickbacks from firms trading through the UN's oil-for-food program between 1997 and 2002 (Andreas 2005). These criminal networks do not "evaporate" once the sanction regimes are lifted but continue to operate in the post-sanction period, adversely impacting peacebuilding, state-building, and reconstruction. A decade later, when IS gained full territorial control over parts of Northern Iraq and adjacent Syria, long-established oil smuggling circuits facilitated the illegal sales of oil that boosted the terrorist organization's war chest. IS gained control of a majority of oilfields in Syria and a few small fields in Iraq, giving it an estimated production capacity of up to 80,000 barrels of crude a day in 2014, some of which processed in bootleg refineries. The group sold oil at a discounted price—allegedly between $25 and $40 a barrel, while the international price was above $100. The middlemen included Iraqi, Syrian, Turkish, and Iranian "entrepreneurs" who had grown rich, connected, and powerful during the earlier UN embargo against Iraq, and have revived their networks.

Sender countries have become aware of (some of) these pitfalls. They have inserted humanitarian exemptions into sanction regimes and counterterrorism legislation. At times, they have supported relief organizations precisely with the aim of cushioning civilians from the most severe humanitarian consequences of the sanctions, being concerned to render sanctions more acceptable to their own domestic constituencies. Yet, the same sender countries have made the effective cushioning of civilians from the humanitarian consequences of sanctions much harder through the enactment of counterterrorist legislation. Donor countries such as the United States, the United Kingdom, Canada, and Australia have adopted a battery of administrative, civil, and criminal laws to ensure that no taxpayer money ends up in the hands of designated terrorist groups. Humanitarian organizations risk being fined or workers imprisoned for the inadvertent transfer of resources to terrorist actors, even if they had no intention whatsoever of supporting terrorist acts. This reinforces risk aversion at the expense of striving to assist those most in need.

In addition, donors have pushed for the inclusion of counterterrorism-related clauses in funding contracts. These require humanitarian organizations to exert due diligence, for example, through careful screening of their staff and of implementing partner organizations against dozens of lists linking individuals and groups to terrorism suspects. Expanded due diligence may even require the screening of aid beneficiaries. Principled humanitarian organizations resist screening ultimate beneficiaries or denying them the right to assistance on the basis of potential sympathy for, or ties with, listed terrorist groups, which would go against the essential principle of impartiality. Finally, the withdrawal of medical assistance to individuals requiring healthcare on the basis of alleged ties to designated groups would violate medical ethics. A way to change the equation is to rely more on carrots and less on sticks and using foreign aid—together with other measures to reduce people's grievances—with a view to making peaceful alternatives more attractive to potential terrorist recruits, increasing the opportunity cost of joining or supporting terrorist organizations. That said, political motivations grounded in specific historical and institutional circumstances cannot be understated and must be factored into the equation as well.

CONCLUSION

Linking theory and practice, the chapter illustrates how economic agendas and financing of non-state armed groups have a direct bearing on humanitarian negotiations and outcomes. Highlighting the scope and relevance of humanitarian economics, it further examines the implications of economic sanctions on war economies as well as the treatment of detainees and the booming kidnap-and-ransom market.

The costs of mobilizing and maintaining fighting capacity determine the number of resources that an armed group must be able to generate to pay for the war. On that basis, three key variables related to conflict finance appear to exert a significant influence on the behavior of armed groups with regard to humanitarian concerns and actors. First, the armed group's economic agendas beyond the sole objective to pay for the war, and the extent to which armed violence serves the purpose of maintaining a climate of impunity propitious to illegal activities. Second, the extent of an armed group's territorial control over people and resources, and in particular over natural resources that it can extract, trade, and/or tax. And third, the type and amount of external resources that a warring party is able to command through foreign aid, third-party state support, diaspora networks, and the likes.

Whether economic activity is a means to support an armed struggle or is an end in itself can make a big difference in the conduct of hostilities, even if the boundary between these two scenarios is often blurred. When war spoils become the aim and violence is perpetuated to sustain profit rather than to challenge the political status quo, a non-state armed group may have less interest in adapting its behavior to the laws of war, especially if the prime objective of violence is to maintain a climate of impunity for criminal activities to flourish. Calling on strictly profit-driven armed groups to respect human rights and IHL may seem *a priori* pointless. In this context, humanitarian economics emerges as largely untapped field dealing with the economic and political economy dynamics of armed conflict and humanitarian action.

Many studies on war economies adopt an anti-rebel bias. There are many risks involved in the tendency to dismiss non-state armed groups as mere criminals while possibly condoning repressive regimes prone to deny non-state armed actors any right and protection that they would be entitled to as party to a non-international armed conflict. Designating and labeling an armed group as "criminal" or "terrorist" may further erode any concern it may have with regard to its reputation and international legitimacy. Under the cost-benefit analysis, stigmatization and international blacklisting reduces the opportunity cost of radicalization; a stigmatized armed group may feel that it has more to lose than to gain by engaging humanitarian organizations and more to gain than to lose by rejecting or grossly exploiting them.

Further research is needed on several fronts, all the more that relief approaches are evolving fast. Smart cards, mobile money, biometric recognition, and other technological innovations lead to expanding cash-based assistance in crisis, including in remote areas where it was previously simply not feasible. The economic literature raises many arguments in support of cash-based programing and a few against it. Cash aid gives beneficiaries a greater say over how to allocate aid according to their needs. Multi-sector cash assistance allows beneficiaries to pay not only for food, but also to cover housing, education, transport, heating, water, and other requirements. It generally cuts down transaction costs compared to in-kind distribution and reduces ensuing grievances. But in some instances, bringing trucks and moving goods into remote areas is important to open up enclaves and reinforce passive protection of conflict-affected communities through greater physical presence. In conflict-ridden areas, research on cash-based assistance could expand beyond cost-benefit analysis and consider the symbolic dimension of heavy logistics and physical field presence of humanitarian agencies via warehouses, distribution sites, local offices and the likes. Further research is required to understand how this shift toward cash-based assistance plays out within specific war economies, and the extent to which the transaction saved are reinvested in effective protection work or result in affected communities being assisted from afar and left unprotected.

We need to better understand the complex dynamics on the humanitarian market itself, shedding light on instances where competition between relief organizations stimulates enhanced humanitarian impact and others where it produces adverse outcomes. Fierce competition in the humanitarian marketplace may stimulate greater and better aid delivery. But it also weakens the sector's position vis-à-vis warring parties, donors, and other key stakeholders. Coordinated humanitarian response remains illusory even in instances where stakes are particularly high for the humanitarian sector as a whole, as is the case of stringent counterterrorist provisions that jeopardize the exercise of impartial humanitarian action. More research is needed to gauge the humanitarian impact of trade and financial sanctions–including "smart" ones. Their long-term criminogenic influence on war economies deserves further scrutiny as it can have a significant bearing on the transition from war to peace.

NOTES

1. Development Initiatives adopts the standard definition of humanitarian action, shared by the Organization for Economic Co-operation and Development (OECD), whereby its objective is to "save lives, alleviate suffering and maintain human dignity during and after man-made crises and disasters caused by natural hazards, as well as to prevent and strengthen preparedness for when such situations occur," following the principles of: humanity, impartiality, neutrality, and independence (see http://devinit.org/defining-humanitarian-assistance/# <last accessed on March 15, 2018>. The data comes primarily from the OECD's Development Assistance Committee (DAC) and UN Office for the Coordination of Humanitarian Affairs (OCHA)'s Financial Tracking Service (FTS).
2. To address these issues in this chapter, I draw from various chapters of my 2016 book entitled *Humanitarian Economics: War, Disaster and the Global Aid Market* (Carbonnier 2016).
3. See, for example, Viscusi, Kip, and Joseph Aldy, "The Value of a Statistical Life: A Critical Review of Market Estimates Throughout the World," *Journal of Risk and Uncertainty* 27, no. 1 (2003), pp. 5–76.
4. It seems that food and nonfood items were subject to greater duties than medical assistance, food being more valuable and fungible in general than drugs and medical devices. Al-Shabaab drew additional revenue from property rentals, logistics, and transport. The diversion of food aid by Al-Shabaab was at times quite significant (Ashley and Aynte 2013: 18).
5. See https://www.theguardian.com/society/2008/aug/01/internationalaidanddevelopment.netherlands.

REFERENCES

Andreas, Peter. 2005. "Criminalizing Consequences of Sanctions: Embargo Busting and Its Legacy." *International Studies Quarterly* 49, no. 2: 353–60.

Biersteker, Thomas, Eckert, Sue, and Marcos Tourinho, eds. 2015. *Targeting Sanctions: The Impacts and Effectiveness of UN Action.* Cambridge: Cambridge University Press.

Carbonnier, Gilles. 2015. "Reason, Emotion, Compassion: Can Altruism Survive Professionalisation in the Humanitarian Sector?" *Disasters* 39, no. 2: 189–207.

Carbonnier, Gilles. 2016. *Humanitarian Economics: War, Disaster and the Global Aid Market.* London and New York: Hurst and Oxford University Press.

Dietrich, Christian. 2000. "UNITA's Diamond Mining and Exporting Capacity." In *Angola's War Economy: The Role of Oil and Diamonds*, edited by Jakkie Cilliers, and Christian Dietrich, 275–94. Pretoria: Institute for Security Studies.

Development Initiatives. 2017. *Global Humanitarian Assistance 2017.* London.

Dunant, Henry. 1862/1959. *A Memory of Solferino.* Reprinted in Geneva: ICRC.

Fassin, Didier. 2012. *Humanitarian Reason: A Moral History of the Present.* Berkeley: University of California Press.

Frey, Bruno, and Heinz Buhofer. 1988. "Prisoners and Property Rights." *Journal of Law and Economics* 31, no. 1: 19–46.

Hartley, Aidan. 2001. "The Art of Darkness." *The Spectator*, January 27.

Humanitarian Outcomes' Aid Worker Security Database. 2014. https://aidworkersecurity.org/, accessed on November 25.

Jackson, Ashley, and Abdi Aynte. 2013. "Talking to the Other Side: Humanitarian Negotiations with Al-Shabaab in Somali." ODI HPG Working Paper, p. 18.

Jackson, Stephen. 2003. "Fortunes of War: The Coltan Trade in the Kivus." *Background Research for HPG Report 13.* London: ODI.

Kalyvas, Stathis. 2006. *The Logic of Violence in Civil War.* Cambridge: Cambridge University Press.

Keynes, John M. 1919. *The Economic Consequences of Peace.* New York: Harcourt, Brace, and Howe, Inc.

Keynes, John M. 1940. *How to Pay for the War.* New York: Harcourt, Brace, and Howe, Inc.

Maxwell, Daniel, and Nisar Majid. 2014. "Another Humanitarian Crisis in Somalia? Learning from the 2011 Famine." Feinstein International Center, Tufts University.

Meron, Theodor. 1999. "International Humanitarian Law from Agincourt to Rome." *International Law Studies* 75: 301–11.

Olson, Mancur. 1993. "Dictatorship, Democracy, and Development." *The American Political Science Review* 87, no. 3: 567–76.

Pigou, Arthur C. 1921. *Political Economy of War.* London: Macmillan and Co.

UNODC (United Nations Office on Drugs and Crime). 2013. "Afghanistan Opium Survey 2012."

UNSC (United Nations Security Council). 2002. "Letter Dated 15 October 2002 from the Secretary-General Addressed to the President of the Security Council." UN Doc. S/2002/1146, October 16, para. 88.

Weinstein, Jeremy. 2006. *Inside Rebellion: The Politics of Insurgent Violence.* Cambridge: Cambridge University Press.

Wennmann, Achim. 2009. "Grasping the Financing and Mobilization Cost of Armed Groups: A New Perspective on Conflict Dynamics." *Contemporary Security Policy* 30, no. 2: 265–80.

World Bank. 2014. *World Development Report 2015: Mind, Society, and Behaviour.*

Chapter 4

Rebel Taxation

Between the Moral and Market Economy

Zachariah Mampilly

Can a non-state armed group ever engage in taxation? Or, as a non-state actor, is it axiomatically engaged in extortion? Among the more enduring tropes in literature on organized violence is that taxation by a rebel group is no different than a protection racket. Consider these statements on the Islamic State's finances by CNN: "The main reason ISIS is still making billions is *taxes*. The Islamic State's *extortion* of the people living inside its territory in Iraq and Syria has skyrocketed from $360 million in 2014 to $800 million in 2015 (emphasis mine)" (Pagliery 2016). The reporter slips easily between taxation and extortion, suggesting that taxation by rebels is by definition a criminal act. Academic studies of the subject frequently rely on a similar slippage. For example, a 2014 study in the influential *Journal of Conflict Resolution* is titled, "*Extortion* with Protection: Understanding the Effect of Rebel *Taxation* on Civilian Welfare in Burundi" (emphasis mine) (Sabates-Wheeler and Verwimp 2014).

Two core assumptions undergird this paradigm. First is the belief that rebels only engage in taxation to generate revenue. Second is that while such groups might offer protection in exchange for payment, the rebellion is the source of the threat. Hence rebel taxation is a form of racketeering in which an actor demands payment for protection from itself, in other words, a protection racket. But if so, why apply the term "tax" to non-state armed groups at all?

In this chapter, I argue that such economic instrumentalism is inadequate for understanding the logic of rebel taxation. Of course, taxation is always concerned with revenue generation. But rebel taxation is also overlaid with political and social valences that rarely draw mention from scholars, in contrast to studies of state taxation where such logics are often foregrounded. I review recent studies of rebel taxation and show that authors dwell on the economic logic of taxation while ignoring its political dimensions. Studies of rebel taxation would benefit from a closer understanding of the literatures on rebel governance as well as on studies of state taxation practices which can provide insights into the political motivations for taxation that commonly elude analyses of rebel behavior. Building from these literatures, I introduce several potential noneconomic logics for rebel taxation. Some of these have no direct economic benefit, while others are secondary to the economic rationale. I illustrate these dynamics drawing on examples from recent conflicts. I conclude that rebel taxation should be understood as a technology of governance, potentially even more so than its immediate economic purpose.

ECONOMIC INSTRUMENTALISM AND THE CRIMINALIZATION OF REBEL GROUPS

In the late 1990s and early 2000s, a new research paradigm on the political economy of war spread through the halls of academia before spilling over into the policy and cultural realms. Shaped by the ideas of the Oxford economist Paul Collier and various collaborators, these studies argued that insurgent organizations were not motivated by injustice or other political grievances (Collier and Hoeffler 1998). Instead, armed groups should be understood as profit-seeking firms whose true motivation could be discerned by applying sophisticated statistical analyses to their finances. In this view, rebellion was the product not of politics but rather rational cost-benefit analyses by profit-seeking individuals who create armed organizations to pursue their economic objectives.

This conception of rebellion as a "quasi-criminal" (Collier 2000) activity led directly to influential policy interventions as the World Bank embraced these ideas, even commissioning a widely circulated study by Collier and several collaborators in 2003 (Collier et al. 2003). The Kimberly Process Certification Scheme endorsed by United Nations General Assembly Resolution 55/56 in 2004, for example, was designed to regulate the sale of so-called conflict diamonds based on their perceived role in fueling a civil war. Treating rebels as criminals even crossed into popular culture with the release of the song "Diamonds from Sierra Leone" by Kanye West in 2005 and the film *Blood Diamond* starring Leonardo DiCaprio in 2006.

Comparing rebellion to a criminal enterprise reached its apogee in 2009 when the Stanford political scientist and former Obama State Department official, Jeremy Weinstein (2009), wrote in *Foreign Policy* that "initiating a rebellion may be easier than starting a business" and that to prevent people from rebelling against their government, "War must be made more expensive." That same year, Sam Brownback, a conservative senator from

Kansas, introduced the Congo Conflict Minerals Act, showing the paradigm's bipartisan appeal. Though the legislation initially died in committee, in 2010, Obama signed into law the "Dodd-Frank Wall Street Reform and Consumer Protection Act" which included a specific section that adopted Brownback's legislation and sought to regulate so-called conflict minerals that were claimed to "finance conflict" producing "extreme levels of violence."

What is striking is how few rebel groups actually adhered to the "rebellion as criminality" model in the real world. In Africa in the mid-2000s, the focus of Weinstein's polemic, older groups with clear political objectives like the Sudan People's Liberation Army (SPLA) were still active while newer groups such as the Justice and Equality Movement and the Sudan Liberation Army were emerging in response to the political conflict in Darfur. In Somalia, the Islamic Courts Union was dominant until its defeat in 2006, which eventually produced Al-Shabaab. Boko Haram was founded in Nigeria in 2002 and turned to violent insurgency in 2009, the same year Weinstein's op-ed appeared. Though not a comprehensive list, these were among the most prominent insurgencies operating in the African context during that time. None fit the mold of apolitical profit-seeking criminal enterprises.

Of course, certain groups do appear to function as criminal enterprises, at least during different phases of their lifecycle. The Revolutionary United Front in Sierra Leone and Charles Taylor's National Patriotic Front in Liberia during the 1990s are often presented as paradigmatic, though even here, extractive logics coexisted alongside and were shaped by deeper political dynamics (Reno 2015). Today, numerous militias that plague the Democratic Republic of Congo (hereafter Congo) are commonly framed as mafias. Yet even as certain small militias which control the informal mining sector may be productively viewed as criminal (Sanchez de la Sierra, Unpublished manuscript), it is much harder to suggest that more prominent groups like the FDLR, M-23, or the CNDP were primarily motivated by profit.

Numerous critiques of the rebellion as criminality paradigm have been put forth, pointing out both the conceptual weakness and political naivety inherent to this approach (McGovern 2011). Mkandawire's (2002: 185) prescient takedown suggests that its bipartisan appeal lay in its ability to offer relatively painless policy responses: "The view of some policy-oriented researchers seems to be that if the nature of the conflict were posed in an understandable (read "rational") way, potential for its rational resolution would elicit international support because the cause-effect nexus would be obvious." Since rebels were economic not political actors, reducing the profitability of conflict minerals would remove the underlying motivation for insurgency itself. Contrasted against the messy, large-scale nation-building efforts in Afghanistan and Iraq unfolding at the same time as the paradigm's emergence, placing sanctions on conflict minerals was a much easier pill to swallow for neo-cons and liberal internationalists alike.

Despite the failure of the policy interventions that emerged out of the war as criminality paradigm (Seay 2012), it still casts a large shadow. Many studies continue to assume that the point of rebellion remains profit-seeking, as I discuss below. These studies have moved away from the model of apolitical, greed-based rebellions advanced by Collier and his followers. Yet they still treat taxation by rebels as a form of extortion, though now emphasizing an earlier sociological lineage derived from the theoretical and empirical work of Charles Tilly (1985) and especially Mancur Olson (1993) instead.

Tilly and Olson were concerned not with groups violently challenging state authority per se but rather the protogenitors of the modern state. Both focus on the emergence of the state system in Western Europe, emphasizing its origins among the banditry that characterized the medieval period. In this view, bandits engaged in looting eventually embraced regularized taxation as a more reliable method for extracting revenue. As rational actors, violence is deployed as a mechanism to facilitate extraction, but only to the point that it does not undermine revenue generation. As groups face structural logics that curtail their deployment of violence, they unintentionally initiate a process of state formation. In other words, rather than turning rebels in to profit-seeking criminal enterprises, Tilly and Olson were concerned with the "criminal" logics that undergird processes of modern state formation. They challenged the liberal understandings of state construction, emphasizing instead the ways in which legitimacy is derived from violence and economic need. Neither Tilly nor Olson understood their work as applying to contemporary conflict processes, yet their ideas have remained foundational in shaping how scholars understand rebel taxation.

STATE FORMATION, TIME HORIZONS, AND THE SHADOW OF MANCUR OLSON

Applied to a civil war, Olson's argument seems to provide a clear logic for why some armed groups seek to engage in an exchange relationship with the local population. But often overlooked is Olson's emphasis on the time horizons that shaped his predictions. A core assumption is that bandits face severe constraints on their financing. They only have two options to raise funds, either pillaging or consensual taxation, which is determined by their time horizon. Rulers with short-term horizons possess incentive structures similar to that of roving bandits:

> suppose that an autocrat is only concerned about getting through the next year. He will then gain by expropriating any convenient capital asset whose tax yield over the year is less than its total value. He will also gain from forgetting about the enforcement of long-term contracts, from repudiating his debts, and from coining or printing new money that he can spend even though this ultimately brings inflation. At the limit, when an autocrat has no reason to consider the future output of the society at all, his incentives are those of a roving bandit and that is what he becomes. (578)

In contrast, in the long run, Olson argues that that taxation is better than violent predation both for the ruler and the ruled. He suggests that "the rational stationary bandit will take only a part of income in taxes, because he will be able to exact a larger total amount of income from his subjects if he leaves them with an incentive to generate income that he can tax." For Olson, a rational autocrat will provide public goods when it is in their economic interest to do so: "Since the warlord takes a part of total production in the form of tax theft, it will also pay him to provide other public goods whenever the provision of these goods increases taxable income sufficiently" (568).

According to Olson, would-be rulers without prospects of establishing a long-term durable social order, one capable of engaging in regularized taxation, have no incentive to become stationary bandits and will remain roving bandits. The transformation from warlord to state formation via taxation is a long-term process. The question is how long? Unfortunately, Olson's work is unclear when describing the difference between short- and long-term time horizons. While short term seems to imply less than a year, as the quote above makes clear, he portrays the stationary bandit variously as "taking a long view" or that "they have an indefinitely long planning horizon" and that the process of state formation he describes unfolds in the "long run" (571). At a minimum, a long run time horizon in Olsonian terms seems to refer to an individual concerned about the well-being of his or her future generations: "If the king anticipates and values dynastic succession, that further lengthens the planning horizon and is good for his subjects" (571).

Do leaders of rebel groups calculate over the "long term" and determine their taxation strategy accordingly? While Olson does not specify the actual length, it is clear from the above passages that he is thinking in terms of decades rather than weeks or months. Tilly is similarly vague on the time horizon by which states gain legitimacy, but makes it clear that it took a "long time" for these processes to play out (1985: 173). While many armed groups profess their interests over the long run, even the most durable forms of rebel rule are characterized by shifting and fragmentary forms of control (Kalyvas 2006). If rebels do express intergenerational aspirations, it is likely to refer to vague hopes for their children's futures more than a specific ambition to ensure their family wealth through favorable taxation policies in the manner of Olson's rational autocrat. Raeymaekers (2010: 575), for example, quotes an official from a Congolese armed group that typifies the short termism inherent in rebel fiscal strategies: "We didn't have any budget, so the money earned from tax duties was immediately used." Indeed, it would be irrational for armed groups to behave as if territorial control can ever be stable over the long run. As Mao made clear, territorial control must be understood as a contingent strategy, and any armed group with long-term aspirations must be willing to cede control over territory as necessitated by the military struggle.

A second concern is drawn from studies of state taxation practices. Olson's framework presumes that the logic that shapes bargaining between the ruler and the ruled over taxation can be discerned in both the short and long run. A rational autocrat will set tax rates at the maximum possible level without introducing disincentives that reduce income generation and hence the amount of tax collected: "the rational self-interested autocrat chooses the revenue maximizing tax rate" (570). Civilians, in exchange, receive public goods up to the point where a dollar invested in welfare benefits by the rational autocrat increases his share of income by more than a dollar. However, most studies of actual state taxation practices emphasize that while "tax bargaining" is inevitable, the results are rarely apparent in the short term or even easily discernable in the long run. For example, Prichard (2015: 2) writes, "explicit tax bargaining . . . speaks to the potential for conflict over taxation to spur broader governance gains." But he warns "the connections between taxation, responsiveness and accountability have been comparatively implicit, indirect and long-term." At best, it is unclear whether armed groups would ever meet Olson's criterion for long-term horizons that is at the heart of his thinking, or that such long-term planning is even possible in the context of violent conflict.

A third concern is that lacking any sort of international recognition of their territorial claims, rebel leaders differ markedly from leaders of recognized state sovereigns, even where the latter may be unable to exercise their full claim. For both Tilly and Olson, a core feature of the world they imagine is its anarchic structure, a reality that requires armed groups to emphasize their coercive abilities. In their conception, there is no difference between the recognized sovereign and challengers to its authority. But is this an accurate description of the world in which civil wars unfold today? Governance by armed groups is predicated on control of territory, a phenomenon determined primarily by the military strength of the combatants, though reinforced by the strategic needs of the incumbent. Lacking a basis in international law for their status, armed groups' territorial claims mean little without empirical control (Mampilly 2011). This is in contrast to recognized state authorities who benefit from juridical recognition even when their empirical abilities lag. In other words, even where rebels and states may possess equivalent empirical control, it is incorrect to assume that their logics of rule and taxation would be the same as incumbents who benefit from the juridical status granted to them by international law. Put simply, even in weak states, governments might possess long-term time horizons simply because international law grants them this privilege in ways armed groups can never enjoy.

In contrast, for rebels, lacking any juridical standing, their sole nonmilitary claim to territory is defined by their *socially constructed relationship to a distinct civilian constituency*. As such, their ability to tax civilians is far more precarious than incumbent governments. From the perspective of civilians, the fact that states enjoy juridical recognition even where they lack empirical control means that they are obliged to pay taxes to the incumbent even if they are victims of government coercion. Indeed, not paying taxes is widely considered an acceptable basis for punitive measures by the state. In contrast, rebel organizations that impose punishments on civilians for not paying taxes face the dual risk of civilian defections and condemnation by the international community for engaging in "extortion." Few analyses of rebel taxation fail to consider these limitations of applying the Olsonian framework in their analysis.

REBEL TAXATION: A BRIEF EXAMINATION OF THE LITERATURE

Much like Olson's rational autocrat, studies treat rebel taxation as a top-down dynamic with rebels offering public goods in exchange for payments with civilians grateful to receive such offerings rather than facing more coercive options.[1] Such a top-down approach to taxation is surprising, considering most scholars of state taxation have long argued that the payment of taxes is a key mechanism that civilians deploy to articulate demands on their government. Yet, almost no studies of rebel taxation address civilian agency in their analyses. The question is: how does such "tax bargaining"—often prolonged, usually interactive, and rarely direct—shape rebel taxation practices? I suggest that both rebels and civilians are participants in a specific wartime political and economic order that can reinforce, and potentially legitimize (or delegitimize), rebel rule. In this view, beyond its immediate economic benefits, taxation is a technology of governance that rebels deploy to resolve a variety of political, economic, and organizational challenges.

Existing studies treat rebel taxation as a revenue generation mechanism enforced through the superior coercive capacity of the armed group, in Tillyan terms, a protection racket. In this conception, rebel taxation is always extortion. It is essential to delineate the particular incentives and constraints that shape rebel taxation practices rather than relying on an outdated economic determinism. Yet, few studies apply insights regarding how taxation mediates the relationship between rulers and the ruled to the study of rebel taxation. They also do little to examine the highly constrained space in which rebel institutional development takes place.

Writing about the FARC in Colombia, Weinstein's political economy of rebellion provides a paradigmatic example: "The FARC took up the charge of policing criminal and delinquent activity in an attempt to minimize the negative ramifications of the drug trade. *To pay for these services on behalf of the peasantry* [emphasis mine], the FARC implemented a system of taxation that became increasingly formalized and wide-ranging over time" (2006: 291) Considering the central role revenue generation plays in shaping organizational behavior in his model, the application of an explicit logic of economic exchange to taxation is unsurprising.

Yet, even scholars who do not rely on the model of a criminal enterprise for comprehending rebel behavior revert to an Olsonian framework to comprehend taxation. For example, when writing about "security governance" in eastern Congo, Garrett et al. (2009: 14) provide the following description of why armed groups provide security: "The relatively secure environment allows for the concentration on more productive work on the side of the miners and traders, instead of being permanently on guard against existential threats. The growing productivity leads to a higher income in tax collection for the armed group." Sabates-Wheeler and Verwimp (2014: 1475) provide a similar logic in a study of rebel taxation in Burundi: "payments to powerful groups—government forces, rebels, militia, and mafia—can be extorted or given over voluntarily in exchange for protection, or insurance, against a range of negative outcomes, including death."

Even where studies situate taxation within a broader political competition, they fail to extend this logic to rebel groups. For example, in a study of the Colombian civil war, Rodriguez-Franco identifies a core political logic of taxation, showing how conflict can "stimulate patriotism among elites," thereby leading to increased taxation (2015: 5). In this conception, building on the work of Margaret Levi (1988), conflict leads to increased identification with, and trust in, state institutions, thereby increasing taxation. However, while she suggests that "insurgents share similar consequences for state taxation: they compete with the state for the taxable resources of elites," she does not apply the same logic to insurgent taxation. Yet, insurgents similarly engage in taxation to enhance civilian trust in their governance institutions. By performing a core routine associated with the state—taxation—insurgents promote a sense of "state-ness" among civilians, fostering a sense of identification with the nascent rebel authority. For example, the NSCN (I-M) claim that "paying tax to NSCN is in itself a political demonstration of indicating that Naga people pay tax to Naga government and not the occupying force" (*The Morunga Express* 2016).

Each of these studies treats the payment of taxes as a revenue generation mechanism, enforced through the threat of coercion. Taxation allows rebel groups to generate popular support, or at least to prevent defection, through the provision of a broad array of public and private goods. In other words, taxation is a function of a rebel organization's ability to wield violence, while simultaneously reducing the insurgency's need to rely on coercion. Taxation is treated as part of a purely exchange relationship, comparable to other market transactions, though with the threat of force favoring the rebels in the imagined negotiation. Such an approach ignores the importance of popular support in the construction of a legitimate authority, the essential point of distinction between taxation and mere extortion, a point I will return in the next section. As a result, they provide little context for the political bargaining inherent in any form of taxation and say little about civilians' capacity to shape their relationship to armed groups in meaningful ways.

Most studies of rebel taxation also suffer from a significant empirical blind spot, that is, focusing on only the most visible cases of payment to the rebel authority and eliding payments, including nonpecuniary forms, made by rural farmers, small traders, and ordinary civilians. In their search for an Olsonian mechanism, most studies only examine specific economic classes capable of making meaningful payments, usually traders or business elites rooted to specific territorial concerns. Matsuzaki (2019) explains the logic that undergirds this bias: "it is easier to collect taxes on goods and activities that are geographically concentrated or must be transported through a limited number of access points, such as ports and highway toll stations"—activities primarily engaged in by traders and business elites operating in dense, urban environments. Sabates-Wheeler and Verwimp's (2014: 1476) findings wherein taxation only follows an instrumental logic when considering the class position of the contributor is exemplary: "persons owning an enterprise are more likely to make cash contributions to rebel groups. This means that rebels know whom to target, or in alternative wording, persons with this profile know that they have to contribute." Rodriguez-Franco (2016) similarly emphasizes elite loyalties in her analysis of Colombia as does Sanchez de la Sierra (unpublished) in his work on informal miners in Congo.

Titeca's (2011: 56) study of the FAPC in Congo relies on a similar focus on a specific class, arguing that protection was only offered to elite traders but not to smaller traders: "The result of this militarized and brutal means of conflict resolution was that the major traders felt they were operating in a (more or less) secure economic environment, while the smaller traders lived in fear." FAPC territory was particularly well suited for trade, located as it was on the Ugandan border where a robust Nande trading community had long dominated transborder commerce. But even here where conditions produced a high degree of symbiosis between trading elites and the rebel leadership that might support a purely exchange logic, the FAPC demonstrated substantial concern for public welfare building a football stadium, co-funding a university and creating a local development fund that demonstrate a more political purpose than a purely exchange dynamic might suggest (Reyntjens 2014: 533).

A similar narrow focus characterizes Aisha Ahmad's (2014/15) work on the relationship of the business community to Islamist armed groups in Somalia. Ahmad's study correctly links the logic of Olson and Tilly with the ideas of Paul Collier. Her focus on the lower rate of taxation offered by the Union of Islamic Courts as the reason why the business community chose to support the rebels is convincing as compared to explanations that emphasize Islamist- or clan-based identities. But it also raises a basic question regarding all such studies that focus on the relationship of elite traders with armed actors: How else would we expect a community defined by its pursuit of economic profits to behave?

Innate to this approach is a focus on visible types of taxation, particularly those related to large-scale resource extraction and/or cross-border trade. While framed as studies of rebel taxation generally, they rarely address contributions from low-income groups. Sabates-Wheeler and Verwimp's inclusion of coerced labor as a form of taxation is an exception and raises an additional concern. Rebels frequently do not take pecuniary contributions but rely on in-kind donations whether labor, food, or some other nonmonetary good. As Che Guevara prescribed in his manual on how to fight a guerrilla war (1968: 76): "Taxes may be collected in money in some cases, or in the form of a part of the harvest." A whole range of in-kind contributions including agricultural products, food and shelter, various forms of labor including sex acts, as well as, more dramatically, offerings of individual family members should be included in our understanding of rebel tax practices, especially in a context where those with fiscal means often are the first to flee a rebel-controlled territory.

Such forms of tax payments can be especially hard to observe and quantify, leading analysts to ignore them altogether. Yet by ignoring nonpecuniary forms of taxation that remain outside our view, whether due to their low potential to generate revenue or the difficulty of quantifying their value, scholars reinforce the biased understanding of rebel taxation that prevails. In particular, this approach positions the relationship between rebels and civilians as dominated by an elite trading and business class. Unintentionally, this suggests that individuals with little wealth, despite their prevalence within rebel-controlled territories, have no mechanisms through which to influence the behavior of armed groups. More problematically, it ignores the actual empirical evidence that "token" or "head" taxes on low-income groups by rebels are surprisingly commonplace. For example, in India, the NSCN-IM imposes a Rs. 100 tax (approximately US$1.25–1.50) on all villagers, an amount unlikely to cover the costs of collection (Santoshini 2016). Similarly, in South Sudan, rebels imposed a symbolic tax on market women that was openly acknowledged by rebel administrators as bringing in little to no revenue (Mampilly 2011).

Beyond Economic Instrumentalism

If we return to the example of the FARC, we can see some of these noneconomic dynamics at work. A quote from a FARC leader regarding the rebellion's "war tax" seems to offer support for taxation as a revenue generation mechanism: "We didn't do this before because we needed to eat. And this isn't a matter of feeding one or two people. There are thousands of guerrillas who need food, clothing, and everything that you need to live day to day" (Hernández 2016.)

However, both economic and political logics are necessary to understand FARC taxation practices. Consistent with its Marxist ideological orientation, the organization focused its taxation efforts on large-scale coca growers, landowners, and industrial interests (Cala 2000: 59). At one level, these actors are most likely to possess economic resources that can be taxed—justification for the focus on them in the studies cited above. But at another level, it is impossible to disentangle the targeting of elites from the rebellion's ideological position. Targeting a specific class of actors explicitly reinforced the organization's redistributive message, a point frequently invoked in its ideological appeals. This logic is clear in the directive the group released announcing its tax policy in 2000, "Ley 002: Sobre la Tributación." Framing their policy as a response to the behavior of the Colombian government, which had recently received an infusion of cash from its U.S. government patron through "Plan Colombia," the document makes clear that taxation was simultaneously part of its perceived struggle against the Colombian state, U.S. imperialism, and global capitalism. Toward this end, the "Peace Tax" (el impuesto para la paz) would only be levied on those whose wealth exceeded US$1 million.[2]

The FARC was not unique in its approach to taxation as an expression of its ideological position. Other Marxist groups have long paid close attention to the class dimensions of their tax policies in order to reinforce their ideological agenda. Guevara (1968: 104) articulated this logic most clearly: "If conditions continue to improve, taxes can be established; these should be as light as possible; above all for the small producer. It is important to pay attention to every detail of relations between the peasant class and the guerrilla army, which is an emanation of that class."

Taxation must also be understood as a mechanism of social control. While initially the FARC limited its taxes to "owners of large extensions of land, merchants, and large companies," over time they extended this practice to "peasants who owned small farms" (Arjona 2016: 182–83). Did taxing peasants really increase revenue for the organization? It is unclear whether the revenue generated offset the costs of collecting taxes. A different explanation is that the extension of taxation was a product of the competition the organization faced from paramilitary groups. These paramilitaries "taxed every worker in town; from those selling coffee in carts on the street to taxi drivers to shop owners—all had to pay" (Arjona 2016: 183). Taxation may not merely be about raising revenue nor simply an expression of ideological positioning. Instead, it is also an important site in the contest for civilian loyalty and a claim to legitimacy by both sides.

Few studies have attempted to break out of the Olsonian box and situate rebel taxation in relation to broader social and wartime contexts. One exception is a recent study by Mara Revkin, who demonstrates that purely economistic approaches cannot account for how rebel organizations devise their taxation practices. Drawing on a unique dataset of taxation in ISIS-controlled territories of Iraq, she shows that rather than varying by the potential revenues the organization could have generated within specific provinces, the insurgents impose standardized taxation practices even in those provinces where such taxation might have a negative impact on the fiscal situation. She suggests that taxation must then be motivated by something more than the material payoff, suggesting "that the tax policies imposed by insurgent groups may promote state-building through three non-economic mechanisms: social control, collective identity formation, and demographic engineering" (Revkin Forthcoming).

Ultimately, a purely Olsonian approach cannot fully account for the nature and range of rebel taxation practices. The lack of empirical evidence provides some justification for the limited attention to taxation's broader registers. But at the core, reducing rebel taxation to a purely economic bargaining logic fails to situate it within the broader social and political contexts that many scholars of taxation and state power emphasize. These include taxation as a symbolic component of stateness, the role it plays in reinforcing the rebel's ideological position, its capacity to define a particular social constituency, as well as its regulatory dimensions, all essential concerns for any political authority seeking legitimacy.

Taxation and Rebel Governance

By reexamining existing studies, we can identify places in which the regulatory and ideological dimensions of rebel taxation appear even when not explicitly theorized. I argue that understanding the fiscal relationship between rebel rulers and their civilian subjects is essential to grasp the nature of rebel governance and the broader wartime order they put in place. In other words, understanding rebel taxation as a technology of rebel governance can tell us much about the authority relationship between a rebel regime and its subjects.

Rebel governance refers to the development of institutions and practices of rule to regulate the social and political life of civilians by an armed group. Such rebel "governments" commonly come to attention for engaging in the provision of public goods, including things like health and educational systems, a system of food distribution, and so on. But governance extends beyond an explicit exchange relationship. It includes regulatory activities such as land-use policies, issuing of permits and licenses to commercial and nonprofit actors, and social and moral prohibitions. In addition, armed groups often devise symbolic practices, such as the adoption of flags and anthems in order to lend the rebel government an air of legitimacy (Mampilly 2015).

Assessing rebel governance then is no simple task. One approach is to think of rebel governance as a basket of goods that can be enumerated and measured. Armed groups are commonly treated as providing such goods in exchange for material and other support, a quasi-social contract consistent with the Olsonian logic described above. But this assumes that the quality of rebel governance is merely a function of the degree of governance. In other words, the more governance, the better.[3]

Beyond things that can be enumerated, assessing rebel governance entails the more challenging task of teasing out the *texture* of the rebel/civilian relationship, in other words, the way in which civilians feel about their system of rule. Put differently, governance is an innately intersubjective process, one that can only be understood as contingent and dependent on the social relationship between a political authority and its constituency.

Understanding rebel governance then necessarily entails examining whether civilians accept the *legitimacy* of the rebel political authority, by which I am referring to how civilians react to the wartime political order established by the would-be rebel rulers. Taxation provides one opportunity to do this. While taxation does provide material resources to a rebellion, this is not the only purpose it serves. I suggest that in order to understand rebel taxation, it is necessary to comprehend it as both a mechanism for raising revenue and equally as an expression of the sovereign aspirations of the rebel governance system. In addition to its fiscal functions, taxation is a regulatory technology deployed to delimit, control, and sustain a subject population as well as an ideological tool designed to facilitate order by promoting identification and adherence to the rebellion's political project. As such, alongside violence and ideology and interrelated with both, taxation is an integral field of struggle within the broader competition over civilian (and other) loyalties between belligerents.

In the next section, I discuss three separate dimensions of rebel taxation that go beyond economic instrumentalism. These include political logics that have to do with a rebellion's attempt to construct a legitimate authority, organizational dimensions that have to do with strengthening the rebel organization, and economic dimensions that go beyond the simple exchange logic of most extant studies.

Political Dimensions

Many studies of taxation by armed groups do not discriminate between different forms of payments to rebel groups nor the different types of actors involved in such activities. Only rarely do scholars attempt to draw a line between political and economic activities, thereby reducing rebel taxation to other forms of criminal extortion and hence comprehensible through Olson's instrumental logic. Is it possible to draw a line between extortion and taxation in the context of armed groups? While there is no accepted approach, one way to separate extortion from taxation is to ask: from whom is the payer being protected? Protection from the payee can be appropriately described as extortion, while protection from a generalized system of disorder might more accurately be described as taxation (c.f. Tilly 1985).

Thus, a starting point for any inquiry must recognize that rebel taxation is always situated within a broader wartime social context. It is always a political as well as economic process and should not be reduced to mere criminality. In order to do this, it is first necessary to distinguish between taxation by armed groups that seek to tax as part of a broader effort to govern territory from those that deploy it for purely extractive purposes. We can then identify several potential mechanisms that link taxation with the construction and expression of political authority. These operate at multiple levels within the organization and are targeted toward different categories of actors. What they share is their systemic relationship to bolstering the wartime political order constructed by the rebel group. In other words, rather than simply a revenue generation mechanism, taxation serves multiple noneconomic functions that may even surpass its fiscal effects.

Scholars have long noted the role that taxation plays in identifying and surveilling a domestic population. Among other things, tax agencies collect data on an individual's work, professional abilities, place of residence, marital status, gender and sexuality, number of children and other dependents, religious views, ideological beliefs (through donations to charitable organizations) and even whether one is engaged in an extramarital affair (if it involves any regular payment to the unrecognized partner) (Hatfield 2015). Indeed, tax agencies are often privy to more information about a larger portion of the population than agencies explicitly designed to engage in surveillance.

This is not merely an offshoot of taxation but central to it. A political authority cannot engage in effective taxation without extensive demographic information regarding the population it seeks to tax. Civilians wary of the encroaching power of a political authority may choose to shirk or deceive such efforts requiring the authority to increase their monitoring capacity in order to define a tax-paying public. Such efforts may require extensive collaboration with civilians and their various representatives to identify would-be absconders. Put differently, effective taxation requires a would-be political authority to make legible the civilian population, itself a barometer of government strength.

Taxation is also an expression of the ideological orientation of a regime. A core debate that divides political parties in democracies is the level of "appropriate" taxation. Agreement on the level of taxation often unites political parties that may feature considerable internal disagreement around almost every other issue. Similarly, a politician's position on taxation is arguably the strongest indicator of their ideological position. Even autocratic regimes often decide on taxation levels based not on economic but political factors, with many levying suboptimal rates (i.e., rates below what the population could afford and below what a government might need without turning to external loans) in a tacit exchange for political support (Ross 2012).

How a regime chooses to levy taxes—on whom, at what rates, in what manner—often reflects political as much as economic choices. In other words, while all regimes may prefer to maximize their revenues from taxes, these choices do not occur in a politically neutral vacuum but rather reflect central ideological and normative preferences of the regime itself. Historically, in many Islamic polities, taxes called *jizya* were levied on nonbelievers for the privilege of living within the realm, for example. ISIS was reported to offer Christian residents of Mosul the opportunity to pay the tax in order to remain in the city (*Reuters* 2014). In a related fashion, regimes use taxation as a mechanism to sort who should receive social welfare benefits.[4]

Scholars of state taxation position it as a mechanism through which a government seeks to create reciprocal bonds that tie it to a civilian constituency. From the perspective of civilians, paying taxes is often understood as an indicator of their support for a regime. Even where they may disagree with a specific level, tax compliance is often understood by both the regime and its constituents as an indicator of the legitimacy of the regime itself. Leaders of the NSCN (I-M) in India have suggested that "taxation is imposed to show loyalty to the outfit's authority and legitimacy" (*The Telegraph* 2013).

In a context of internal war, in which sovereignty itself is contested, fostering such identification with the local authority is a crucial component of the struggle for dominance. Rebel theorists have long noted how civilians' feelings about different taxations can shape the conflict in determinative ways. For example, Amilcar Cabral suggested that "the colonial authorities have to tolerate this refusal to pay tax from fear that enforcement will cause the populations to flee into our liberated areas or into neighbouring countries" (Quoted in Davidson 2017: 101). In this way, rebels may use taxes not to generate resources but rather to reenforce existing social norms that can ideally increase identification with the local community. Governments frequently levy such "vice" or "sin" taxes to discourage activities deemed at odds with community standards, such as drinking or gambling (Kim 2020). If effective, the purpose of such taxes is not to increase revenue, but ideally, to cancel out a specific revenue source by making it prohibitively expensive. In Colombia, for example, rebels levied sin taxes on beer to discourage alcohol consumption that was claimed to lead to increased episodes of domestic violence.

Organizational Dimensions

Scholars of state formation have long examined the interrelationship between development and taxation. Taxation requires that a political authority develop a bureaucratic capacity both to monitor the population and enforce punitive measures for nonpayment. While some taxes are relatively easy to implement—such as custom duties and sales taxes or the imposition of commercial licenses—others require more complex structures. Income taxes require some basic knowledge of individual's earning potential forcing a political authority to develop expertise in labor economics. Taxes on productive assets such as land require the capacity to do land surveys. The presence of both are generally understood as indicators of the bureaucratic strength of a governing authority (Matsuzaki 2019).

In these ways, taxation can serve as a mechanism for building organizational capacity and relatedly, ensuring organizational discipline. Formalizing a taxation regime can minimize graft by developing specialized structures within a rebel organization to solicit resources from civilians in regularized fashion. It transforms petty graft, a common struggle for most armed groups, into a disciplinary infraction with important implications for popular support. The need to crack down on petty bribery and graft by members of the organization emerges frequently in conversations with both leaders of armed groups and members of the civilian community. Perceptions that a group lacks internal discipline or that it intentionally facilitates the taking of bribes or other forms of corruption among its cadre can fundamentally undermine faith in the rebel political project. Rebel groups, whose leaders are perceived as cracking down on cadre indiscipline and extortion benefit from the perception that they are fair governors, are unafraid to deploy coercive measures against their own for infractions of shared rebel-civilian norms. These are old admonitions first articulated by both Mao and Che in their seminal guerrilla manuals. Rebel taxation provides a bureaucratic solution to the challenge of cadre indiscipline by demanding the establishment of internal organizational structures or regulations capable of ensuring economic discipline throughout the organization.

Taxation may also serve as a mechanism that links local leaders with a national cleavage. In Kalyvas's influential account of the local/national or micro/macro split inherent in civil wars, violence is the primary mechanism that connect local actors with national leaders leading to the "joint production of violence" (2006). But taxation can also be used to resolve the tensions between the two levels. Leaders at the national level may empower local leaders with the authority to tax civilians as a mechanism through which to bring in alignment the often private agendas of local leaders with the interests of leaders at the national level. In this way, the power to delegate who can engage in taxation is a key mechanism that may further the alliance between rebel leaders focused on a national struggle and local elites. Many groups including the SPLA relied on traditional leaders to collect taxes on its behalf, thereby ensuring a privileged position for a potential source of opposition. Yet, this strategy may have its own risks as empowering traditional leaders to raise revenues might allow them to raise their own militias that ultimately challenge the domination of the rebel group itself, a frequent occurrence in South Sudan during the war.

Economic Dimensions

Taxation is obviously concerned with revenue generation, but its economic effects require a more nuanced understanding than normal market transactions, especially when considering non-state actors. A core assumption for both Olson and Tilly is that the spending of rulers is constrained by their capacity to generate revenue through taxation. But is this true? Perhaps it was during the period of European state formation in the early seventeenth century that Tilly focuses on. But as Miguel Centeno (2002) has shown in Latin America, by the nineteenth century, elites could turn to easy financing from the nascent transnational banking sector to borrow money that would allow them to spend beyond their short-term capacity to generate revenue. It is true that borrowing is not an efficient strategy in the long run as lenders will eventually seek to collect their debts. However, there are important exceptions. First, Michael Ross (2012) demonstrates that resource-rich countries can indefinitely avoid this logic by subsidizing their spending with non-tax revenues. And second, some sources of lending may not be driven by a desire to earn interest but rather by a part of a strategy for a country to gain political influence or leverage over another. Or because such support might lead to mutually beneficial gains, either political or economic, that is, money is given with no expectation of economic gains on an investment.

Does their ability to tax constrain the spending of armed groups? There is little reason to think that it does. Rebels can avail numerous sources for funding their activities beyond taxation in ways that most scholars acknowledge including "voluntary or forced contributions from civilians; racketeering, kidnapping, and/or looting of local businesses and civilians; payoffs from multinational corporations; diversion of humanitarian aid from international agencies and nongovernmental organizations (NGOs); patronage from foreign governments; aid provided by international solidarity organizations; contributions from diasporic communities; the sale of drugs and other illicit goods; systematic mineral expropriation; and revenue from controlling key customs checkpoints" (Mampilly 2011: 14).

Even where their fiscal activities resemble state taxation, it is doubtful whether they are similarly constrained. While rebels frequently receive financing from external sources, there is little to no expectation that this money will be returned to the primary state patrons who provide it. Instead, states understand their "investment" in rebellion primarily as a means of engaging in political conflict without direct confrontation and can avail of the significantly lower costs, both financially and reputationally, compared to direct military action. Even where the money is derived from private sources with an explicit expectation of a return on their investment, any investor putting money into a rebellion must calculate the significantly higher probability of default even compared to the riskiest investment in the government of the weakest state. In other words, rebels are more likely to treat taxation in the manner of resource-rich autocrats rather than resource-constrained democracies.

If taxation is not simply about revenue generation, what are the other economic-related uses for which it can be productively deployed by rebels? Some rebel groups use taxation as a mechanism for ensuring the provision of basic goods and building trust in the rebel authority. In this way, rebel taxation might be more productively understood as part of a moral economy built on notions of trust, fairness, justice, and collective survival in contrast to the market economy's focus on free-market competition, individual risk and profit.

Populations living within war zones require basic goods such as food and fuel for survival. Failing to ensure the provision of basic goods may lead to substantive consequences in regards to civilian support. Carolyn Nordstrom (2004: 92) shows how the trade in such goods is a constant concern in areas outside the control of the state. Rather than an anarchic free for all, she suggests that a cohesive network built on trust and involving a wide variety of actors move goods from legal to illegal and back again (See also Meagher 2014). Rebel organizations are an essential node within this network and must work with a variety of actors, including state forces and other non-state groups, to ensure the flow of goods or face civilian discontent. Each actor within the network plays a specific role, and control over taxation is the central mechanism through which rebel organizations link to this broader network. On the other side, local government representatives, both from neighboring states and the incumbent regime, must be sated to facilitate cooperation. All kinds of novel taxation arrangements emerge as a result.

In South Sudan, an interview with a founder of the SPLA customs authority revealed that the primary concern for adopting specific taxation policies during the second civil war was to ensure that basic goods like butter and salt were available to the civilian population. The goal was to reassure traders that they could sell their goods without harassment from the multiplicity of actors that often proliferate in the context of state withdrawal. Traders are anxious about entering rebel-controlled spaces due to a reasonable assumption of anarchy. But the rebels sought to mitigate this anxiety by building a bureaucratic system that provided a degree of certainty. For the SPLA, the task was to ensure that traders only pay customs duties one time upon entering rebel territory so as to ensure the collective survival of their civilian constituents.

Over time, the establishment of regularized system of taxation may even build affection for the rebel regime and translate into political support. The FAPC in Congo seems to have benefited from this dynamic. Returning to Titeca's study, he suggests that the political value of taxation extended beyond the specific class of traders who benefited from direct rebel protection. Instead, it was also a method for the armed group to build trust with other social groups that did not pay taxes by demonstrating the fairness of the rebel regime: "This did not mean that the major traders were protected at all costs. Smaller traders perceived Jérôme's regime to be relatively fair because any misbehaviour by the major traders was also punished."

Even where taxation serves more overt revenue generation functions, the relationship may not be as direct as commonly portrayed. Adopting a particular approach to taxation can be a signal to an external audience, which is trying to slot an organization into various categories based on their perceived fealty to broader ideological concerns. Successfully wooing external actors, whether nongovernmental organizations, international organizations, multinational corporations and, of course, potential state sponsors, can produce substantive revenue benefits for an armed group. For example, in South Sudan, numerous informants confirmed that the original impetus for initiating a system of taxation came not from any ambitions to generate revenues internally. Rather, following the fall of the Marxist Dergue regime in neighboring Ethiopia, the rebellion's original sponsor, the SPLA, was left searching for a new partner to fund the rebellion. The U.S. government stepped into this void offering to serve as the rebellion's new patron, if rebel leaders were willing to shift their rhetoric from socialism to free-market capitalism. As part of this reorientation, the rebels were provided technical expertise and the necessary materials to establish a customs authority, the first step toward establishing a market economy.

Finally, taxation can serve as a mechanism to ensure diasporic support and engagement. According to leaders of the NSCN (I-M), taxation helps "to mobilise support across the world" (*The Telegraph* 2013). Cut off from the immediate costs of the war, many members of the diaspora seek ways to proffer their support to violent movements in their homeland. Often, providing support to the governance activities of armed groups with the intention of supporting kith and kin left behind is the only way for diasporic members to contribute to the struggle in the homeland. In this way, taxation is a "commitment mechanism" that allows members of the diaspora to demonstrate their support for the cause and their concern for those left behind. For the armed group, collecting taxes from the diaspora brings representatives in close contact with civilians who are outside of their direct military control. This requires them to deploy other, nonmilitary appeals that emphasize the political objectives of the group.[5]

But diasporic support is not simply political. Many who have fled their homelands seek to retain direct material ties to the land they left behind. As the sovereign power within these territories, rebel organizations may seek to reassure diaspora members (and internally displaced populations) that their private material interests will be protected by the group during the conflict. For example, the LTTE allowed diaspora members to register property claims in specially created "land courts." Members of the diaspora were then allowed to pay land taxes to ensure that their ownership claims were protected during the conflict and that they would be allowed to reclaim their lands following the end of the fighting. In short, both private and public logics motivated individual civilian behavior in ways that demonstrate the importance of civilian agency in shaping rebel tax practices.

CONCLUSION

Much more needs to be said about taxation in relation to the broader dynamics of rebel governance, particularly its ideological and regulatory dimensions. Taxation by rebels should not be understood solely as an instrumental fiscal concern but rather as part of the larger political project of gaining popular support and controlling the civilian population. Taxation policies in a contested environment reflect the broader struggle for authority between the state and non-state actors. This can produce countervailing logics, such as establishing a taxation apparatus that does little to bring in revenue and more to resolve challenges inherent in the rebel/civilian relationship by symbolically reinforcing an armed group's claim to authority. In other words, whether or not it provides substantive resources, the fact that civilians and businesses are willing to pay a tax is an important indicator of their willingness to accept the sovereign claim of the armed group. By rejecting a narrow economic instrumentalism as the sole logic driving rebel decisions to impose taxes, scholars can open up the possibility of numerous political logics that more accurately account for the behavior of violent groups.

NOTES

1. A similar logic of "competitive state-building" also undergirds much of the thinking on counterinsurgency with states encouraged to build school and hospitals or otherwise provides services in order to compete or outadminister rebel governance provision.
2. FARC-EP. 2000. "Ley 002: Sobre La Tributación."
3. As we know, there are both normative and political reasons why this assumption rarely holds true in the real world. Politically, a more expansive state apparatus is also likely to be less efficient, a key concern for many in regard to how they assess governance performance. Normatively, many resent governments that are seen as too expansive and hence capable of interfering too much in private life.
4. In the United States, for example, resident aliens who pay social security taxes are eligible for the benefits as citizens as long as they remain in the country. However, if they choose to retire abroad, they are subject to a complex set of requirements that their citizen counterparts living abroad are not required to meet. See, for example, "Social Security Payment Requirements for Most North, Central And South American Citizens Living Outside The United States." https://www.ssa.gov/international/61-011.pdf
5. Certainly, armed groups may occasionally reinforce this with force but this is more challenging in foreign countries where the groups lack military power.

REFERENCES

Ahmad, Aisha. 2014/2015. "The Security Bazaar: Business Interests and Islamist Power in Civil War Somalia." *International Security* 39, no. 3: 89–117.

Arjona, Ana. 2016. *Rebelocracy: Social Order in the Colombian Civil War*. New York: Cambridge University Press.

Cala, Andres. 2000. "The Enigmatic Guerrilla: FARC's Manuel Marulanda." *Current History* 99, no. 634: 56–59.

Centeno, M. A. 2002. *Blood and Debt: War and the Nation-State in Latin America*. University Park: Penn State University Press.

Collier, Paul. 2000. "Rebellion as a Quasi-Criminal Activity." *Journal of Conflict Resolution* 44, no. 6: 839–53.

Collier, Paul, and Anke E. Hoeffler. 1998. "On the Economic Causes of Civil War." *Oxford Economic Papers* 50: 563–73.

Collier, Paul, V. L. Elliott, Håvard Hegre, Anke Hoeffler, Marta Reynal-Querol, and Nicholas Sambanis. 2003. *Breaking the Conflict Trap: Civil War and Development Policy*. A World Bank Policy Research Report. Washington, DC: World Bank and Oxford University Press.

Davidson, Basil. 2017. *No Fist Is Big Enough to Hide the Sky: The Liberation of Guinea-Bissau and Cape Verde, 1963–74*. London: Zed Press.

Garrett, Nicholas, Sylvia Sergiou, and Koen Vlassenroot. 2009. "Negotiated Peace for Extortion: The Case of Walikale Territory in Eastern DR Congo." *Journal of Eastern African Studies* 3, no. 1: 1–21.

Gowrinathan, Nimmi, and Zachariah Mampilly. 2019. "Resistance and Repression under the Rule of Rebels: Women, Clergy and Civilian Agency in LTTE Governed Sri Lanka." *Comparative Politics* 52, no. 1 (October): 1–20.

Guevara Ernesto. 1968. *Guerrilla Warfare*. New York: Vintage Books.

Hatfield, Michael. 2015. "Taxation and Surveillance: An Agenda." *Yale Journal of Law and Technology* 17: 319–67.

Hernández, Alan. 2016. "Colombia's Largest Rebel Group Will Stop Collecting War Taxes." *Vice News*, July 5. https://news.vice.com/article/colombias-largest-rebel-group-will-stop-collecting-war-taxes.

Kalyvas, Stathis. 2006. *The Logic of Violence in Civil Wars*. Cambridge: Cambridge University Press.

Kim, Diana. 2020. *Empires of Vice: Opium and the Rise of Prohibition across Southeast Asia*. Princeton: Princeton University Press.

Levi, Margaret. 1988. *Of Rule and Revenue*. Berkeley: University of California Press.

Mampilly, Zachariah. 2011. *Rebel Rulers: Insurgent Governance and Civilian Life during War*. New York: Cornell University Press.

Matsuzaki, Reo. 2019. *Statebuilding by Imposition: Resistance and Control in Colonial Taiwan and Philippines*. Ithaca: Cornell.

McGovern, Mike. 2011. "Popular Development Economics—An Anthropologist among the Mandarins." *Perspectives on Politics* 9, no. 2 (June): 345–55.

Meagher, Kate. 2012. "The Strength of Weak States? Non-State Security Forces and Hybrid Governance in Africa." *Development and Change* 43, no. 5: 1073–101.

Mkandawire, Thandika. 2002. "The Terrible Toll of Post-colonial 'Rebel Groups' in Africa: Towards an Explanation of the Violence Against the Peasantry." *Journal of Modern African Studies* 40, no. 2: 181–215.

The Morunga Express. 2016. "NSCN (IM) Affirms Position on Legitimacy and Taxation." June 18. http://morungexpress.com/nscn-im-affirms-position-legitimacy-taxation/

Nordstrom, Carolyn. 2004. *Shadows of War: Violence, Power, and International Profiteering in the Twenty-First Century*. Berkeley: University of California Press.

Olson, Mancur. 1993. "Dictatorship, Democracy, and Development." *The American Political Science Review* 87, no. 3: 567–76.

Pagliery, Jose. 2016. "ISIS Makes Up for Lost Oil Cash with Rising Taxes and Fees." *CNN Money*, May 31. http://money.cnn.com/2016/05/31/news/isis-oil-taxes/index.html

Prichard, Wilson. 2015. *Taxation, Responsiveness and Accountability in Sub-Saharan Africa: The Dynamics of Tax Bargaining*. Cambridge: Cambridge University Press.

Raeymaekers, Timothy. 2010. "Protection for Sale? War and the Transformation of Regulation on the Congo–Ugandan Border." *Development and Change* 41, no. 4: 563–87.

Reuters. 2014. "Convert, Pay Tax, or Die, Islamic State Warns Christians." July 18. https://www.reuters.com/article/us-iraq-security-christians/convert-pay-tax-or-die-islamic-state-warns-christians-idUSKBN0FN29J20140718

Reyntjens, Filip. 2014. "Regulation, Taxation and Violence: The State, Quasi-state Governance and Cross-Border Dynamics in the Great Lakes Region." *Review of African Political Economy* 41, no. 142: 1–15.

Rodriguez-Franco, Diana. 2016. "Internal Wars, Taxation, and State Building." *American Sociological Review* 81, no. 1: 190–213.

Ross, Michael. 2012. *The Oil Curse: How Petroleum Wealth Shapes the Development of Nations*. Princeton: Princeton University Press.

Sabates-Wheeler, Rachel, and Philip Verwimp. 2014. "Extortion with Protection: Understanding the Effect of Rebel Taxation on Civilian Welfare in Burundi." *Journal of Conflict Resolution* 58, no. 8: 1474–99.

Sanchez de la Sierra, Raul. Unpublished manuscript. "On the Origin of States: Stationary Bandits and Taxation in Eastern Congo."

Taylor, Brian and Roxana Botea. 2008. "Tilly Tally: War-Making and State-Making in the Contemporary Third World." *International Studies Review* 10, no. 1: 27–56.

Tilly, Charles. 1985. "War Making and State Making as Organized Crime." In *Bringing the State Back In*, edited by Peter Evans, Dietric Rueschmeyer, and Theda Skocpol, pp. 169–91. Cambridge: Cambridge University Press.

Titeca, Kristof. 2011. "Access to Resources and Predictability in Armed Rebellion: The FAPC's Short-lived 'Monaco' in Eastern Congo." *Africa Spectrum* 46, no. 2: 43–70.

Weinstein, Jeremy. 2009. "Africa's Revolutionary Deficit." *Foreign Policy*, October 13. http://foreignpolicy.com/2009/10/13/africas-revolutionary-deficit/

Part II

HISTORICAL PERSPECTIVE

Chapter 5

The War Economy of Nomadic Empires

Nicola Di Cosmo

INTRODUCTION

The history of Eurasia, from antiquity to the modern era, would be inconceivable without the inclusion of nomadic peoples, whose migrations, conquests, and interactions with every major civilization transformed cultures, societies, and ecologies. Yet, the basic mechanisms through which steppe nomads achieved historical prominence have not been sufficiently understood, or even investigated. Most often they are represented as cyclical occurrences caused by events such as climatic crises that pushed nomads out of their natural environment, or the appearance on the scene of a charismatic leader who unified various ethnic and political groups and, on the strength of that unity, embarked on campaigns to raid, invade, and conquer other peoples. In fact, steppe nomads were only occasionally able to transcend the limitations of their economy and environment, and the empires they formed were all different from one another: some were limited in scope and duration, some more eventful and consequential.

One question that seems to be at the heart of the formation of nomadic empires is that each one of them was born in war and nourished by war, first of all among the nomads themselves (Di Cosmo 2002). But intra-nomadic warfare by itself surely cannot account for the upward trajectory that took such nomadic formations to a level of supremacy and complexity that challenged the richest and greatest of coeval powers. To grasp how nomads managed to undertake political and social transformations on their path to statehood, the economic aspects appear both crucial and elusive (Di Cosmo 1999).

The term *state*, one should note from the start, here simply means a political structure inclusive of a body of "subjects" that recognizes a central sovereign authority and is, in different degrees, dependent upon the gradual institutionalization of certain government functions, such as judicial, fiscal, and administrative tasks. More specifically, gradual institutionalization and bureaucratization of a steppe empire always found their roots in a war economy that had to supply the means to sustain the territorial and demographic expansion of the state as well as its increasing complexity while continuing to maintain an efficient army and reward a sprawling aristocracy. It is therefore essential, in order to understand the historical import of steppe nomads, to consider how their war economy was able to supply the means to make a "state" possible. With that overarching goal in mind, this chapter aims to describe the ways in which nomadic empires could only be sustained by seeking to procure resources from outside their original productive basis (pastoralism) and how their war economy was, at different stages of the empires' life, inextricably linked to their growth and success. War economy was, in fact, one of the key drivers of political and social transformations that allowed nomadic rulers to hold together a diverse population, retain a highly centralized leadership, and overcome the centrifugal tendencies typical of societies based on tight kinship and territorial bonds.

A NOTE ON METHOD

A methodological point is in order. Only in a few cases we gain a glimpse of how nomadic empires (or "polities") came into being, and any attempt to hypothesize a pathway to state-building common to all nomadic empires depends upon a combination of data from scant textual sources, uneven archaeological finds, as well as, on a more removed evidential plane, paleoclimatic, genetic, and other scientific data. Moreover, we need to consider that, while it has long been assumed that nomadic empires constitute a separate category of empires, it is unclear why that should be the case, that is, what makes them into a separate category of historical analysis. To wit, the fact itself that discrete nomadic empires have been treated as isolated instances, which lacked continuity and only entered history episodically, militates against a holistic view of the "nomadic empire" as a distinct "historical type." And yet, when historians look for state formations that may be analogous or comparable with that, for instance, of the Mongol Empire (c. 1206–1368), they are far more likely to consider the Xiongnu Empire, established in the third century BCE, than coeval medieval empires such as the Byzantine, Holy Roman, or Mamluk. The reasons why Inner Asian empires are so often placed in a single basket is only one, namely, that they were created by steppe nomads, and therefore are presumed to belong to the same political species, based mainly on shared economic practices—that is, pastoral production—and forms of social organization.[1]

While such, mainly anthropological, perspectives can be useful to question our sources, if taken as the predominant interpretive strategy they can also introduce analytical biases. One of these biases, for instance, is that these empires ipso facto share not just economic and social traits but also political features and traditions that come "with the territory" of being a nomadic empire. The notion that nomads have their own ways, and are, as such, incommensurable with other political formations, if taken as an axiom, renders opaque if not invisible aspects of governance and institutions that may be shared with or borrowed from outside a nomadic milieu. Such approaches also tend to produce circular arguments, to the extent that nomadic traditions are then established on the basis of the very similarities attributed to them. In reality, it is the variety, dynamism, and flexibility of these empires that is most interesting when studying them as expressions of a special type or historical manifestation and human experience, rather than the ageless and static attributes they seem to share.

With that caveat in mind, we can nonetheless readily see that, even in cases in which two nomadic empires behave and evolve in profoundly different ways, their genesis remains remarkably similar and is rooted in a particular type of process that transforms endemic low-grade violence into gradually more organized violence, whereby the whole of society becomes increasingly more militarized, armies grow in size, and war becomes the chief means of transformation of the social and political order. Such turning points in steppe history are generally shrouded in mystery and can be perceived only through faint signs left in the sources of literate neighbors or in the writings (including myths and epics) written down after they attained a mature imperial condition.

A VERY BRIEF SURVEY OF NOMADIC EMPIRES

Notorious for their destructiveness, nomads were structured, from the time of Herodotus down to the dawn of the modern age, in ethno-political groups, defined sometime as nations or tribes. At times they were unified under a single ruler that engaged in long-range predatory raids, territorial expansion, conquest, and, in the most successful cases, formed massive empires and lasting dynasties.[2] Their political culture left deep, if often unacknowledged, grooves in the organization and culture of sedentary empires, from China (Ming and Qing dynasties) to Central Asia (Timurids), India (Mughals), and the near east (Ottomans). Moreover, the empires they founded were transnational, multicultural, polyglot, and able to organize commercial and cultural exchanges over long distances. As such, they also played a significant role in premodern transnational and "trans-civilizational" connectivity, and have been regarded as predecessors of modern phenomena of "globalization."

How they achieved such heights of sway and power is a matter of debate, but a critical and thus far unanswered question surely regards the economic sphere, and more precisely the resource basis that permitted the "quantum leap" from a state of political fragmentation to one of political centralization, based on top-heavy command structure, permanent army, and incipient bureaucracy. The starting point of the investigation, however, is quite clear. Empires started in wars whose "economy" can be reasonably assumed to have been the key mechanism that ignited the systemic transformations leading to state formation—whether we call the resulting product a "state," an empire, or a "supercomplex chiefdom" (Kradin 2004).

When nomads formed their first large political unions and polities has not been determined. The first historically documented nomads are the Scythians found in Greek sources from the fifth century BCE, but how "imperial" they were is unclear. Surely archaeology bears witness to the power and prowess of their aristocracy, but we do not have a record of an "empire" that could be regarded as comparable to that created by later nomads. The information in the sources is more ethnographic than political: various Scythian groups are documented, but their structure is rather loose, and it appears that they were not unified politically. On the other hand, their large burials and rich material culture seem to indicate an abundance of wealth and power that belies political complexity.

It is on the other side of Eurasia, in China, that we find the first full-fledged description of a nomadic empire, that of the Xiongnu (or "Asiatic Huns"), which emerged around the end of the third century BCE. Taking this as a departure point is a useful device, even though we must assume that the foundations of their political culture were laid long before. The Xiongnu are described by the Chinese historian par excellence, Sima Qian, with many details that allow us to follow their trajectory from a state of disunity and crisis to the achievement of imperial status, massive territorial expansion, and superior status in foreign relations with the Chinese empire.

The weakening and demise of the Xiongnu Empire around the first to second centuries CE were followed by an extraordinary period of change and transformation on the northern frontier of China, which made several nomadic groups prominent politically. Their dynasties, established in areas straddling the steppes of Mongolia and Manchuria, and the agricultural areas of northern China, were politically hybrid, but also transformative of both the Inner Asian and the Chinese previous traditions. The Northern Wei dynasty (386–534 CE) claimed nomadic origins but transitioned toward more Sinitic forms of political and administrative organization, while the nomadic Rouran became masters of the steppe region, from the fourth to the early sixth century.

The political dynamism of the steppe was heightened in the sixth century, when the early Türk Empire emerged as a phenomenon that encompassed East and West, expanding to the point of reaching Byzantium and Iran, and thus playing an unprecedented role in commercial and diplomatic relations across Eurasia. Their expansion in also connected to expansion of the Avars, a steppe people who attacked the Byzantine Empire. Their empire had roots that have been traced back to the aforementioned Rouran who, defeated by the Türks, migrated westward. Migration, like conquest, is the result of political events that are difficult if not impossible to detect with the diagnostics instruments currently available to historians—perhaps genetics will one day offer better tools—and therefore we are often compelled to resort to speculative hypotheses. However, there is no doubt that intra-nomadic wars played a large role in causing the political instability behind migrations and regime changes. Surely the events leading to the fall of the Second Türk Empire in the eighth century, and eventually to the rise of the Uighur Empire (744–840 CE), were the result of internecine wars among nomadic groups, whose power bases were in Mongolia.

Mongolia and Manchuria remain for the following centuries the places that generate a succession of increasingly more articulate and expansive empires, long characterized in historical writing as "conquest dynasties" because they ruled over parts of China, where they established their own ruling dynasties, and because to a degree they fashioned themselves as Chinese dynasties, and were regarded as such in Chinese historiography. The Khitan and Jurchen peoples established respectively the Liao and the Jin dynasties, both nomadic, quite different from each other, and pitched against the native Chinese dynasty of Song. These, too, emerged from times of violent struggles within an Inner Asian milieu, and the Jin itself successfully defeated the Liao, thus once again emerging after a period of intra-nomadic power struggle.

The "apotheosis" of nomadic power was reached by the subsequent Mongol conquest and empire (c. 1206–1368), encompassing most of Eurasia, which established Mongol rule over China, Russia, Iran, and Central Asia. Here we are not interested specifically in what made the Mongols successful, but we should note that, once again, the Mongol conquest was preceded by much political turmoil and thirty years of tough, merciless wars within Mongolia, which transformed the political landscape. The unprecedented success of the Mongols may have been the result of special circumstances, but the manner in which it emerged and evolved is consistent with the experience of other empires, namely, after a long period of internal nomadic wars.

Finally, the last dynasty in China (Qing 1644–1911) was created by the Manchus, another Inner Asian people whose rise to glory and construction of a state able to challenge the Chinese empire, and then conquer it, is the product of approximately fifty years (1580s to the early 1630s) of wars against

Inner Asian foes, both Manchu and Mongol ones. The creation of a Manchu state, and its conquest of China, show in sharp detail the connections between economy and warfare and the efforts made by its leaders to transcend the limits of their economic basis as a key feature of their military success and state-building.

What emerges from such a cursory survey is that, while these empires were all very different in terms of ethnic makeup, territorial extension, political structure, and international relations, an investigation of the role of their "pre-state" war economy can focus on one remarkably similar and in my view truly comparable feature. This feature can be described as the economic requirements generated by the inter-nomadic wars in order to establish and maintain a new political order, which is predicated upon union and centralized rule.

WAR IN THE RISE OF A NOMADIC EMPIRE

To my knowledge, the only specific study on the war economy of nomadic empires is by two economic scholars, Ronald Findlay and Mats Lundhal (Findlay and Lundhal 2006). Their work contains many important insights, especially in relation to the formalization of the relationship between labor force, wages, taxes, and nomadic conquests. The connection between the size of territory conquered and the fiscal yield, as well as the economic "productivity" of the army by increasing the territorial extension of the empire, are questions that historians need to pay close attention to, and Findlay and Lundhal ought to be praised for singling out economic mechanisms that would be invisible to anthropologists and historians. However, the study also raises questions. For instance, several assumptions are not examined in a long-term historical context. The assertions that "no artisan activities could be developed on a large scale in nomadic societies" or that "trade could not yield such benefits as plunder" (26) are generic and not grounded in a historical context. What "large scale" means should be related to the size of a society and its needs, and steppe archaeology shows considerable variety and "scale." Likewise, the profits yielded by trade *vis-à-vis* plunder, while hard to quantify, also depend on the historical period in question. It is exceedingly difficult to say, for instance, that in the relations between the Ming dynasty and the Mongols trade was less profitable than plunder.[3] Going from generic assumption about the nomadic economy to the economics of the Mongol conquest, the authors essentially bypass the long history of state and empire building of nomadic empires, missing, in my view, the political dimension of the climactic transformation from a series of small polities into a large "imperial" polity. The notion that "the steppe empire was the creation of its emperor, not the other way around, and when he died, his successor would have to create his own structures and allegiances—again on a completely personal basis" (28) is a generalization that finds little historical support. But it is true and worth reflecting on the conditions that made each steppe empire a new "creation." Even if this was the product of a "singular figure" (28)—a statement that most historians of Inner Asia would dispute—the resulting political structure would have requirements that far exceeded those of smaller, regional polities.

Indeed, a highly centralized political structure under a single overarching authority is far from being the most common condition for pastoral nomads, whose environment and mobile activities favor fragmentation, with relatively small social units dispersed over a large territory. This lifestyle is often subject to internal feuds and endemic low-intensity violence, although this rarely rises to the level of large-scale conflicts. Under certain circumstances, however, the level of violence can increase dramatically, as can, with it, the size of armies and the degree of militarization. Once the political landscape begins to change from a balance of power among internally cohesive groups to a state of war that gradually envelops the whole society, a situation of "warlordism" emerges. Successful military leaders are compelled by the logic of competition to increase their armies or risk destruction.

War, in the case of nomadic empires, was not just critical to their formation but seems to be a sine qua non of their very existence. On the economic side, running a nomadic empire was more expensive than the nomadic economy could pay for, no matter how much wealth was extracted from the common members of society, because the cost of the state apparatus far outstripped the productive base. On the political side, the legitimacy of a steppe ruler was not based on the prestige of the office (such as a divine right to rule) but on personal charisma and on a logic of redistribution of wealth throughout the body politic. Both charisma and the acquisition of wealth were inseparably tied to attaining success in war. In other words, war provided the only means through which the ruler could keep whatever "state" was being built both fiscally viable and politically stable. In-built centrifugal pressures made war not just a choice but a necessity, because the nomadic empire was born hungry and required a constant influx of resources—riches, land, and people. In sum, war was key to supporting the army, keeping the loyalty and privileges of an expanding elite, and protecting the leadership of the khan from internal challenges; and while most premodern empires are created by conquest and war, nomadic empires have in war the only safe way to arise and survive.

The causes that ignited the intra-nomadic wars, that often led to the formation of empires, are difficult to identify and surely cannot be reduced to one single factor, but have been mostly discussed in terms of widespread crises linked to pressures from foreign invaders, or environmental breakdowns, such as droughts. Speaking of environmental hazards, contemporary ethnography has demonstrated the high degree of vulnerability of economies based on rangelands, in particular in Mongolia and semiarid zones where animal husbandry is the chief form of production, to environmental changes. In nomadic economy, an optimal equilibrium between land resources and animal resources is, under normal circumstance, extremely difficult to achieve (Vetter 2005). For instance, if the herds exceed the carrying capacity of the land, overgrazing can deplete the supply of grass, and require changes in the exploitation of pastures. Climatic variability and sudden disasters can affect the mortality rate of animals, and reduce, sometimes dramatically, the food supply for human beings, inducing social crises due to famine and migrations. It, therefore, cannot be excluded that the vulnerability of the nomadic economy may be at the root of periodic crises that ignited conflicts over access to resources, be these pastures, animals, trade routes, or people. However, such vulnerability is not, per se, the cause that pushes nomads beyond the steppes. This needs to be searched for, rather, in the new political order that protracted warfare created.

Whatever small or indirect information we have about the period that preceded the formation of nomadic empires, there seems to be a constant pattern. In each case, society is stressed by longer conflicts, and conflicts involve increasingly larger armies. It is not an extraordinary stretch of the imagination to say that at such times both the destructive effects of war and its underlying causes (especially in the case of environmental crises) severely reduced production, whose downward trajectory in turn intensified competition over dwindling resources. This cycle of increasing violence for the control of diminishing resources can be identified, possibly, as key toward the creation of unified polities, whereby small groups faced extinction unless their leaders allied themselves with larger groups and subordinated their status as minor aristocrats to the fortunes of a more powerful leader. As time went on, and the vicissitudes of war pruned the pool of contestants, the various groups were reduced to a few warring parties and competing leaders.

Eventually, a single leader emerged as victorious and obtained the surrender or alliance of the others. In the process, however, the political establishment was turned into a much more vertical structure in which key positions were occupied by members of the royal family and also members of aristocratic lineages who typically rose through the military ranks, by forging a personal bond of fealty with the sovereign. Land and privileges were conceded to them, but the central power claimed a monopoly over resources, the right to go to war, and to conduct the foreign policy of the state. Arguably, such a "state" came into existence out of two concurrent mechanisms. The first was the assimilation of conquered tribes, whose members could be either recruited or enslaved after their leaders had been defeated. The second was a voluntary act by lesser aristocrats and local commanders to lead their people and join the camp of the "unifier-to-be." In either case, these people would have had to undergo a process of redefinition of their social status, which could be severely decreased in the first case, or stay the same and even increased in the second. The main trade-off of this arrangement was that it protected society as a whole from a cycle of unending violence that threatened everyone's livelihood.

However, a major change occurred in the distribution of economic resources. The old tribal aristocracy relied on the surplus production of their immediate subjects, which was occasionally taxed, to retain its position of privilege. On the contrary, the new leadership regarded the state, and the people, as personal patrimony and thus acquired a "redistributive" role so that positions, honors, rewards, and land grants all flowed from a single center. Such an arrangement was usually consolidated during the initial "civil war" period, when the warring groups raided each other's camps, and appropriated the enemy's livestock, people, and whatever valuables. To the extent that the rival parties had access to trade, wars were also fought over access to commercial centers. All of this could not but cause the relentless militarization of society, which also meant subtracting producers from the economic base. As we see from a number of cases, and possibly most clearly in the case of the early Mongol Empire, at the moment of "confederation," the size of the army increased dramatically, as did the court apparatus, even as economic resources most likely dwindled. How could the army and court be supported?

What I argue here is that the new political order came with a steep "sticker price" which the nomads simply could not afford with the economic resources at their disposal. The threat that such a bitterly fought over new order might rapidly collapse was real. In order to prevent that the well-known centrifugal tendencies of nomadic politics might be reignited, the "supratribal" leader—the political unifier, the khan, the sovereign—could not establish a firm control on the army and government without finding ways to pay for them. Supporting a large personal army, rewarding loyal commanders, preserving the loyalty of family members, developing new institutions (judicial, fiscal, and administrative) and financing state-building projects such as sponsoring religious clergy, expanding handicraft production (i.e., metallurgy for military supplies) and increasing the general pastoral and agricultural productivity required people (slaves), and revenues from outside the steppe economy. Hence, the process of state-building had to rely on strategies for raising revenues from outside the nomadic society. Note that this is not a general requirement of the pastoral economic, but rather a special requirement that stems from political, rather than merely economic, conditions.

The extraction of resources was based on various methods that changed over time, and depend on the nomads' ability to modify their state-building process by deploying increasingly more sophisticated economic strategies. These strategies or revenue extraction can be grouped in four categories, some of which appeared at an earlier historical stage, while others developed later: raiding, tribute, trade, and taxes. Their historical evolution bespeaks not only of the diversified nature of imperial nomadic economies, but also of changes in their political culture. Indeed, the transition from the direct application of violence to more complex forms of extraction marks the particular and essential dynamism of nomadic empires and their main forms of economic and political interaction with sedentary societies.

ECONOMIC STRATEGIES

Raiding and Pillaging

The primary form of subsidy for the newly minted leader and his court and military apparatus consisted of booty from incursions and raids into sedentary areas. The central principle of this strategy was simple, and consisted of using the military superiority of nomads as a predatory mechanism. When we speak of raids by a centralized army, we should clarify that these are not small war parties but rather expeditionary armies numbering in the tens of thousands, which had the potential to devastate a large territory, assault border towns, and occupy a given region for months. The raids by Xiongnu or Türk armies into Chinese territory could easily number more than 30,000 soldiers, while Khitan and Mongol armies were even larger. The collection of booty was centrally organized, and the spoils were redistributed both among the aristocracy and to the rank-and-file soldiers in the form of "rewards" that included slaves, livestock, and various commodities. The border defenses of agrarian states, even those as rich and powerful as China, were typically no match for nomadic warriors, hardened by a lifetime of battles, highly mobile, and organized into an effective and highly disciplined fighting force.

Over time, however, counting exclusively on looting could prove unsustainable. Spoliation of the frontier regions through repeated pillaging had two effects. On the one hand, the constant threat of raids could cause the gradual abandonment of the frontier by settlers, resulting in depopulation and impoverishment. On the other hand, if more muscular policies prevailed among the victims of nomadic raids, the latter might proceed to step up their defenses, leading to the progressive militarization of the frontier. For instance, during the Former Han dynasty (206 BCE–9 CE), the Chinese authorities progressively built defenses and moved armies to the frontier for the protection of those border regions that were exposed to attacks by the Xiongnu. These developments meant that the "booty economy" of the nomads produced diminishing returns, while becoming costlier. As a source of state financing, a strategy based on predation was eventually bound to fail or at the very least to produce extremely unreliable results.

More critically, from the point of view of the preservation of the ruling elite, in the long run this strategy could produce destabilizing political effects. The sovereign, while theoretically in charge of the whole army, could not prevent his own commanders and aristocrats from engaging in raiding for their own personal gain, in order to strengthen their own position within the state, potentially mount a challenge to the authority of the ruler, or constitute an alternative center of power.[4] The existence of a "supratribal" leadership required that profits from booty were theoretically controlled solely by the ruler, and indiscriminate pillaging damaged his authority as well as the economic foundations of the empire. Therefore, already with the first historical nomadic empire (the aforementioned Xiongnu), raiding was in part replaced by the exaction of a "tribute" paid through treaties and official agreements negotiated directly by the ruler and backed by his military power.

Tribute

Tribute is to be understood as a payment extorted in exchange for peace, that is, essentially, protection money. Compared to a purely predatory strategy, tribute obtained by diplomatic means had the advantage of replacing irregular spoils of war with regular yearly collections. It consisted of various forms of wealth, mostly luxuries and precious materials such as silk, gold, silver—that is, commodities that could also be monetized. The nomadic leader both negotiated and monopolized the tribute subsidies, which could be invested in consolidating his power, strengthening the army, and expanding the empire's influence and territory. The amount of tribute was fixed by treaties negotiated between rulers, which were periodically renewed either when a new ruler succeeded to the throne or after a war disrupted the agreement and required a renegotiation.

Even in a treaty regime, conflicts may erupt either because nomads wanted to increase the payment or because the party that paid tribute wanted to sever that obligation. If we take into consideration the empires that most consistently relied on tribute—the Xiongnu, the Türks, and the Liao dynasty—we see that treaties were periodically disrupted, although they may also produce fairly long spells of peaceful relations. By monopolizing the collection of tribute, the "khan" was able to maintain his redistributive role, pay for the government and personal army, and keep the loyalty of the military aristocracy.

In Chinese history, the first sustained economic strategy that relied on the extraction of tribute for the financing of a nomadic empire was promoted by the Xiongnu Empire in the second century BCE. The threat of violence was initially sufficient to persuade China to pay, but eventually China turned to a more offensive stance, based on ceasing the payment of tribute, deploying a larger and more effective military force, and pursuing a shrewd "divide and rule" policy aimed to incite internal divisions in the nomadic camp. Civil war, the lack of revenues, and rivalries in the succession to the throne weakened and eventually destroyed the Xiongnu as a unified polity.

The Xiongnu also present the opportunity to examine in depth the failure of treaty relations because of the debates that accompanied the Chinese decision to cease the payment of tribute and embark in a long and expensive war. In a nutshell, the Chinese decision was not simply caused by the humiliation of paying a tribute to barbarians, or by the excessive economic burden it constituted. Rather, paying tribute did not guarantee peace because the sovereignty of the nomadic ruler was not sufficient to guarantee that the terms of the treaty would be respected. If some of his generals still engaged in raids and predation, then paying a tribute did not guarantee peace. In fact, from a Chinese point of view, the tribute might have had a more positive effect, had it consolidated and strengthened the position of the nomadic ruler as the sole sovereign. As this was not the case, the requests of tribute increased, the burden grew, and to keep paying the tribute became politically and economically unsustainable (Di Cosmo 2002: 209–27). The Xiongnu, for their part, found it difficult to overcome one of the major pitfalls of their political culture, viz., the inherent weakness of the ruler relative to the military aristocracy.

The Türk Empire, established in the sixth century CE, in its initial phase also extracted a large tribute mostly in silk from the short-lived Western Wei and Northern Zhou Chinese dynasties, before China was reunified under the Sui and Tang dynasties. Shortly after the Tang came to power (618 CE), the Chinese emperor ceased paying tribute to the nomads, and responded militarily to the threat posed by the eastern Türk Empire. In a few years, the empire collapsed. Although there were various reasons that accelerated the crisis, the lack of revenues was a key factor leading to its collapse. Without external revenues the Türk *qaghan* was left with very limited options, when his economic basis was ravaged by a climatic crisis, famine spread across his lands, his commanders defected, and other subject peoples also refused to pay tribute (Graff 2002; Di Cosmo et al. 2017).

More successful was the treaty negotiated between the Liao and the Song dynasty in 1004–1005—the Treaty of Shanyuan—which included, together with a host of other provisions, a hefty annual payment to the Liao. This treaty marked a turning point in Liao-Song relations, which had been until then especially bellicose. The Treaty of Shanyuan provided a framework for peaceful relations, but above all provided the Liao with a steady stream of revenues. As Twitchett and Tietze pointed out, the subsidies paid by the Song in silk and silver constituted a small amount for the very wealthy Chinese dynasty, but were a substantial sum for the Khitan, "whose revenues were comparatively meager" and "used the silk for their own major internal expenses, for instance, in building the new Central Capital immediately after the treaty"; in addition, the "Khitan acquired a steady source of additional revenue and were able to reduce their southern border defenses to some degree and to concentrate on internal developments" (Twitchett and Tietze 1994: 110). The effects of the revenues provided by the treaty were especially significant in stabilizing the central leadership, and, in the case of the Liao, also providing a precious commodity, silk, that could be traded to other people, thus stretching further the financial significance of the payment (Twtchett and Tietze 1994: 110). The success of the treaty relationship between Liao and Song, and the relative importance of the tribute that nomads were cashing in, must be placed in a context in which additional forms of income were also being pursued, such as trade and taxation, as we shall see below.

On the contrary, in cases such as the Xiongnu and the Türk, who operated under different historical circumstances, tribute relations had pitfalls that undermined its usefulness. While the extortion of tribute might have seemed an efficient way to procure the revenues needed to feed the empire, ultimately it was a strategy based on a delicate balance that could be easily disrupted if the tribute's amount exceeded the ability of the payee to satisfy the request, or if it did not preserve peace and security on the frontier. The pressures on the nomadic leaders to request increasingly greater payments came from the proliferation of aristocratic privileges and growth of the army, which are physiological processes in a nomadic empire, whose political survival is predicated on the preservation of aristocratic entitlements and constant military success. Such a parasitic strategy could be acceptable to the payer only as long as it did not threaten its survival. Once the price of peace exceeded that limit, nonpayment, even at the risk of war, became a preferable option.

Note that an excessive economic dependency on tribute also exposed the nomadic leader to various perils. While military pressure could be applied to enforce payment, and looting also could be resorted to, the success of such tactics depended upon the relative strength of the nomads, whose military superiority was only assured as long as they remained united. China indeed resorted to threats and blandishments of its own, offering political alliances and economic inducements to subordinate leaders in order to break the unity of the nomadic leadership. Special rewards, protection, and land deals were given to tribal leaders that turned against the "khan" in exchange for submission and loyal service. In Chinese, this strategy was often referred to as *yi yi zhi yi* "using the barbarians to rule the barbarians."

Because the redistribution mechanisms were not straightforward, and the sovereignty of the "khan" was above all linked to the charismatic nature of his power, the treaties could be easily challenged by other members of the aristocracy, who could resort to "private" pillaging of the sedentary areas in case of disaffection, just as in the case of a policy based exclusively on predation. The ruler's inability to preserve peace or the hostile party's inability or unwillingness to pay indefinitely eventually resulted in a breakdown of the treaty system, and resumption of war at times when the nomads, because of internal crises, could ill afford it, causing in most cases its demise.

While the "supratribal" sovereign could revert to a policy of pillaging to maintain its government financially viable, for the reasons mentioned above, this strategy would eventually become unsustainable, and the centralized state would eventually crumble under internal and external pressures. Under such circumstances, defecting nomadic chieftains might seek refuge and protection in China, and accept Chinese terms of surrender according to which they would be relocated along the frontier and employed as a military resource to protect China's borders. Eventually, the military machine of the nomads would no longer exist and its unified leadership would vanish.

Trade

A very important economic instrument that could guarantee long-term support for the nomadic aristocracy was trade. The nomads' control of long-distance overland trade routes allowed them to capitalize on the exchange of goods that, from the early centuries of the Common Era, began to circulate across Eurasia, among which silk was especially relevant, as both commodity and currency. Controlling these routes meant controlling international trade. By forming partnerships with merchants, the nomadic aristocracy could rely on a regular income and at the same time acquire goods that were prized within their own society, and could be used as means of exchange or to store value.

What nomads brought to the table was political weight and military muscle. In order to flourish, ancient trade required a secure, low-risk environment, which could be guaranteed by the military power of the nomads. Politically and diplomatically, strong steppe leaders could use the threat of war to pry open trade routes and markets with agricultural regions. For the nomadic ruler, the ability to monopolize the profits and redistribute them to the aristocracy helped increase his charisma, political clout, and wealth. More importantly, trade had a transformative effect on nomadic society, far more so than pillage and tribute, since trade is not just exchange of goods. Not only were commercial networks created, but market towns flourished on the margins of the steppes and even within it, and merchant communities were allowed to reside safely in nomadic territory.

Probably from the fifth or sixth century CE, with the development of long-distance trade across Eurasia, this new revenue stream could be accessed and integrated in the economy of the nomadic militarized and centralized state, as the aristocracy forged special ties with the commercial houses that controlled transnational trade. The first instance of a clear engagement of nomads with international commerce was with the Türks, who inserted themselves in the silk trade between China and Byzantium. However, their diplomatic overtures did not lead to concrete results (Stark 2016).

The successor to the Türks, the Uighur Empire—established by the Uighurs in 744 CE—made explicitly trade the mainstay of its economy. Ordo Baliq (or Karabalghasun), the capital of the Uighur Empire, was located in the heart of Mongolia, and included markets, temples, government buildings, workshops, and agricultural fields. The court resided there at times but remained, in nomadic fashion, an itinerant one. Key to the Uighurs' engagement with trade was their positioning themselves between China and Central Asia. The steppe economy produced a surplus of horses, which cost them very little but which China needed for military purposes, and China produced a surplus of silk, which the Uighur coveted for internal consumption but also for sale throughout Eurasia, via the commercial networks of Central Asian merchant houses. The partnership between nomads and merchants allowed the silk exchanged for horses to be resold or used as currency in transactions across Asia (Beckwith 1991). Flowing into the networks of international trade controlled by Sogdian merchants, silk sales generated revenues that would be shared between the political (Uighur) and the commercial (Sogdian) elites. This system required a centralized government and a court that functioned as a hub for collecting horses, redistributing silk, and conducting political relations with China. Such a symbiotic relationship between Uighur rulers and Sogdian merchants favored not just trade but also peace between the nomads and China, so that the last forty years of the Uighur Empire were remarkably free from military ventures (Kovalev 2016).

Was trade part of the nomadic "war economy"? In the Uighur Empire, trade was connected to war in two specific ways, quite different from previous nomadic empires. First, military force was necessary to protect trade routes and to compete over trade routes against other empires, states, and so on. Without a centralized military force, trade revenues could not be guaranteed, given that commercial relations could only flourish under conditions of reduced risk, secure roads, and reliable access to markets. Second, the military power of the Uighurs was used as a mercenary army to protect China against other external enemies, such as the Tibetans, who had repeatedly invaded and threatened Tang territory, including the imperial capital Chang'an. The "payment" for these mercenary services was the horses-for-silk trade that guaranteed a regular supply of silks to the Uighur Kaghan and the commercial elites associated with the Uighur court. There is, therefore, a clear and direct connection between the upkeep of a centralized army by the Uighurs and commerce with China and internationally.

What is also remarkable is that the "tribute" mechanism with China that prevailed with the Xiongnu and Türk Empires was transformed under the Uighurs into a system of forced political trade. The silk obtained by such means would then flow into the networks of international trade controlled by Sogdian merchants, generating revenues that would be shared between political (Uighur) and commercial (Sogdian) elites. This system required a centralized government and a court that functioned as a hub for collecting horses, redistributing silk, and conducting political relations with China, and continued to function as long as the Uighur army was able to maintain its strength. Once it was attacked and destroyed by a hostile force, not just the Uighur Empire collapsed, but also trade, as the two systems were codependent.

Commerce, markets, and urbanism are trademarks of the relationship between the nomadic Khitan and the Song dynasty, too. Once a comprehensive peace treaty was signed between the two powers in 1005, commerce developed on a grand scale and contributed to the flourishing of an urban culture, exotic taste, and a general openness to foreign goods in Chinese cities. In their empire, the Khitan established multiple capital cities and a stable administration (Shiba 1983; Wright 1998).

It is with the Mongol conquest, however, that vast, comprehensive, transnational Eurasian trade networks achieved their maximum premodern expansion. Judged in terms of commercial prowess, the Mongols were by far the most successful nomadic conquerors. Trade developed in the wake of massive territorial conquest and of the imposition of Mongol rule over a myriad different people. It may be intriguing to speculate that the success of the Mongols may stem in part from their inability, for three generations (the reigns of Chinggis, his son Ögödei, and the grandsons Güyük and Möngke), to move from a state of war to a state of peace (Allsen 2004). The Mongol juggernaut barreled on for six decades, notwithstanding internal conflicts, and expanded far beyond the Mongols' ability to maintain a unified empire. Such an expansion could not be sustained without the adoption of a variety of economic strategies, of which trade was the most successful exactly because they could unify so many regions into a single trading system.

Under the Mongols the routes of continental Asia joined the other large world market, Europe, through the hub of the Black Sea, where ships and caravans met. The role of the Mongols as active trading agents and not just as "facilitators" of commercial connections between faraway markets was critical. Circulation and redistribution of goods reached unprecedented proportions because the Mongols enabled the link between the continental Asian trade routes and the Mediterranean seafaring traffic by establishing relations with maritime powers, such as Genoa and Venice. The convergence of commercial interests between Mongol rulers and European merchants made the fourteenth century the most "networked" system that had ever existed till then.

The opening of the Mongols to commerce and the inauguration of a period of peace sometime referred to as *pax mongolica* was based at least in part on institutions that were developed during the conquest, such as the postal stations that allowed for the rapid spread of information and communication throughout the empire. Financial innovations adopted by the Mongols, albeit with mixed success, such as new coinages and the issuance of paper money, were aimed to facilitate commercial transactions. Formal treaties with foreign merchants stipulated low tariffs and opened new markets. The formalization of a system of partnership between merchants and members of the Mongol aristocracy generated demand for luxury goods and increased the volume of commercial activities (Allsen 1989). All these policies functioned as incentives and accelerators of trade, and, by and large, dissuaded the Mongol rulers from engaging in military activities that would have kept merchants away.

The significantly interconnected Eurasian space that trade created was key to stopping or at least scaling down wars, limiting further territorial conquests, and transitioning to regimes that were able to support themselves with a combination of fiscal and commercial policies, but commercial revenues were sought long before peace was established. The very beginning of the Mongol expansion into Central Asia, which posed the foundations for the later waves of conquests of Russia and Iran, was caused by a crime committed against the Mongols in the Muslim empire of Khwarazm, which included the whole of Iran and Central Asia. As Chinggis Khan was expanding his military operations in northern China, it is understandable that international trade could be seen as a means to gather additional revenues. It is in this context of seeking commercial openings that we need to see the merchant caravan that reached the frontier city of Otrar in 1218 (May 2016: 35–36, 219–20). The massacre of the merchants by the governor of Otrar precipitated the Mongol invasion of Central Asia, and can be seen as a catalyst of war. Behind the Mongol retaliation for the "insult" of killing Mongol envoys, we can see the desire to insert themselves into international trade as one of the objectives of Chinggis Khan, and the reason why a diplomatic and commercial embassy was sent to the Khwarezmian Empire in the first place.

Finally, we should stress that an excessive dependence on trade as a main source of revenue also had drawbacks. Throughout the history of China-Inner Asian relations, the closure of border markets was used whenever possible by the Chinese authorities as an economic weapon to weaken the power of the nomadic ruler. Reliance on trade and markets was also open to the vagaries of prices, climate (which may affect both travel and production) and the willingness of the various parties to accept risks that at times of political instability were quite high. Trade also required a specialized knowledge that was often foreign to the nomads themselves, and, therefore, depended on the intermediation of a class of merchants that was not (as far we can tell) fully integrated with the nomadic elites—with the possible exception of the Uighur Empire—and whose interests may not be fully aligned with those of the nomadic elites.

Taxation

Ultimately, it was only with territorial conquest and the direct extraction of wealth from the subjects by fiscal means that nomads developed as a more stable and regular revenue stream. One of the most successful and important strategies for a nomadic empire to acquire economic viability was through the development of institutions that provided a regular fiscal extraction. Such institutions required the expansion, and in many cases the creation *tout court*, of a civilian bureaucracy. This included a daunting series of innovations, such as the adoption or invention of scripts that could be used to carry out government functions. A natural choice in this direction was to acquire the tools of written administrative records from the more literate countries that were conquered, whose elites were co-opted into the government apparatus with a variety of roles, but especially to discharge administrative functions, such as population censuses, public works and especially tax collection.

According to an established, if outdated, historiography, the first actual conquest (and occupation) of a settled population by nomads can be dated to the Khitan's Liao dynasty (907–1125) who ruled over the northern "Sixteen Prefectures" that had been part of China since olden times (Wittfogel and Feng 1949: 2–20). They also ruled over a large number of settled people in the northeast of China and Korea. The expansion of nomadic rule over a large sedentary population marked a giant leap from a largely military and nomadic sociopolitical organization to one that required a civilian government able to take care of the administration of the sedentary population, and above all to collect taxes for the central treasury, of course controlled by the nomadic ruler and aristocracy.

The Liao dynasty can be regarded as the first fully nomadic "steppe" empire that developed a state organization expressly meant to extract resources from an agrarian population, and to have coined a model of rulership that, at least in East Asia, was followed (with variations) by all other three dynasties that originated in an Inner Asian context, namely the Jurchen, 1115–1234, Mongol (1206–1368), and Manchu (1644–1911) all of which established dynasties in China (respectively Jin, Yuan, and Qing). Each of them relied to an even greater extent on direct taxation and forms of extraction of wealth typical of Chinese governments.

The Liao government was split into two branches, a northern government in charge of nomadic affairs, where the imperial military force was concentrated, and a southern government in charge of agricultural regions, and included a system of multiple capitals, with different sets of offices with specialized functions depending on the type of people that inhabited a given region. The Liao continued to rely, as we have mentioned before, on tribute and trade, but were able to add significant layers of complexity to their sociopolitical organization, including a trained bureaucracy. The Liao attempts to create their own written languages were however not sufficient to replace the language of the dominant cultural power, China. The diversification of the streams of revenues contributed to stabilize the empire and to weather the various crises that periodically shook the leadership.

Seen from a larger perspective, the advantages of conquering areas whose subjects can be taxed offers obvious advantages. While predatory practices depleted the local economy, reduced the producers into extreme poverty, or forced them to flee, taxes generated a regular income. A convenient way to express the shift from a predatory to a fiscal collection is by reference to the distinction between the "roving bandit" and the "stationary bandit" in Mancur Olson's well-known theory: the roving bandit was only interested in theft and destruction, which left the country devastated, while the stationary bandit was interested in preserving and exploiting the local economy (Olson 1993). The roving nomad plunders without regard to the welfare of the people, while the stationary nomad establishes a government that can foster local production and, in this way, obtains the surplus that ensures long-term stability. The difference between a nomadic "bandit" and a regular bandit is, however, that a nomadic stationary government, in order to control and foster production among a sedentary population, must acquire the cultural means that make it possible.

Nomads, as a rule, had little knowledge of the technical requirements of fiscal administration, from fixing rates to collecting revenues and maintaining bureaucratic agencies. A successful transition, therefore, required not just a change in the way revenues were acquired, but also the incorporation of new classes of people within the state machinery, which in turn generated civilian elites alien to the nomadic body politic. The introduction of foreign bureaucracies and administrative cadres created cultural and political tensions that often endangered the very existence of the state. A constant theme in the history of steppe empires is, the opposition between groups defined sometimes as "nativists" and the need to rely on an "intelligentsia" able to fill the ranks of the civil administration. This tension was especially visible, of course, in the dynasties that pursued the most wide-ranging programs of "modernization." The nativists came, typically, from the ranks of the military aristocracy, including the royal clan, who wanted to stay loyal to ancestral traditions and opposed the corrupting influence of foreign cultures.[5] Nomadic emperors often accessed tools of government deriving from multiple traditions of statecraft to suit the governance needs of empires that had grown to be multinational, multiethnic, and multilingual. The degree to which nomadic states were able and willing to accept large doses of Chinese institutional culture—what is often mistaken for Sinicization—complicated internal nomadic politics. Cultural changes within nomadic empires must be related to the fundamental question of economic changes that are part of a long history of searching for solutions to the chronic deficiency of revenues to sustain large political and military establishment and gradually more complex and sophisticated forms of governance.

CONCLUSION

Machiavelli paid some attention to war practiced by Central Asian nomads, which he identified by the generic and archaizing name of Scythians, but did not investigate the type of war they practiced or its economic foundations. What may nonetheless be relevant is what Machiavelli says about the relationship between money and war, and in particular his claim that money was not the *nervus belli*, that is, the muscle (or sinews, or nerve) of war. Instead, he claimed that the loyalty of the troops was far more important, because loyal troops enable the collection of booty while disloyal troops may cost more than they were able to rake in (Tilly 1979). In sum, the quality of the soldiers and the relationship between the prince and the army is more important than the money that needed to be raised for war. If we were to indulge in historical playfulness, we might surmise that Machiavelli would have found a sympathetic audience in Chinggis Khan, or some Türk *qaghan*, since loyalty was highly prized in a nomadic setting. However, the close connection between money and war would not have been lost on nomads. On the one hand, it is true that pillage and the "spoils of war" might buy the loyalty of soldiers, provided that the leader has the proper virtues, such as the ability to win battles and fairness in the allocation of booty. On the other hand, in intra-nomadic wars, the amount of booty likely to be acquired, mainly cattle and slaves, was only barely sufficient to keep the loyalty of retainers, and utterly insufficient to finance a "supratribal" state.

The periodic emergence of large nomadic polities under a single authority out of relatively sparse social groups bound by ethnic, kinship, and territorial bonds, is grounded in a dynamic of expanding militarization. The causes for the increase in violence are difficult to locate exactly and require a case-by-case study. The most probable causes are, however, a depletion of the environment that forced competition over scarce resources, or some external stimulus that altered the existing political equilibrium. In any case, a spiral of increasing violence was ignited, and overtime it further eroded the wealth of the people and the natural resources, while, on the political level, it created the conditions for the emergence of a centralized political power.

The end result was, occasionally and each time in a different form, the formation of a militarized, vertically organized, centrally ruled political structure that relied heavily on war or the threat of it to access and appropriate resources without which the new regime would not be able to maintain itself. Hence, several modes of extraction were devised by the nomadic leadership, attaining even more sophisticated levels of government, social organization, economic and commercial management, and diplomatic activity. Over the course of approximately 2,000 years (200 BCE–1800 CE), the tradition of nomadic rulership evolved in the direction of creating more stable structures that would support a centralized power, and counter the centrifugal tendencies inherent to steppe politics.

The primary objective of the "war economy" was, therefore, to feed and stabilize the overextended military apparatus that had come into existence during the "crisis" that generates the new order. The territorial expansion in which many nomadic empires engaged also responded to the need to increase revenues. The vicious circle of having to increase revenues further and further in order to support an ever-growing military apparatus could only be broken once the economic basis of the empire allowed for an accumulation of resources equal to the needs of the court and army. Since such a balance was almost always impossible to achieve, nomadic regimes were plagued by chronic instability. Only a deep transformation from a mostly military to a mostly civilian administration could eventually break the vicious circle by guaranteeing a steady stream of resources and by curtailing the continuous growth of a no longer functional and largely parasitic military class. The empires that were able to survive the longest were those that tried to find ways to overcome a state of permanent war. The more farsighted rulers were conscious of the fact that survival required more than war, and I would contend that the evolution of steppe political culture revolves around a central problem: *how to stop war and move to peace without committing political suicide in the process*. Many of the political innovations developed by nomadic rulers can be seen as attempts to resolve this conundrum, and in the process transformed not only their societies, but also those of the people with which they interacted, across Eurasia.

NOTES

1. The question of social organization, and especially of the "tribe," in an Inner Asian context has been a hotly contested topic. The discussion around David Sneath's

The Headless State (Sneath 2007) has been especially useful in clarifying the terms of the debate. For various interventions, including by Sneath himself, see *Ab Imperio* 4(2009): 80–175.

2. One of the most popular books in this mode remains Grousset (1970) (originally published in French on 1941 as *L'empire des steppes*).

3. There is a vast literature on nomadic trade and its economic and political implications. See, for instance, Serruys (1975), Jagchid and Van Symons (1989). The relationship between war and trade on the Chinese frontier is often established in binary terms, and for this reason theories based on an assumed single overarching factor (the chronic non-sufficiency of the nomadic economy) suffer from different degrees of underdetermination, since they tend to focus exclusively on economic exchange between "steppe and sown" and to underplay internal steppe political and economic dynamics, so that causation for war and trade is attributed to a range of factors that is most likely too narrow.

4. The most critical moment in the political life of a nomadic empire was that of succession to the throne, which was often contested. Possible candidates, in order to succeed, needed their own economic basis to be viable candidates (Fletcher 1979).

5. On "nativist" political factions under the Liao see Twitchett and Tietze, 114–32. On political struggles in the Liao and Jin dynasties see (Tao 1976: 63–83; Chan 1984).

REFERENCES

Allsen, Thomas T. 1989. "Mongolian Princes and Their Merchant Partners, 1200–1260." *Asia Major* 3rd series, 2.2: 83–126.

Allsen, Thomas T. 2004. *Culture and Conquest in Mongol Eurasia*. Cambridge: Cambridge University Press.

Chan, Hok-Lam. 1984. *Legitimation in Imperial China: Discussion under the Jurchen-Chin Dynasty (1115–1234)*. Seattle: University of Washington Press.

Christopher I. Beckwith. 1991. "The Impact of the Horse and Silk Trade on the Economies of T'ang China and the Uighur Empire: On the Importance of International Commerce in the Early Middle Ages." *Journal of the Economic and Social History of the Orient*, 34.3: 183–98.

Di Cosmo, Nicola. 1999. "State Formation and Periodization in Inner Asian History." *Journal of World History*, 10.1: 1–40.

Di Cosmo, Nicola, ed. 2002a. *Warfare in Inner Asian History (500–1800)*. Leiden: Brill.

Di Cosmo, Nicola. 2002b. *Ancient China and Its Enemies*. Cambridge: Cambridge University Press.

Di Cosmo, Nicola, Clive Oppenheimer, and Ulf Büntgen. 2017. "Interplay of Environmental and Socio-Political Factors in the Downfall of the Eastern Türk Empire in 630 CE." *Climatic Change*, 145.3–4: 383–95.

Findlay Ronald, and Mats Lundahl. 2006. "The First Globalization Episode: The Creation of the Mongol Empire or the Economics of Chinggis Khan." In *Asia and Europe in Globalization: Continents, Regions and Nations*, edited by Göran Therborn and Habibul Haque Khondker, 13–54. Leiden: Brill.

Fletcher, Joseph. 1979. "Turco-Mongolian Monarchic Tradition in the Ottoman Empire." *Harvard Ukrainian Studies*, 3: 236–51.

Graff, David. 2002. "Strategy and Contingency the Tang Defeat of the Eastern Turks, 629–630." In *Warfare in Inner Asian History: 500–1800*, edited by Nicola Di Cosmo, 33–71. Leiden: Brill.

Grousset, René. 1970. *The Empire of the Steppes: A History of Central Asia.* New Brunswick: Rutgers University Press.

Jagchid, Sechin, and Van Jay Symons. 1989. *Peace, War, and Trade along the Great Wall: Nomadic-Chinese Interaction through Two Millennia.* Bloomington: Indiana University Press.

Kovalev, Roman K. 2016. "The Uyghur Empire." In *The Encyclopedia of Empire*, 1st ed., edited by John M. MacKenzie. DOI: 10.1002/9781118455074.wbeoe093

Kradin, Nikolay N. 2002. "Nomadism, Evolution and World-Systems: Pastoral Societies in Theories of Historical Development." *Journal of World-Systems Research*, 8.3: 368–88.

May, Timothy, ed. 2016. *The Mongol Empire: A Historical Encyclopedia]: A Historical Encyclopedia.* Vol. II, pp. 35–36, 219–20. Santa Barbara: ABC-CLIO.

Olson, Mancur. 1993 "Dictatorship, Democracy, and Development." *The American Political Science Review*, 87.3: 567–76.

Serruys, Henry. 1975. "Sino-Mongol Trade during the Ming." *Journal of Asian History*, 9.1: 34–56.

Shiba, Yoshinobu. 1983. "Sung Foreign Trade: Its Scope and Organization." *China among Equals: The Middle Kingdom and Its Neighbors, 10th–14th Centuries*, edited by M. Rossabi, 89–115. Berkeley: University of California Press.

Sneath, David. 2007. *The Headless State: Aristocratic Orders, Kinship Society, and Misrepresentations of Nomadic Inner Asia.* New York: Columbia University Press.

Stark, Sören. 2016. "Türk Kaghanate." In *The Encyclopedia of Empire*, 1st ed., edited by John M. MacKenzie. DOI: 10.1002/9781118455074.wbeoe430

Tao, Jing-shen. 1976. *The Jurchen in Twelfth-Century China: A Study of Sinicization.* Seattle: University of Washington Press.

Tilly, Charles. 1979. *Sinews of War.* CRSO Working Paper no. 195, University of Michigan.

Twitchett, Denis, and Klaus-Peter Tietze. 1994. "The Liao." In *Cambridge History of China vol. 6: Alien Regimes and Border State, 907–1368*, edited by Herbert Franke and Denis C. Twitchett, 43–153. Cambridge: Cambridge University Press.

Vetter, Susanne. 2005. "Rangelands at Equilibrium and Non-Equilibrium: Recent Developments in the Debate." *Journal of Arid Environments*, 62.2: 321–41.

Wittfogel, Karl August, and Chia-sheng Feng. 1949. *History of Chinese Society: Liao, 907–1125.* New York: American Philosophical Society.

Wright, David C. 1998. "The Sung-Kitan War of A.D. 1004–1005 and the Treaty of Shan-yüan." *Journal of Asian History*, 32.1: 3–48.

Chapter 6

Non-State War Economy in Renaissance Italy

William Caferro

Renaissance Italy offers a unique historical vantage from which to examine non-state war economy. The peninsula was the site of perpetual conflict, famously associated with the activities of mercenary soldiers. According to Machiavelli's enduring interpretation, Italian states abandoned native martial spirit in the fourteenth and fifteenth centuries in favor of using "greedy," "disloyal," and ultimately ineffective mercenaries, who formed the core of local armies.[1] The great Swiss historian Jacob Burckhardt (1818–1897) depicted the mercenaries, or *condottieri* as he called them, as the embodiment of "individualism" and "unbridled egotism" that defined the Italian Renaissance and reflected a "modern political spirit" (Burckhardt 1860). The powerful construct placed mercenaries at the center of discussion of the meaning and political developments of the era, while at the same time removing them and the wars they fought in from any worthwhile economic analysis.[2] Scholars know precious little about the financial implications of the use of private, professional soldiers, a lacuna that stands in sharp contrast with the overall study of the economy of the era, which is voluminous. As David Parrott has recently argued, the lack of scholarly study is not restricted to Italy. Preoccupation with early modern European "military revolutions" and the "evolution of state control of coercion" has obscured the overwhelming evidence that the predominant form of warfare throughout the period involved the use of private military entrepreneurs. As a result, premodern mercenaries have been consigned to the "dead-end" historical category of "popular history" (Parrott 2012). The consensus is particularly unfortunate given the modern-day parallels with the use of mercenaries and private companies in south-central Africa and in Afghanistan and Iraq (Kinsay 2006; Percy 2007).

A workable methodology to study the economy of Renaissance Italian war must take into account several basic features of the Italian situation.[3] First,

Italy is and was geographically small, and consisted in the fourteenth and fifteenth centuries of numerous independent and economically potent city-states in close proximity to each other, particularly in the northern and central regions associated with the Renaissance. These "capital-intensive" entities, to use the language of Charles Tilly, fought each other frequently, indeed so frequently that it is difficult to separate one conflict from another (Tilly 1992). Inter-state wars were accompanied by infra-state conflicts between cities and independent rural magnates, who populated the Italian countryside. These contests, wholly overlooked in the Anglophone scholarship, rendered war more pervasive, and more problematic as an object of study owing to the inconsistent contemporary language that alternately describes them as *guerre* (wars) and *cavalcate* (police actions). The line between "civil" and external war is blurred. And at the end of conflicts, soldiers often banded together and harassed the countryside and extorted bribes from towns with which they had no ostensible quarrel.

In any case, the geographic constraints of the peninsula meant that conflict in one place necessarily affected another place, whether or not a state was directly involved. Italian communes were thus always on a defensive footing and always had, despite Machiavelli's statements (and those of modern scholars) to the contrary, men-at-arms on their payrolls. Wars meant the reallocation of economic resources within the peninsula, which stood at the root cause of the wars in the first place. This was reflected in the mode of fighting, which was primarily in the nature of raids aimed at wearing down opponents financially, interrupting trade and stealing livestock, burning structures rather than pitched battles in the field. Success and failure of Italian city-states were therefore intrinsically linked (Caferro 2008).

In this respect, the Italian experience differed fundamentally from that of nomadic empires like the Mongols, outlined by Professor Di Cosmo, which expanded externally. It differed also from Italy's ancient Roman past, which Machiavelli pointedly compares to his own day. The Romans expanded beyond the peninsula; Italian communes built territorial states within the peninsular boundaries. Venice and Genoa, perpetual adversaries, appear at first glance as exceptions, with their contests on the seas and protectorates in the East. But the latter development dated to the thirteenth century; Genoa was always involved in internal conflicts within Italy, and Venice turned forcefully inward in the fifteenth century. Italy was more acted upon from the outside than vice versa. The papacy, an international entity with its own territorial state in central Italy, and the German Holy Roman emperors, who held legal claims to northern Italy, were two uniquely destabilizing entities. Their long-standing opposition to each other stood at the root of the famous Guelf and Ghibelline contest that has defined Italian political rivalries in the popular imagination. The pope's "exile" in Avignon (1309–1378) and the Great

Schism (1378–1415) exacerbated violence in the already fractious papal state. Meanwhile, Holy Roman Emperors routinely descended upon Italy to bestow titles (for fees) on political leaders and legitimate political authority in return for cash payments, which served only to intensify antagonisms. In the process, the papacy and empire both injected and extracted enormous sums of money from the peninsula, much of it in turn used to hire mercenary soldiers to fight wars. The papacy lacked sufficient recruiting grounds in his small Italian state and relied by necessity on such soldiers. The German emperors physically brought with them men-at-arms, who stayed in Italy and hired themselves out as mercenaries, often to the papacy and other entities that they had initially opposed.

The last point underscores the diversity of mercenary service in Italy. It involved both local soldiers and foreigners from outside the peninsula, complicating still further the distinction between state and non-state economy. Foreign or *ultramontane* soldiers (as they were known) were especially numerous in the fourteenth century and were wholly non-state actors, accruing, where possible, personal fortunes, much of which was sent back home. Native mercenaries, who became more prominent in the fifteenth century, served one state as an outsider, but often seized by force the lordship of another state. They were thus non-state economic actors in one place and state players—the state itself—in another. The careers of the Italian mercenaries Braccio da Montone (1368–1421) and Sigismondo Malatesta (1417–1468) are instructive in this regard. The former fought as a mercenary captain for Florence and the Kingdom of Naples before ultimately taking over his native city of Perugia. The latter fought for the papacy, Venice and Florence before installing himself as lord of Rimini. Their success and earnings as *condottieri* allowed them to establish rule in these places, where they also became patrons of Renaissance art (Philip Jones 1974). The investment of their war profits into art, architecture, and "conspicuous display" (as recent scholars call it) adds an economic/material aspect to Burckhardt's otherwise political and psychological interpretation of such men. It raises the intriguing question of whether the famous cultural developments associated with a "Renaissance spirit" were more a matter of private, non-state wealth derived from a military context than public state wealth, as is currently believed, and that the distinction itself is problematic.

CRISES, TAXATION, AND INEQUALITY

The economy of Italian war, therefore, presents varied and often contradictory patterns that require careful future study. The vast quantity of surviving archival material—far more than for any other topic of inquiry—has rendered analysis more difficult. Armed conflict coincided with the well-known cycle of plague and famine, from the mid-fourteenth (Black Death 1348) to the mid-fifteenth century, whose effects economic historians have treated in great detail, but in isolation. The phenomena must necessarily be integrated. Indeed, the pace of conflict increased during the crises, suggesting that states sought to take advantage of them to press their own causes. The movement of armies meanwhile helped spread disease. And there may have been, as I have argued elsewhere, a causal link between plague and war. Plague reduced land values and increased the cost of labor on it, which struck hard at aristocrats, who owned land and for whom war, notably cavalry service, was a class-bound obligation. They may have turned to war to bolster both their flagging profits and social status. War was by its very nature an ennobling activity. The thesis may explain the large presence in Italy in the middle years and later years of the fourteenth century of foreign mercenaries—German, English, Burgundians, and Hungarians in origin—who came to the peninsula in search of profits, but largely disappear by the middle of the next century, when the crises subsided (Caferro 2008).

The point need not be extended too far. It minimizes the importance of concurrent political events—the outbreak of the Hundred Years' War between England and France and the ongoing civil war in Naples involving Hungarian kings—which brought foreign men-at-arms. In addition, little is known—and likely will ever be known—about the actual backgrounds of the soldiers, who are steadfastly described by contemporaries, angered by their inconstancy and marauding ways, as the "dregs of society." What is abundantly clear, however, is that war was expensive. Communal budgets show that 70–80 percent of revenue was devoted to the pay of soldiers, a percentage that declined only slightly in periods of ostensible peace.

The papacy deserves especial attention in our analysis. It was not a "state" in the manner of its Italian counterparts. It was an international entity that brought in tax revenue from throughout Europe and from the Italian states with which it fought on the peninsula. The papacy assessed a variety of imposts on Christendom, including the clerical tenth (on annual income of a benefice or religious house), annates (on the first fruits of ecclesiastical holdings), tithes, and others that became more regularized in the fourteenth century. The papacy also possessed the unique spiritual weapon of excommunication, which it leveled against those who did not pay taxes and adversaries who opposed them on the battlefield. The English scholar Norman Housley has estimated that during the tenure of the first legate, Betrand du Poujet, to the papal state in Italy, the pontiff spent from July 1324 to July 1327 1,164,363 florins on mercenaries for its local wars (N. J. Housley 1982). The average was roughly 388,000 florins a year and exceeded the ordinary revenue of most Italian states at the time. Florentine revenue in the middle years of the century has been estimated at between 250 and 350,000 florins; Siena and Pisa raised 80–100,000 florins a year, respectively, and Lucca took in 60,000–75,000 florins a year. The small town of Bagnacavallo, on the edge of the papal state in the Romagna, earned a mere 5,000 florins a year (Vaini 1966; Molho 1971; Partner 1972; Meek 1978; Caferro 2008).

Raising large sums of money fell hard on fiscal bureaucracies. Italian states relied on a combination of interest-bearing loans and indirect taxes known as gabelles (on consumption and services) to meet the burden. The two were intrinsically linked in that revenue from the latter was used to pay back money for the former. Italian public finance has been the subject of distinguished scholarly study, particularly for the cities of Venice, Genoa, and Florence and their use of public-funded debts, which are treated as precocious instances of economic modernity (Sieveking 1905; Luzzatto 1963; Molho 1971). But war, which was responsible for the establishment of public debts in the first place, exposes the ad hoc and decidedly non-modern aspects of Italian finance. Fiscal apparati were inherently ill-suited to the speedy collection of large sums of money necessitated by war. Requests for loans required an *alliramento* or assessment of wealth, which was often a protracted process, rendered more problematic by plague which famously rearranged financial portfolios. Meanwhile, war itself interfered with collection of taxes and inhibited movement of goods through town gates, a major source of revenue, and damaged fields, which affected revenue from gabelle on wine, another lucrative source of revenue.

It is important to understand that taxation did not affect all citizens the same way. There was an inherent bias in Italian public finance favoring wealthier elements over middle- and lower-level ones. The recourse to loans and potential returns on investments was generally restricted to well-to-do citizens, who could provide the money. Each request for loans necessarily involved a rise in gabelle rates, the revenue used to repay the loans. Gabelles were regressive taxes on consumption and service that burdened those of lesser means, who could not avoid them. At the approach of an enemy army, states usually undertook as a first step to double gabelle rates across the board. Charles M. de La Roncière has shown how gabelles increased five to ten times in Florence from the beginning of the fourteenth century to the end (Charles M. de La Roncière 1968; Ryder 1977). Studies elsewhere in Italy reveal similar trends and a conscious policy of sustained taxation on consumption and steadfast avoidance of direct tax on capital (Barbieri 1938; Knapton 1985). Elites were not only able to gain return on their tax investments, but also had access to lucrative tax farms that increased remuneration. International merchants who worked abroad were notoriously successful at hiding their assets from tax officials and avoiding taxation altogether (Caferro 1995).

A comprehensive analysis of Italian taxation is muddied, as Patrizia Mainoni notes, by wide-ranging inconsistencies in assessment among states (Mainoni 1997). Scholars must also take into account the economic effects of plague, which, according to the classic formulation, was a boon to the salaried sector of society, particularly those who sold their labor.[4] The relentless nature of war, however, and the relentless taxation that accompanied it, renders problematic any roseate portrait of a "golden age" for working classes. Indeed, the reduction of the tax base attendant the plague alone made wars more burdensome for surviving citizens and compelled states to expand their tax bases, which in turn gave impetus to war. The establishment by wealthier communes such as Milan, Florence, and Venice of territorial states is an egregious example of this. On the more local level, states expanded their tax bases by including outgroups such as Jews, who appear more prominently in economic registers in the later fourteenth century. Officials allowed Jews to settle in towns by means of formal contracts known as *condotte*, which obligated Jews to provide money to the state in times of need, such as war. The appeal for the state was that Jews could be more forcibly coerced and offered inferior terms than their Christian counterparts (Toaff 1975; Boesch-Gajano 1983; Muzzarelli 1984; Luzzati and Veronese 1993; Pini 1996).

The bias inherent in Italian tax policy resembles in general outline that which Christopher Friedrichs described for German towns during the Thirty Years' War (Friedrichs 1980). Fiscal systems created a "spiraling upward" of money in favor of wealthier citizens, which ran counter to the well-known "downward movement" of wealth in favor of the lower classes that resulted from plague. War created profits for wealthy merchant bankers, who served as intermediaries in hiring troops and issued bills of exchange to transfer money to diverse regions to pay soldiers. To be sure, merchants often complained that their assessments cut into profits and that loans went unpaid. And, indeed, many merchants suffered damage, and rarely welcomed war. But the decision by states to tax consumption rather than capital was deliberate. The Milanese ruler, Bernabò Visconti of Milan (1323–1385), openly stated that hikes in gabelles and indirect taxes would raise less meaningful opposition than the alternative. Studies of the Tuscan countryside reveal that the fiscal burdens of war increased the indebtedness of rural dwellers to urban lenders, resulting in an increase in urban ownership of rural land. Large Florentine banking houses often filled the void, collecting interest from their loans to rural communities.

The peasant in the field suffered the most from war. In addition to taxes, he stood directly in the path of the raids that characterized contemporary war. The rules of chivalry—which were operative even in Italy—favored capture and ransom of equals in the field, but did not apply to social inferiors in the countryside.

MIGRATION AND ABANDONMENT OF VILLAGES

The plight of peasants is clear from copious archival evidence showing that, in the face of armed threat, they abandoned their homes and fled elsewhere. The evidence is overwhelming and highlights a crucial and overlooked aspect of the economy of Renaissance warfare: the migration of people and transfer of human capital. In the case of Italy, we see, again, a reallocation of resources within the peninsula. One commune's loss was another's gain. Indeed, given the heavy tax burdens, migration did not only involve the farmer in the field but also skilled urban workers, who sought relief from imposts. The archives contain numerous petitions from workers seeking tax relief in order to remain home. In a time of demographic crisis, government officials were willing to negotiate to preserve their most precious commodity, the tax payer. The desertion of only a handful of people in rural towns left the remaining residents to make up tax shortfalls, which increased the likelihood that they too would move elsewhere.[5]

It is important to stress the role of migration in understanding the economy of Renaissance Italian warfare. The migrations have largely passed under the scholarly radar on account of a teleological tendency, particularly in the Anglophone academy, to minimize the effects of warfare on the countryside, which has been viewed anachronistically as lacking sufficient capital investment to constitute a major economic factor (Goldthwaite 1995). But enemy armies stole cattle and animals and burned houses and barns, which constituted substantial investment for locals. Studies of contemporary France during the Hundred Years' War show that the burning of farms and the stealing of livestock had lasting economic effects on the countryside. Robert Boutruche argued forcefully against those who would compare the costly reconstruction of rural lands in France after the First World War with the seemingly "sluggish" measures taken by the French crown to repair damage in the fourteenth and fifteenth century. He noted that the economic impact of the two were proportionate and thus equally devastating. The government in the medieval instance lacked both the funds and the will to ameliorate the situation (Boutruche 1947). Rural devastation was, in any case, not all the same. Fields trampled by armies could be replanted, but vines took much longer to regrow. And the sale and taxation of wine was a leading source of revenue for Italian states.

The copious evidence of migration warrants more detailed study by scholars. The war between Milan and Florence in 1369–1370 was limited in comparison to the more famous and dramatic contests between the two states at the end of the century. But it caused a great many residents, particularly from the town of San Miniato, a key strategic outpost for Florence, to flee. The town became nearly deserted. After peace was made, mercenary soldiers, freed from service, banded together and undertook raids in the region, leading to migrations from numerous small towns in the environs of Pisa, Florence, and Siena. Siena, with its ample hinterlands and proximity to the via Francigena, a major medieval highway that connected Rome to Avignon (and upon which lay San Miniato), proved a frequent target of raid by "free" companies. In 1398, the Sienese city council complained of forty years of ravages by soldiers such that the Maremma region, an important source of grain, had become "sterile," production reduced by 80 percent. To solve the problem, the Sienese government passed legislation offering settlers grants of tax immunity for five years (Archivio di Stato di Siena, Consiglio Generale 180 fol. 88v; Consiglio Generale 181 fol. 46v).

This was a standard response among Italian states, which appear to have competed with each other to attract villagers displaced by war and/or overburdened by taxation related to it (Caferro 1998, 2006, 2008). What is not clear, however, is precisely who left the towns and where they went. Robert Fossier, in his studies of abandoned villages in Normandy and Champagne during the Hundred Years' War, showed that the emigres were mostly young people between the ages of twenty and thirty, leaving behind an older, less productive, populace, which slowed recovery in those regions (Fossier 1964). There is evidence for Italy that skilled laborers left their homes and attempted to negotiate their tax burdens. This may be because such people are more visible in the sources. But the most notable example is the flight of silk workers from Lucca in 1314 on account of the sack and seizure of the city by the mercenary captain Uguccione della Faggiola (d. 1319). The Lucchese silk industry was a lucrative business and had helped propel the small Tuscan city into the forefront of luxury production in late thirteenth century Italy. In 1314, the workers dispersed, seeking peace and better financial terms in other urban centers, particularly Florence, Bologna, and Venice, who actively sought their services (Molà 1994; Louis Green 1986, 1995).

The impact of the workers on Venice is well known. They have been credited with helping establish the high-end craft in that city. But the flow of skilled workers was, as Louis Green and others have shown, more continuous (Louis Green 1995; Stuard 2006). Silk workers continued to leave during the lordship of Uguccione's violent successor, Castruccio Castracane (1316–1328), who terrorized much of Tuscany and central Italy. Florentine raids in the region in 1329 led to the departure of Lucchese goldsmiths. The nineteen goldsmith shops in the city in 1329 fell to just six in 1330. In 1336, the city of Pisa tried to profit from the war between Florence and Mastino dell Scala of Verona by offering Lucchese workers a five-year moratorium on taxes to settle there. On the eve of war with Milan in 1351, Florence offered tax relief for the inhabitants of the town of Scarperia, which lay on a vital trade route through the Apennines, to ensure that the locals would remain in the fortified village, which was also important for the defense of the northern part of the Florentine state. During the War of Eight Saints (1375–1378), when Milan, Florence, and much of Umbria fought against the papacy, Lucca offered skilled foreign workers five years of tax exemption to settle there, while Pisa offered skilled workers ten years (Silva 1912; Caferro 1998).

City officials were well aware of the stakes. They passed legislation prohibiting the movement of skilled workers, while at the same time demonstrating a willingness to negotiate tax burdens. The surviving evidence, admittedly still sketchy at this point, suggests that wealthier cities such as Bologna, Venice, Florence, and Milan were able to offer better deals to emigres, giving the cities an edge in the competitive market in human beings and human capital. Adding to this subterranean contest was the founding and refurbishing of local universities, which aimed to attract students and their money to cities, with the intention of helping the local economy and improving human capital. This was in fact the stated aim of the Florentine *studio*, founded just after the outbreak of the Black Death in 1348. The city sought to bring in students to mitigate the losses attendant the contagion. Officials even appealed to its exiled native son, Francesco Petrarca, to take up a position at the institution to attract attention to it. Petrarch ultimately declined. Neighboring Siena, whose university dates back to the thirteenth century, responded by appropriating more money to spruce it up and improve the faculty with similar economic goals in mind. Meanwhile, the cities of Pavia (1361), Turin (1411), and Ferrara (1442) established new universities, as did numerous cities in German lands.

WARS AND STATE-MAKING: BALIE AND TAGLIE (CITY-LEAGUES)

The general trend thus far is that wealthier states held the advantage over poorer ones. They were better able to attract migrating workers by offering more favorable terms. In addition, they possessed the economic wherewithal to hire larger armies, more successful and desirable mercenary captains, whom they gave longer, more lucrative contracts, not only improving the quality of forces, but reducing the risk of betrayal and with it the recourse to looting, which was pure loss economically. The most obvious evidence of this was the formation by the leading cities of territorial states and the subjugation by them of formerly independent neighboring cities. The portrait lends support to Charles Tilly's notion of the advantages of "capital-intensive" states. But his conclusion that "war makes states" is not applicable to the Italian context. Any direct connection is rendered problematic from a bureaucratic/institutional perspective. Close examination of the structures shows that they were porous, personal, and inchoate (Caferro 2018). Few states were more "capital intensive" than Republican Florence, which created a territorial state and whose bureaucracy and division of powers has been compared by Guido Pampaloni to that of a modern democracy (Pampaloni 1953). But in times of war, Florence, like other republics, resorted to *balie*, ad hoc committees of prominent citizens with short-term executive powers, to direct the military effort. The *balie* allowed the city to make quick decisions and quick appropriation of funds to avoid the usual ponderous political and deliberative machinery of the state. As a consequence, the machinery remained unchanged, intentionally protected from the mutative effects of war. But *balie* did not protect the financial apparatus of state, which lay exposed. As we have seen, the mechanism of assessment, collection, and payment of taxes was cumbersome even in the best of times. War confounded the system, exposed the limits of the coercive power of states, and rendered the fisc still more confused. The recurrent plague exacerbated the problem. Innovations of the traditional structures were in fact rare (Petralia 2009).

The point bears emphasis, as the scholarship has steadfastly searched for the genesis of the "modern state" and the development of Weberian rational, impersonal bureaucratic forms in Renaissance Italy. Participants in the discussion reflexively stress the nexus between military spending and state-building, assuming the alteration of one entailed an adjustment of the other. Marvin Becker argued that military expenditure directly transformed political institutions throughout Italy, an interpretation that still hovers over the field (Becker 1970). While it is true that the office of *balie* ultimately became a more permanent one in Florence and elsewhere by the latter fifteenth century, changes in political power were primarily the result of usurpation by powerful individuals—who, as Burckhardt stressed, were often mercenaries and thus non-state actors.

Concurrent statist notions of "a growing monopoly of coercive force" are equally problematic in the Italian context. The frequency of wars and persistent threat of violence throughout the peninsula led states to form city leagues, known as *taglie*, for mutual defense. *Taglia* referred to the cut (*taglia*) or share of troops that each participating city provided for a fixed number of years for a joint army. The leagues have received little attention in the discourse on war and states, in large part because nineteenth-century Italian military historians (Ercole Ricotti and Giuseppe Canestrini) treated them as "proto-national" organizations that augured the nineteenth-century *Risorgimento* and reunification of Italy. More recent scholarship has viewed them as a principal cause of the recourse to mercenary soldiers, who staffed league armies, and were an egregious symptom of decay of native Italian military militias and, indeed, the very antithesis of them (Mallett 1974; Waley 1968).

From the perspective of state and non-state economies, the *taglie* are critical, however, because they make clear that Italian communes perceived defense against enemies as a *joint* venture not an individual one. And the league tradition ran deep on the peninsula, back to the famous "Lombard" league of 1167 and its subsequent incarnations that opposed the German emperor Frederick I Barbarossa (d. 1190) (Bordone 1987; Raccagni 2010). The arrival in Italy of the Frenchman Charles of Anjou (brother of the king of France) as king of Sicily in 1266 inaugurated a tradition of "Guelf" leagues based primarily in Tuscany among city-states there. The regional associations meant that armies were not the domain of individual cities. Indeed, Daniel Waley argued that Florence's involvement in leagues during the second half of the thirteenth century was so frequent that it is difficult to "identify a specifically Florentine army." He saw local forces as less "the expression of the city's power" and more part of the "wide framework of regional military policy" (Waley 1968).

The same is true of the subsequent period. Giuseppe Canestrini described the leagues of the fourteenth century as "partial," "insincere," and infrequent (and thus unable to unify Italy). But they were in fact just as common as earlier, and no more or less effective. Florence joined at least twenty leagues during the years from 1330 to 1400 (ASF, Capitoli, 27 fols. 101r–107r; 136r–138r). The *taglie* were typically contracted for five years among participants, but they were often adjusted as political conditions changed on the peninsula. For example, Florence initially joined a league in 1347 with Perugia and Siena, which was revised in 1349 to include Arezzo and several smaller neighboring towns, and revised again in 1351 to include Bologna, and yet again in 1354 to involve still more allies. The signatories were primarily from Tuscany, but other leagues were more ambitious. The so-called *lega lombarda* of 1332 that opposed the entry of the German duke John of Bavaria's into Italy included Florence, Verona, Milan, Mantua, Ferrara, and Naples. The league spearheaded by the papacy in 1366 against marauding bands of mercenaries included kingdom of Naples, Florence, Pisa, Perugia, Siena, and Arezzo (Bayley 1961).

The key point is that local defense was not perceived as the responsibility of individual state armies. This is noteworthy because scholars associate the period with "the flowering of civic life" in Italy and development of civic patriotism (J. K. Hyde 1973). But "vita civile" and civic patriotism did not depend on a civic army. The status quo on the Italian peninsula thus stands in sharp contrast with the trajectory outlined by scholars for elsewhere in Europe, where patriotism and state formation are intrinsically linked to the development of state armies and coercive political, institutional power. The leagues also contradict Machiavelli's famous indictment of Italy for failure to unite in the face of foreign military danger. Italian states were clearly accustomed to joining together. It is with the growth of territorial states in the fifteenth century that the recourse to leagues became less frequent. The peace of Lodi in 1454 created a more lasting arrangement, until the famous French invasion in 1494.

The *taglie* also shed basic light on the economy. They not only distributed the costs of joint armies, but they included provisions for setting up free trade zones among their members. They granted exemption from local tolls (*pedaggi*) on goods traded among them and suspension of all reprisals (*rappresaglie*) (Archivio di Stato di Firenze, Capitoli, registri 12 fol. 105v; Capitoli registri 27 fols. 71v, 77r). *Rappresaglia* was the practice of one city holding another liable for the debts and misdeed of their merchants (Tognetti 2012). The concession was a major one, as reprisals were a frequent weapon used during wars to inflict economic damage on an opponent. The policies need to be studied more closely by scholars alongside concurrent economic fiscal measures, outlined by Stephan R. Epstein, that promoted greater "market integration" and, with a nod to Joseph Schumpeter, "creative destruction" in response to the plague. Epstein's thesis does not account for the *taglie* or in fact for warfare (Stephan Epstein 2000).

It needs be stressed again that scholars must devote greater attention to the political implications of the leagues and integrate them into the current, and abundant, literature on territorial states. Henrik Spruyt, who has studied city leagues in their Italian, German and pan-European context, has argued that the associations represent the opposite political trajectory from that of territorial states. "The city league," he wrote, "lies in starkest contrast to the territorial state" (Spruyt 1994). But Florence and Milan, which built territorial entities, did so while still joining *taglie*. Meanwhile, D. M. Bueno de Mesquita portrayed Milan's involvement in leagues as a cynical device to gain "a friendly hearing" from states it ultimately sought to conquer and subjugate—a judgment that contemporaries applied also to Florence (D. M. Bueno de Mesquita 1941). If, as Giorgio Chittolini argues, territorial states represent the unique trajectory of state-building in Italy, it appears more useful to treat the *taglie* as a factor in their formation rather than the opposite of it (Chittolini 1989). The answer will inevitably be a nuanced and complicated one, but nevertheless an important corrective to pervasive and overly simple notion that "wars make states."

PUBLIC AND PRIVATE WEALTH; CONSPICUOUS CONSUMPTION AND RENAISSANCE

A final tally sheet for the economy of Renaissance Italian is not possible. Scholars need to examine more closely the effects of war on trade routes and transaction costs; on the manufacturing and industrial sector; on money supply and the recycling of wages; and military expenditure back into local economies. Above all, there is need to look more closely at the mercenaries themselves, to move beyond moral and psychological issues to careful consideration of questions relating to their organization, financial portfolios, and spending habits. It is here that we may most readily assess the relationship between non-state and state economies, private and public wealth (Caferro 2008).

The tendency of mercenaries to coalesce into bands is itself noteworthy. The so-called companies of adventure (*compagnie di ventura*) of the fourteenth century in particular represent an intriguing non-state phenomenon. Their private nature has led military historians to depict them as the very antithesis of standing state armies, while their colorful names—the Great Company, the White Company, the Company of the Star, Company of the Hat, and the Company of St George—colorful deeds and personnel have consigned them to David Parrott's "dead-end" category of popular history. The novelist Sir Arthur Conan Doyle, of Sherlock Holmes fame, relayed the exploits of the White Company in all their romantic and fictional glory. But the bands were, in their nonfictional historical context, first and foremost business ventures. Their structure was corporate in nature and they pointedly referred to themselves as "societies" (*societates*), the same term used by contemporary Italian businesses including cloth and silk firms and banks (Caferro 1998, 2006). They maintained a hierarchy of officials, including treasurers to keep accounts and distribute money and notaries to send letters and to draw up legal documents. The dealings of the societies with states were legalistic, the distribution of profits from looting was done according to contractual agreement, in a manner that evokes Somali pirates of the present day. The captain of the society/mercenary band was elected by the rank-and-file soldiery and when he left the band, it retained its "corporate" name and elected another captain. Comparison between a mercenary captain and a modern CEO is not off the mark. The Great Company, active during the mid-fourteenth century, was led respectively by the mercenaries Werner of Urslingen, Montreal d'Albarno, and Lutz von Landau over a span of more than twenty years. The Florentine chronicler Matteo Villani described it as its own species of state, which also included women, who ground grain and tended domestic chores (Matteo Villani 1846). The financial account books of the company led by the Italian mercenary captain Micheletto Attendoli (1424–1448) have survived in the archives of the *Fraternità dei laici* in Arezzo and attest to their fiscal and bureaucratic sophistication. They were kept by Francesco Viviani, a cloth merchant from Arezzo, who joined the company as treasurer. They employ the complex integrated accounting technique of the day, with cross-listings to a set of interlocking ledgers.[6] There is evidence that the books may be double entry, although not enough of them survive to be sure.

A fundamental question is then: what do the companies say about state formation in Renaissance Italy? To the extent that scholars have advanced beyond popular history, they have viewed the mercantile aspect in opposition to feudalism, which, according to that line of reasoning, was the basic military organization of the day in Europe. The opposition is, however, too facile. Despite the business features of the bands, their "corporate" names had intentional chivalric/feudal overtones (St George, so often used, was the patron saint of chivalry). Indeed, feudalism in its characteristic medieval European form (if indeed it existed there) is notably difficult to find in urbanized Italy. Moreover, the companies often grouped themselves around nationalities. The German captain Werner of Urslingen built the original Great Company around a core of German soldiers. The Italian mercenary Alberigo da Barbiano relied primarily on Italians for his band in 1379 and the Hungarian captain John Horvath formed his company around fellow Hungarians in 1380 (Caferro 2006). May we then speak of the associations as species of foreign states in Italy? If so, however, they did not last and had no fixed territorial locus. The point here is that definitions are complicated in the Italian context and "state-making" deserves closer scrutiny with the above-stated variables taken into account.

The issue of nationalities is also significant from an economic perspective, and returns our discussion back to where it started. Foreign mercenaries sent money home, limiting recycling of money on the peninsula. The famous Englishman John Hawkwood (1320–1394), the most successful and richest captain in Italy in the fourteenth century, bought landed estates in his native county of Essex and neighboring villages, sent funds for the construction of the church of St. Peter's in Sible Hedingham, his home, and endowed a chapel for himself and his wife. His countryman, John Thornbury, who fought alongside Hawkwood in the 1370s, invested his Italian profits in estates near his native village of Little Maldon and, during his service to the papacy, gained a prebend in the English church for his son Philip that had been promised John Wycliff. John Beltoft, whose career flourished in the 1380s, arranged for a lifetime annuity from the pope to be paid directly in England.

German soldiers did likewise. The captains Johann von Rietheim and Konrad Weitingen purchased lands in their respective native towns of Ulm and Radolfzell (Seltzer 2001). Huglin von Schöneck sent money home to Basel, where he subsidized the construction of a chapel in the local church in his own honor and, with papal consent, sent home a relic of St. Theobald that he found in Italy (Gessler 1923; Seltzer 2010). The historian Wolfgang von Stromer has made the provocative argument that German mercenaries also took home with them knowledge of Italian business methods. Bertold Mönch, who led Milanese forces in 1372, worked after his service for the Milanese Del Mayno bank and later set up his own firm on that model in Cologne (Stromer 1970). Thus, there was also flow of intellectual capital.

Little is known, however, about the financial dealings of Hungarian mercenaries and the vast majority of men-at-arms on the peninsula. If Stephen Selzer's estimate of 10,000 German soldiers serving in Italy in the middle years of the fourteenth century is accurate, however, the flow of money from Italy from that sector alone was significant. And while mercenaries, especially those from places close to Italy, likely rode home with their profits, there is evidence that both English and German mercenaries used the Italian banking system, the most advanced of the day, to facilitate transfers back home. Englishmen sent money home via bills of exchange drawn on the Guinigi merchant bank of Lucca, the largest firm in that city, which had interests in England dating back to the thirteenth century. German soldiers used the Del Mayno bank, one of Milan's most important firms. The recourse to bills meant earnings for those bankers who dealt in them, providing another means, as noted above, by which war money returned to the more prosperous classes.

The evidence calls into question William McNeill's statement in his synthetic study of war that the use of mercenaries in Renaissance Italy made warfare "self-sufficing," as money spent by soldiers was recycled back into the Italian economy by purchases of good from merchants (McNeill 1982). At the same time, Fritz Redlich's famous portrait of mercenary "military enterprisers" of the Thirty Years' War, which David Parrott and many scholars use as the standard for the profession, does not quite apply to Italy either (Redlich 1964). Study of mercenaries in Florentine service has shown that the salaries of the men were set by state, not by their captains themselves, and that wages, for all their opportunities of employment elsewhere and supposed greed (see Machiavelli), remained "sticky" over substantial periods of time (Caferro 2018). Indeed, the Florentine army, portrayed by scholars as ad hoc and dismissed after campaigns, was in fact surprisingly organized and continuous, with foreign and Italian mercenaries working faithfully for the city for long stretches of time (Caferro 2008b). The image of the mercenary has been skewed by the examples of famous men who seemingly did as they wanted. In the world of Italian *condottieri*, there were, as in the world of academia, different levels: the star *condottiere* who set his own terms, and the lesser lights, the larger group, who have received little attention, but who stayed with the same employer, married locally, even sought citizenship where it was available.

Difficulties notwithstanding, it is possible, at least prospectively, to trace the movement of soldiers' wages. We have already seen how mercenary money found its way to Jewish money lenders. In 1364, Pope Urban V issued a degree absolving member of the White Company from obligations to Jewish lenders in the hope of inducing the men to go on crusade. Papal budgets in the *Archivio Segreto Vaticano* show that Jews were involved in selling goods to armies, including horses, saddles, and even prayer books. An extant account book of a Jewish banker in the town of Montepulciano from the first decade of the fifteenth century shows that the majority of clients were mercenary soldiers, who pawned their equipment and other valuables, which they bought back later at interest (Carpi 1985). The last example is evidence, confirmed elsewhere, that states often fell into arrears in their payment to soldiers, necessitating recourse to lenders. Soldiers in Tuscany pawned arms to local tavern owners, who then sold them back to the men at a profit. The *Archivio della Fabbrica del Duomo* in Milan contains numerous deeds of loans contracted by German mercenary captains with Milanese and Bolognese bankers (Archivio della Fabbrica del Duomo di Milano, Cartelle 62, 82, Eredita 86)

A basic and notable pattern of soldiers' spending involved "conspicuous" consumption, a term, as noted above, that has been applied to the Renaissance itself. This appears to have been true of both successful and unsuccessful warriors. Nadia Covini has argued that Milanese soldiers patronized the luxury market even when they lacked basics such as food (Covini 1998). An extant Perugian inventory of the possessions taken from soldiers captured during the siege of the city's citadel in 1375 lists silks, gold, and silver cups and dishes, ceremonial armor, and enameled *barbute* (helmets). The English captain William Gold's belongings included high-priced silk cloth as well as rubies, sapphires, and diamonds. The purchases listed in the account books of Francesco Viviani, treasurer of the company of Micheletto Attendoli show that the captain and his men bought silver saltcellars, pearls, precious gems, silks, and other expensive cloths. Micheletto had an ongoing account with the goldsmith Bernardo dei Bardi (1431–1433) from whom he bought silver cups, a golden belt with silver buckles, golden rings, and a silver clock. Viviani himself supplied the band with high-priced cloths made by his own firm (Archivio di Fraternità dei Laici, Arezzo, Libro di entrata e uscita 3569 fols. 79r–80v; Testatori, 3357). Meanwhile, the battlefield served as a theater of display. Contemporary accounts of Italy, France, and elsewhere show that soldiers came festooned with their valuables and dressed in colorful expensive cloths (Wright 1998; Stuard 2006; Caferro 2008).

It is with respect to conspicuous consumption that state and non-state economies converge most closely with notions of Renaissance. The use during the fourteenth century of non-Italian mercenary soldiers limited the degree of luxury spending within Italy, as foreign soldiers, using the advanced banking system of Italy, sent money back home. The shift to mostly native soldiers in the fifteenth century, a phenomenon currently treated wholly in military terms, enhanced the degree of recycling and conspicuous consumption within the peninsula. It is not unreasonable to argue that where *condottieri* seized cities and became lords, conspicuous consumption and display became elevated from the personal (non-state) sphere to a public (state) one (Caferro 2008). C*ondottieri*/rulers like Braccio da Montone and Sigismondo Malatesta (noted above) and Federico da Montefeltro (d. 1482), who took over Perugia, Rimini, and Urbino respectively and used their profits and status as state actors to become famous patrons of art and architecture, securing posthumous status as "Renaissance men."

The evidence raises the question of whether Burckhardt's famous "Renaissance spirit" derives from the battlefield and economic milieu (a subject that did not interest Burckhardt at all). It suggests the possibility that the cultural implications of economy of the Renaissance were as much a matter of private, non-state wealth as public state wealth, or better, were the result of non-state acquisition of resources used in the service of states, a hypothesis that runs counter to current economic interpretations that have stressed the overall performance of state economy in creating "permissive" conditions for conspicuous consumption associated with the Renaissance.

NOTES

1. This appears in Niccolò Machiavelli, *The Prince*, trans. and ed. David Wooten (Indianapolis, 1995), pp. 38–45; *The Discourses*, trans. Leslie J. Walker, ed. Bernard Crick (New York, 1970), pp. 339–41; *Art of War*, trans. and ed. Christopher Lynch (Chicago, 2003), pp. 13–32.

2. The tradition of Italian scholarship on Renaissance war is highly nationalistic in nature and connected to the *Risorgimento*, during which academic study first began. Ercole Ricotti, a professor of Turin, who fought in the First Italian War of Independence (1848–1849) looked specifically to the political disunity and military devolution of the fourteenth and fifteenth centuries as a "distant mirror" of Italy's modern-day lack of military strength. His influence on the field remains surprisingly strong. See William Caferro, "Individualism and the Separation of Fields of Study" in *The Routledge History of the Renaissance* (London and Routledge Press, 2017), pp. 62–74. Ercole Ricotti, *Storia delle compagnie di ventura in Italia*, 2 vols. (Turin, 1844–1845); Giuseppe Canestrini, "Documenti per servire alla storia della milizia italiana dal XIII secolo al XVI," *Archivio Storico Italiano*, Vol. XVI (1851); Piero Pieri, "Alcune questioni sopra fanterie in Italia nel periodo comunale." *Rivista storica italiana* (1933), pp. 561–614 and *Rinascimento e la crisi militare italiana* (Turin, 1952).

3. An attempt at this is in William Caferro, "Warfare and Economy in Renaissance Italy, 1350–1450," *Journal of Interdisciplinary History*, Vol. 39, No. 2 (Autumn, 2008), pp. 167–209.

4. A general study of the effects of plague on labor is in Christopher Dyer, *Standards of Living in the Later Middle Ages: Social Change in England, 1200–1320* (New York, 1989). See also Giuliano Pinto, "I livelli di vita dei salariati fiorentini (1380–1430)" in *Toscana medievale* (Florence, 1993).

5. For emigration in Tuscany, see Samuel K. Cohn, *Creating the Florentine State: Peasants and Rebellion, 1348–1434* (Cambridge, 2000), pp. 35–38, 67–72, 84, 90, 94–95, 108–9, 268; Christine Meek, *Lucca*, pp. 88–89; William Caferro, "War and Economy," p. 187; Gene Brucker, *The Civic World of Early Renaissance Florence* (Princeton, 1977), pp. 142, 146, 223–25, 402–3; Charles M. de La Roncière, *Prix et salaries à Florence au xive siècle, 1280–1380*, pp. 750–52; Molho, *Public Finance*, pp. 37, 40–42. For studies of emigration and war in France during the Hundred Years War, see G. Fourquin, *Le campagnes de la région parisienne à la fin du moyen âge* (Paris, 1964), p. 250; J. Monicat, *Les grandes companies en Velay, 1358–1392* (Paris, 1928); Guy Bois, The *Crisis of Feudalism: Economy and Society in Eastern Normandy, 1300–1550* (Cambridge, 1984).

6. Viviani was in the service of the captain for more than twenty years, until the band was dispersed after the defeat at the battle of Caravaggio in 1448. See A. Antoniella, *L'Archivio della Fraternità dei Laici di Arezzo*, vol. 2 (Florence, 1985); Mario del Treppo, "Gli aspetti organizzativi economici e sociali di una compagnia di venture italiana," *Rivista Storica Italiano*, Vol. 85 (1973), pp. 253–75.

REFERENCES

Archivio della Fabbrica del Duomo di Milano, Cartelle 62, 82, Eredita 86.

Archivio di Fraternità dei Laici, Arezzo, Libro di entrata e uscita 3569 fols. 79r–80v; Testatori, 3357.

Archivio di Stato di Firenze, Capitoli, registri 12; Capitoli registri 27.

Archivio di Stato di Siena, Consiglio Generale 181.

Armstrong, Lawrin. *Usury and Public Debt in Early Renaissance Florence.* Toronto: University of Toronto Press, 2003.

Barbieri, Gino. *Economica e politica nel ducato di Milano, 1386–1433.* Milan: Vita e Pensiero, 1938.

Bayley, C. C. *War and Society in Renaissance Florence: The De Militia of Leonardo Bruni*. Toronto: University of Toronto Press, 1961.

Becker, Marvin. *Florence in Transition.* Vol. 2. Baltimore: Johns Hopkins University Press 1968.

Boesch-Gajano, Sofia. "Aspetti e problemi della presenza ebraica nell' Italia centro-settentionale (secoli XIV e XV)," in *Quaderni dell'istituto di scienze del Universita di Roma.* Rome, 1983.

Boutruche, Robert. "The Devastation of Rural Areas during the Hundred Years' War and the Agricultural Recovery," in in Peter S. Lewis (ed.) and G. F. Martin (trans.), *The Recovery of France in the Fifteenth Century* (New York, 1971): 23–59.

Bueno de Mesquita, D. M. *Giangaleazzo Visconti, Duke of Milan (1351–1402)*. Cambridge:Cambridge University Press, 1941.

Burckhardt, Jacob. *The Civilization of the Renaissance in Italy*. Translated by S. G. C. Middlemore. New York: Modern Library, 2002.

Caferro, William. "Continuity, Long-Term Service and Permanent Forces: A Reassessment of the Florentine Army in the Fourteenth Century," *The Journal of Modern History*, Vol. 80 (2008): 219–51.

———. "Individualism and the Separation of Fields of Study," in *The Routledge History of the Renaissance*. London and Routledge Press, 2017: 62–74.

———. *John Hawkwood: An English Mercenary in Fourteenth Century Italy*. Baltimore: Johns Hopkins University Press, 2006.

———. *Mercenary Companies and the Decline of Siena*. Baltimore: Johns Hopkins University Press, 1998.

———. *Petrarch's War: Florence and the Black Death in Context*. Cambridge: Cambridge University Press, 2018.

———. "Warfare and Economy in Renaissance Italy, 1350–1450," *The Journal of Interdisciplinary History*, Vol. 39, No. 2 (Autumn, 2008): 167–209.

Canestrini, Giuseppe."Documenti per servire alla storia della milizia italiana dal XIII secolo al XVI," *Archivio Storico Italiano*, Vol. XVI (1851).

Carpi, Daniel. "The Account Book of a Jewish Moneylender in Montepulciano (1409–1410)," *Journal of European Economic History*, Vol. 14 (1985): 501–51.

Cassandro, Michele. G*li Ebrei e il prestito ebraico a Siena nel Cinquecento*. Milan: A. Giuffre, 1979.

Caturegli, Natalie. *La signoria di Giovanni dell'Agnello*. Pisa, 1920.

Chittolini, Giorgio. "City-States and Regional States in North-Central Italy," *Theory and Society* Vol. 18, No. 5 (1989): 689–706.

Covini, Maria Nadia, *L'esercito del duca: organizzazione miltare e istituzioni al tempo degli Sforza (1450–1480)*. Rome, 1998.

"Cronaca della Città di Perugia (Diario Del Graziani)," *Archivio Storico Italiano*, Vol. XVI (1850).

Epstein, Stephan R. *Freedom and Growth: The Rise of States and Markets, 1300–1700*. New York: Routledge Press, 2000.

Fossier, Robert. "Remarques sur les mouvements de population en Champagne méridionale au XVe siècle," *Bibliothèque de l'école des Chartes*, Vol. CXXII (1964): 186–89.

Friedrichs, Christopher R. *Urban Society in an Age of War: Nördlingen, 1580–1720*. Princeton: Princeton University Press, 1980.

Gessler, Eduard A. "Huglin von Shönegg. Ein Basler Reiterfuhrer des 14. Jahrhunderts in Italien. Ein Beitrag zur damaligen Bewaffnung," *Basler Zeitschrift für Geschichte und Altertumskunde*, Vol. 21 (1923).

Goldthwaite, Richard. *Wealth and the Demand for Art in Italy 1300–1600*. Baltimore: Johns Hopkins University Press, 1995.

Green, Louis. *Castruccio Castracani: A Study on the Origins and Character of a Fourteenth-Century Italian Despotism*. Oxford: Oxford University Press, 1986.

———. *Lucca under Many Masters: A Fourteenth-Century Italian Commune in Crisis (1328–1342)*. Florence: Leo S. Olschki Editore 1995.

Holmes, George A. "Florentine Merchants in England, 1345–1436," *Economic History Review*, Vol. 13 (1960–61): 193–208.

Housley, N. J. *The Italian Crusades: The Papal-Angevin Alliance and the Crusades Against Christian Lay Powers, 1254–1343*. Oxford: Oxford University Press, 1982.

Hunt, Edwin. *The Medieval Super-Companies. A Study of the Peruzzi Company of Florence*. Cambridge: Cambridge University Press, 1994.

Hyde, J. K. *Society and Politics in Medieval Italy*. New York: St Martin's Press, 1973.

Jones, Philip. *Malatesta of Rimini and the Papal State*. Cambridge: Cambridge University Press, 1974.

Kaeuper, Richard. *Bankers to the Crown, The Riccardi of Lucca and Edward I*. Princeton: Princeton University Press, 1973.

Kinsey, C. *Corporate Soldiers and International Security: The Rise of Private Military Companies*. London: Routledge Press, 2006.

Knapton, Michael. "City Wealth and State Wealth in North East Italy, 14th–17th Centuries," in *La ville, la bourgeoisie et la genise de l'etat moderne*, edited by Neithard Bulst and J-Ph. Genet. Paris, 1985.

La Roncière, Charles M. de "Indirect Taxes or 'Gabelles' at Florence in the Fourteenth Century: The Evolution of Tariffs and the Problems of Collection," in *Florentine Studies*, edited by Nicolai Rubinstein. Evanston, 1968: 140–92.

———. *Prix et salaries à Florence au xive siècle, 1280–1380*. Rome: L'Ecole française de Rome, 1982.

Larner, John. *Lords of the Romagna*. Ithaca: Cornell University Press, 1965.

Luzzati, Michele and Alessandra Veronese, *Banche e Banchieri a Volterra nel medioevo e nel Rinascimento*. Pisa: Pacini, 1993.

Luzzatto, Gino. *Il debito pubblico della repubblica di Venezia*. Milan: Istituto Editoriale Cisalpino, 1963.

Mainoni, Patrizia. *Le radici della discordia: Ricerche sulla fiscalita a Bergamo tra XIII e XV secolo*. Milan: Unicopli, 1997.

———. *Mutui alle compagnie di ventura al servizio dei Visconti*. Milan: Unicopli, 1980.

Mallet, Michael. *Mercenaries and their Masters*. Totowa: Rowman and Littlefield, 1974.

Martines, Lauro. *Power and Imagination: City-States in Renaissance Italy*. New York: Alfred A. Knopf, 1979.

McNeill, William H. *The Pursuit of Power*. Chicago: University of Chicago Press, 1982.

Meek, Christine. *Lucca, 1369–1400: Politics and Society in an Early Renaissance City-State*. Oxford: Oxford University Press, 1978.

Molà, Luca. *La comunità dei lucchesi a Venezia. Immigrazione e industria della seta nel tardo medioevo*. Venice, 1994.

Molho, Anthony. *Florentine Public Finances in the Early Renaissance*. Cambridge: Harvard University Press, 1971.

———. "Tre città-stato e i loro debiti pubblici. Quesiti e ipotesi sulla storia di Firenze, Genova e Venezia," in *Italia 1350–1450: tra crisi, trasformazione, sviluppo*. Pistoia, 1993: 185–215.

Muzzarelli, Maria Giuseppina. *Ebrei e citta d'ltalia in un eta di transizione: il caso di Cesena*. Bologna: Editrice Clueb, 1984.

Naldini, L. "La 'tallia militum societatis tallie Tuscie' nella seconda metà del sec. XIII," *Archivio Storico Italiano*, Vol. LXXVIII (1920): 75–113.

Pampaloni, Guido. "Gli organi della Repubblica fiorentina per le relazioni," *Rivista di studi politici internazionali*, Vol. 20 (1953): 261–96.

Parrott, David. *The Business of War: Military Enterprise and Military Revolution in Early Modern Europe*. Cambridge: Cambridge University Press, 2012.

Partner, Peter. *The Lands of Saint Peter*. Berkeley: University of California Press, 1972.

Percy, Sarah. *Mercenaries, the History of a Norm in International Relations*. Oxford: Oxford University Press, 2007.

Pieri, Piero. "Alcune questioni sopra fanterie in Italia nel periodo comunale." *Rivista storica italiana* (1933): 561–614.

———. *Rinascimento e la crisi militare italiana*. Turin, 1952.

Pini, Antonio Ivan. *Citta medievali e demografia storica*. Bologna: Clueb Editrice, 1996.

Raccagni, Gianluca. *The Lombard League, 1167–1225*. Oxford: Oxford University Press, 2010.

Redlich, Fritz. *The German Military Enterpriser and his Work Force, A Study in European Economic and Social History*. Vol. 1–2. Wiesbaden, 1964.

Ricotti, Ercole. *Storia delle compagnie di ventura in Italia*. 2 Vols. Turin, 1844–1845.

Ryder, Alan. *The Kingdom of Naples under Alfonso the Magnanimous: the Making of a Modern State*. Oxford: Oxford University Press, 1976.

Selzer, Stephan. *Deutsche Söldner im Italien des Trecento*. Tübingen: Max Niemeyer, 2001.

Sieveking, Hans. "Studio sulla finanze genovesi nel medioevo," in *Atti della società Ligure di storia patria*, translated by O. Soardi. Vol. 35, 1905.

Silva, Pietro. *Il Governo di Pietro Gambacorta in Pisa*. Pisa: Nistri, 1912.

Spruyt, Hendrik. "Institutional Selection in International Relations: State Anarchy as Order," *International Organization*, Vol. 48 (1994): 527–57.

———. *The Sovereign State and its Competitors*. Princeton: Princeton University Press, 1994.

Stromer, Wolfgang von. *Oberdeutsche Hochfinanz, 1350–1450*. Wiesbaden: Harrassowitz, 1970.

Stuard, Susan Mosher. *Gilding the Market Luxury and Fashion in Fourteenth-Century Italy*. Philadelphia: University of Pennsylvania Press, 2006.

The Chronicle of Jean de Venette, translated by J. Birdsall, edited by R. Newhal. New York, 1953.

Tilly, Charles. *Coercion, Capital and European States, 990–1992*. Cambridge: Wiley-Blackwell, 1992.

Toaff, Ariel. "Gli ebrei a Città di Castello," *Bolletino della deputazione di storia patria*, Vol. LXXII (1975): 1–105.

———. *Gli ebrei di Perugia*. Perugia, 1975.

Tognetti, Sergio. "La rappresaglia a Firenze nel secondo Trecento. Due vicende di uomini d'affari in Romagna e a Napoli," in *Mercatura è arte: Uomini d''affari toscani in Europa e nel Mediterraneo tardomedievale*, edited by Lorenzo Tanzini and Sergio Tognetti. Rome: Viella, 2012: 249–70.

Vaini, Mario. "La Spada e l'argento: I Gonzaga nel secolo XIV," in *Guerre, stati e citta: Mantova e Vitalia Padana dal secolo XIII ai XIX,* edited by Carlo M. Belfanti, Francesca Fantini d' Onofrio and Daniela Ferrari. Mantua, 1988.

Valentini, R. "Braccio da Montone e il comune di Orvieto," *Bollettino di storia patria per l'Umbria*, Vol. 25 (1922); Vol. 26 (1923): 65–157; 1–199.

Villani, Matteo. *Cronica*. Vol. 5. Florence, 1846.

Waley, Daniel. "The Army of the Florentine Republic from the Twelfth to the Fourteenth Century," in *Florentine Studies*, edited by Nicolai Rubinstein. Evanston, 1968: 70–108.

Wright, Nicholas. *Knights and Peasants: The Hundred Years War in the French Countryside*. Woodbridge: Boydell and Brewer, 1998.

Chapter 7

The Economy of Warlordism in Early Twentieth-Century China

Edward A. McCord

The military commanders who rose to power following the collapse of China's last imperial dynasty in the early twentieth century are often viewed as classic warlord prototypes. As seen in the Chinese case, the dominant defining element that ties warlords together is the importance of the command of military force as the primary basis of their political power. A less often noted commonality is how this military base of power is perforce dependent on access to economic or financial resources. Beyond these basic commonalities, different economic and political conditions and opportunities determine the particular features of warlordism in specific contexts. Thus, one special feature of warlords in modern China, not necessarily seen in other cases, is the extent to which they actively sought, and wielded power through, claims of political legitimacy, the acquisition of official government positions, and the control of state resources. As such, the character of Chinese warlords does not always align consistently with the broader concept of "non-state" military-political actors under which warlords are often subsumed in contemporary literature. The character of Chinese warlords, then, was grounded in the very specific political and economic conditions that surrounded their rise.

The main event that set the stage for the emergence of warlordism in early twentieth-century China was an anti-imperial revolution that arose in 1911 to overthrow the Qing dynasty. The 1911 Revolution did not create a political vacuum, let alone produce a complete state collapse. Instead, a new, albeit weak, national government continued to operate after the fall of the Qing dynasty. Equally important, civil administration did not collapse, and indeed largely continued to function even amid the ensuing civil wars that facilitated the transformation of military commanders into warlords. This gave Chinese warlords resources not always available to non-state military actors in other contexts. In essence, the control of political offices enhanced the capacity of emerging Chinese warlords to gain access to taxes and to provide legitimate cover for other financial exactions needed to maintain and expand their military forces. Insofar as continued access to such resources were necessary to sustain a warlord's war-making capacity, this also gave China's warlords a stake in the survival of state administrative structures. At the same time, the linkage of political-administrative centers to highly developed commercial networks also increased the importance of these centers for resource acquisition, giving a structure to warlord power that was more nodal than defined by strictly bounded territories.

Given the nature of warlordism as a form of highly personalized military rule, the character, abilities, and motivations of warlords as individuals provide an additional overlay on the social, political, and economic field in which they operated. Some "predatory warlords" used their increased access to state resources not just for the maintenance of their military forces but also for personal enrichment. Even so they had to operate within social and political contexts that often constrained their capacity for autonomous action. Thus, some warlords eventually sought to stabilize their power and legitimacy by seeking the support of public opinion through the provision of public goods. Attempts to enhance the economic development of their domains could serve this legitimating purpose even while enhancing their resource base. In the end, then, warlordism in modern China, despite responding to and fostering a degree of political fragmentation, was embedded in complex social, economic, and political networks and relationships that belies any assumption that the warlord era was a time of complete political or economic disintegration.

Given the inherently fragmented nature of warlordism, it is hardly surprising that studies of China's warlords have often focused on case studies, the biographies of individual military commanders, or the activities of specific warlord cliques. Any examination of particular warlord cases, however, presents a problem for generalization given the different characters of individual warlords and the specific contexts in which they operated. To avoid mistaking unique features for commonalities, this chapter was purposefully devised as an effort to synthesize, and to draw comparative insights from both the author's own research and the best examples of other scholarship to present more effectively the common features of modern China's warlordism as well as the range of behaviors and conditions that could exist within such commonalities.

TWENTIETH-CENTURY CHINESE WARLORDISM

Warlordism may be described as a situation where military commanders exert political authority over a substate region based on their personal control of military force. While this definition provides a foundation for comparative analysis, the specific features of warlordism as it has appeared in particular areas and periods of time are always grounded in contingent social, economic, and political conditions. Warlordism in twentieth-century China thus adapted to both a highly developed commercial economy and a complex political environment, including the continuation of systems of local and central administration and the rise of nationalism. These conditions provided resources that aided in the establishment of warlord power but also placed some constraints on their economic and political autonomy in unique ways. Under these conditions, one distinctive feature of twentieth-century Chinese warlords, in contrast to the warlords that arose in China following the collapse of previous dynasties, was the absence of attempts to establish independent states (which in premodern contexts usually took the form of competing kingdoms or imperial dynasties). The specific characteristics of Chinese warlordism in the early twentieth century thus cannot be divorced from the specific social, political, and economic conditions of this era.

The study of Chinese warlordism has always been strongly framed by contextual interpretations. One early and still often-cited theory traces the rise of China's twentieth-century warlords to changes in military organization in the mid-nineteenth century when massive popular uprising (such as the Taiping Rebellion, 1851–1864) forced the Qing dynasty to allow the organization of "regional" armies led by members of the civil "gentry" elite. These politically influential regional army leaders, with their strongly personalized command structures and largely autonomous local financing systems (based on commercial taxation), bore considerable resemblance, and thus suggested a causative relationship, to later twentieth-century warlords (Michael 1949). Such a direct connection between these regional armies and their leaders to later warlords does not, however, hold up to careful examination. In particular, this theory largely overlooked the wide-ranging military reforms carried out by the Qing dynasty at the turn of the century that eliminated most of the original regional armies, absorbed the taxes that had supported them into regular state budgets, and replaced them with Western-style and bureaucratically organized "New Armies" (Liu 1974; MacKinnon 1973). Ironically, it was these new, and largely professional, military forces that would ultimately provide the main foundation for warlord power.

A more recent theory links the development of these New Armies to the origin of warlordism but with a greater focus on fiscal resources than on military organization. According to Hans van de Ven (1996), the need to fund massive reform projects, including the New Armies, coincided with a drastic decline in central financial resources (arising from many factors, but significantly affected by indemnities imposed on China following military conflicts with foreign powers). As a result, both the Qing imperial court and subsequent Republican governments were increasingly forced to devolve responsibility for reform programs, including the development of modern-style New Armies, to provincial governments. In essence, van de Ven sees the origins of warlordism in a fiscal crisis that led to the devolution of power, including control over military finances, to the provinces.

The decentralization of public finance, and the resulting fragmentation of military organization, certainly had a major impact on the development of Chinese warlordism. At the very least, this situation insured that the rise of military power as a political force took the form of warlordism (with a division of power among competing military commanders) instead of a centralized military dictatorship. What van de Ven is less able to answer, though, is why this fiscal devolution necessarily placed political power in the hands of military men. Explaining this requires an additional understanding of the political context of the era.

I have argued that the acquisition of political power by military commanders was the result of a two-step process: first the politicization of the military and second the militarization of politics (McCord 1993). The politicization of the military occurred when educated young officers, primarily in the New Armies, were drawn into debates over reform or revolution in the last years of the Qing dynasty. This led directly to military participation in provincial uprisings that initiated the revolution against the dynasty in 1911. This participation, however, was also the first step toward the militarization of politics. The main context for this development was a lack of political consensus over the nature of the post-imperial "Republican" government (e.g., whether to establish a centralized or a federalist state, or a presidential or a parliamentary system of government) and who should hold political power. Lacking a consensus on how to resolve these issues, all sides turned to military force to advance their political objectives. In 1913, a small number of "revolutionary" provinces organized a military revolt against the dictatorial tendencies of the first president, Yuan Shikai. Yuan then used military force to suppress this revolt and extend central power more completely over the provinces. When Yuan attempted to strengthen his power further by restoring the monarchy in 1915, with himself as emperor, an even larger number of provinces raised arms against him. Yuan's death in the middle of this conflict did nothing to resolve underlying political issues. Rather a series of conflicts continued to pit Yuan's former generals in North China with recalcitrant southern provinces seeking to maintain a larger degree of political autonomy.

The militarization of politics that occurred over the course of these repeated civil wars produced warlordism—that is, a shift of political power into the hands of military commanders. If nothing else, the very fact that military force became the main political resource automatically increased the political influence of these commanders. At the same time, the need to meet the financial requirements of warfare increased the predilection, as well as the ability, of military commanders to gain control of political and financial resources. Thus, to maintain the support of military commanders for their political causes both Yuan Shikai and his political opponents had little choice but to award them with administrative positions, such as military or even civil governorships, that they could use to provide a financial base for their forces. It is at this point that the decentralization of military finances worked in favor of the emergence of a fragmented system of warlordism. Meanwhile, the emergence of warlordism also changed the nature of political conflicts. Once military commanders gained control over administrative and financial resources, the maintenance of their own power quickly became their main priority. The original issues that had given rise to the Republic's early wars faded into the background, to be replaced by civil wars that were mainly warlord struggles for power.

This explanation of the emergence of warlordism as the result of the steady militarization of politics also challenges another frequent account of the rise of Chinese warlordism that sees military men as simply filling a political and administrative vacuum created by the fall of the Qing dynasty in 1911.[1] As a matter of fact, civil administration did not simply collapse with the establishment of the Republic. Indeed, for the most part, local, provincial, and national administrations, though weakened, continued to function across the Republican era, including the early period that saw the rise of warlordism. Officials continued to be appointed; taxes continued to be collected.[2] Access to these administrative and financial resources were precisely why military commanders sought to gain control of political offices, particularly those with control over appointments and revenues. Maintaining the financial resources that could be derived from these positions (which were necessary to support their armies) also required that these commanders give at least a modicum of attention to the maintenance of administrative systems.

It is difficult, then, to designate Chinese warlords simply as "non-state actors" when they universally sought, and commonly held, official positions such as provincial civil or military governorships. The maintenance of their power actually required Chinese warlords (at least the successful ones) to act not only as military commanders but also as state bureaucrats. The main distinction that needs to be made, though, is that they were not merely functionaries of a central state but rather local or regional power-holders who gained control over pieces of the administrative system that had survived from the imperial state into the Republic.

The political fragmentation and decentralization that accompanied the emergence of Chinese warlordism often leads to an assumption of political autonomy, or even independence, as a key and defining characteristic of warlordism. Thus, one commonly cited definition of warlordism by

James Sheridan, in his introduction to a study of the Chinese warlord Feng Yuxiang, notes, "A warlord exercised effective government control over a fairly well-defined region by means of a military organization *that obeyed no higher authority than himself*" [italics added] (Sheridan 1966, 1). More general definitions of warlordism beyond the Chinese case make the same characterization. Thus, Antonio Giustozzi (2005, 5) notes that the warlord "has full and autonomous control over a military force, which he can use at will."

Although the potential for autonomous action is an important feature of warlord power, an examination of the Chinese case also suggests the constraints under which many warlords were actually forced to operate. First, although a warlord depended on his command of a military organization as the foundation of his power, this command was based in turn on his ability to maintain the support of his military subordinates. Such support might be enhanced by a warlord's personal charisma, but in the end, it mainly derived from his ability to meet the specific needs of his officers and soldiers—with military positions, advancement opportunities, and, most importantly, pay. Control over civil administration also offered warlords the opportunity to reward followers with lucrative civil office appointments (Kapp 1974, 159–60). Second, warlords did not exist in isolation but as part of a competitive warlord system. While certainly free to make independent decisions, most found security in broader factional alliances. These alliances operated with a set of rules that constrained warlord actions, which Hsi-sheng Ch'i (1976) has compared to the working of the international system. Finally, beyond this warlord system, warlords also had to operate within a broader social and political milieu, which often forced compromises with civilian elites or even accommodations with broader popular opinion.

The importance of such constraints is clearly visible in the rise and fall of the Hubei warlord, Wang Zhanyuan. While originally enjoying strong support from his officers and men, over time insufficient financial resources, exacerbated by Wang's efforts to line his own pockets, led to massive arrears in troop pay. When Wang sought to disband his oldest and most loyal troops as a money-saving measure, they mutinied and pillaged Wang's capital city. The public outrage over this incident, and other similar mutinies around the province, led to increased opposition from Hubei's political elites to Wang's continued rule. More importantly, the mutinies suggested to outsiders that Wang was no longer in full control of his own military forces. This created concern among Wang's factional allies that their enemies might seize Wang's territory and upset broader power arrangements. To forestall this outcome, Wang's putative allies took advantage of the popular outcry against him to move their own troops into Hubei, deposing Wang and incorporating his army and his territory into their own (McCord 2014b). Certainly, up to that point, Wang had been an "autonomous" actor in China's warlord system; but that autonomy still operated within numerous constraints.

Among the constraints within which Chinese warlords had to operate was the survival of central government structures that still retained some authority and political power. Some recent scholarship on warlordism has argued that warlords operate "at sub-state level, in regions where state has withdrawn or has lost monopoly of violence." As such, warlords are seen as simply attempting to benefit as much as possible from state disorder (Giustozzi 2005, 5). This reinforces the conceptualization of warlords as non-state actors pursuing their own interests in opposition, or indifference, to the state. An investigation of the relationship between Chinese warlords and the Chinese state, however, suggests a more complicated process at work.

While the Chinese state was clearly weakened following the fall of the Qing dynasty, and provincial warlords steadily undermined the central government's monopoly over military force, central authority did not entirely disappear. At the most basic level, an internationally recognized national government continued to exist in Beijing over the entire warlord period. More to the point, this government was not totally without resources. Indeed, the unwillingness of the foreign powers to see China's complete collapse ensured that all customs revenues (after the fulfillment of foreign loan obligations) were delivered to Beijing. This alone made the Beijing government a prize to be fought over by competing warlord factions. A more subtle resource was the central government's power of appointment that provided political legitimacy for the control of local and provincial administrations—and the revenues they generated. As a result, these appointments were highly sought after. This did not mean that the Chinese state, represented by the government in Beijing, was able to exert much direct control over its "appointees." For example, central ministers frankly admitted to civilian petitioners calling for Wang Zhanyuan's removal that the central government had no effective means to do this (Liu 1922, 132, 137–40). At the same time, over the term of his office, Wang Zhanyuan was engaged in a constant dance with the central government over titles, appointments, and revenues that showed that the central state still maintained some minimal leverage.

The nature of central authority in China during the warlord period was complicated because southern provinces (and their warlord rulers) periodically denied the authority of the national government in Beijing, controlled as it was by their main warlord rivals. Nonetheless, in such cases, they usually collaborated in the recognition of an alternate central government situated in Canton (sometimes headed by the main revolutionary leader Sun Yat-sen) that based its authority on earlier constitutions or national assemblies overthrown by Yuan Shikai or his successors in Beijing. Although never internationally recognized, these Canton governments performed the same legitimating function for southern warlords as the Beijing government did for their northern competitors. None of this denies the substantial political autonomy enjoyed by China's warlords in most contexts. But a decentralized government is hardly the same as the absence of government.

The decisions by warlords, north or south, to offer allegiance, even if largely nominal, to either the central government in Beijing or to a Canton challenger were also a response to other international and domestic constraints. On the one hand, the decision by the international community to recognize only the Beijing government inhibited any movement toward more complete independence by individual warlords (Chong 2009). On the other hand, and perhaps more importantly, any warlord declaring complete independence risked provoking internal patriotic furor. While the direct danger from popular opposition might be limited, this opposition could provide a justification for attacks by warlord competitors. As a result, most warlords at least nominally expressed their support for a unified (or reunified) China as their ultimate political goal. This then was yet another limitation on full warlord autonomy.

The main period of warlord ascendency in China was the decade following Yuan Shikai's death in 1916. In 1926, though, the Nationalist Party government in Canton launched a military campaign, known as the Northern Expedition, dedicated to the overthrow of warlordism and the reunification of the country. The main military resource for this effort was a new professionalized party army meant to break the power of the warlords and end the pattern of personalized military command. The success of this expedition, under the leadership of the commander of this party army, Chiang Kai-shek, was only possible, though, by carefully balancing the defeat of major warlord contenders with appeals for support from other lesser warlords for the party's nationalist cause. The need to rely on military force to achieve political "unification" actually worked to preserve the power of military leaders (both former warlords and new Nationalist Party Army commanders) in the new political system—with many of these commanders holding the same level of military-based authority in the provinces as their early Republican warlord predecessors.[3] As a result, James Sheridan characterized these commanders in the decade of Nationalist Party rule from its new capital in Nanjing (1927–1937) as a period of "residual warlordism" (Sheridan 1966, 14–16).

The main difference between this decade and the earlier period of original warlordism was a slow recovery of central power under the Nanjing government, with some increased constraints on warlord autonomy. One main indicator of this change was the near universal recognition by surviving or new warlords of the ideological legitimacy of the Nationalist Party, to the extent that some scholars argue they might better be identified as "party" rather than "residual" warlords (Lary 1974, 130). Nonetheless, these warlords did not necessarily always recognize the authority of Chiang Kai-shek at the head of the Nationalist Party government. As a result, recurring civil war remained a feature of the period, with various military commanders challenging Nanjing with claims that they were actually more faithful to the ideological aims of the Nationalist Party. In the end, though, none of these challenges stopped the growing power of the Nanjing government. So, while both the period following the death of Yuan Shikai and the Nanjing decade may be considered periods of warlordism, the first period was mainly characterized by struggles among competing warlords amid declining central power, while the second period was marked by increasingly defensive actions by residual warlords against a restrengthened center. In the end, though, the relative autonomy of warlords in both periods relied mainly on their ability to control the financial resources necessary to maintain the military forces that were the main foundation of their political influence.

WARLORD FINANCES

The frequency of warfare in the decades following the 1911 Revolution both reflected and exacerbated the unstable and competitive nature of Chinese warlordism. One result of this situation was to set a process into motion whereby the survival of individual warlords ultimately required the constant expansion of their military forces in order to maintain their competitive edge. The growth of the number of men under arms in Hubei Province provides a good example of this military expansion. In the late Qing, Hubei had what was considered a fairly robust provincial New Army of one division and one independent brigade (in a military system where divisions were normally composed of two brigades, with around 10,000 officers and soldiers per division). By 1920, Hubei's military forces had grown to five divisions and nearly a dozen brigades controlled by the province's main warlord, Wang Zhanyuan, and other affiliated military commanders, totaling over 100,000 soldiers (McCord 1993, 278–82). The main warlord of Manchuria, Zhang Zuolin, commanded a single division when he pressured the central government to appoint him civil and military governor of Fengtian Province in 1916. By 1922, after Zhang had expanded his influence over Manchuria's three provinces, his command grew to over 100,000 soldiers. Before the end of the decade, his army had expanded to nearly 300,000 men (Suleski 2002, 8–10). Likewise, a "party" warlord who ruled over Guangdong Province from 1929 to 1936, Chen Jitang, consolidated his position not only by eliminating military competitors but also by increasing his own army from 50,000 to 150,000 men (Lin 2002, 184). These are but several examples of a continuing process of military growth seen in all areas during China's warlord era.

This rapid military expansion quickly strained the fiscal resources of the Chinese state at all levels. At the beginning of the Republic, military units favored by "national" designations were in theory supposed to be paid directly by the central government, while other forces were paid through provincial budgets. Financial weakness, however, quickly made it impossible for the central government in Beijing to meet its full obligations to national units, whose commanders then tapped into provincial revenues to meet their troop payrolls. Thus, by 1920, the contribution of the central government to Wang Zhanyuan's "national" division in Hubei was reduced to a dribble, while his military expenses grew to claim one-half to two-thirds of the province's budget (McCord 2014b, 58–59). Increasing provincial responsibility for troops payrolls, however, also made the warlords even more reluctant to forward "national" taxes to the Beijing government (even in the provinces where its authority was recognized), thus weakening even further the central government's ability to exert any control, by fiscal means, over the country's growing armies and their commanders.

The ability of Chinese warlords to maintain their military forces, and thus their capacity to wage war, thus came to depend primarily on their capture of, or control over, local or provincial state resources. Warlords like Wang Zhanyuan and Zhang Zuolin sought to obtain official positions precisely because this gave them operational authority over provincial or local administrations, and hence over the financial resources of these administrations. To be more precise, what they sought was not just a specific amount of resources controlled through these positions, but the authority to increase revenues as needed to support their growing armies. In a useful summary of warlord economic capabilities, Hsi-sheng Ch'i divides these resulting revenue streams into two broad categories, "regular" sources of income, mainly taxes, and "special" sources of income including "bonds, loans, currency manipulation, opium profits, and various forms of emergency exactions" (Ch'i 1976, 151).

For most of Chinese history up to the twentieth-century warlord era, the most important source of "regular" state income was the land tax. In theory, all land tax was supposed to be delivered to the central government, making it the main fiscal foundation of the state. Following the 1911 Revolution, though, many provinces began to withhold land tax revenues to pay for the increasing costs of "modern" provincial and local administration. By this means, the land tax also became an important initial financial resource for emerging warlords controlling provincial governments. Recognizing the inability to reverse this devolution of taxing power, the Nationalist government established in 1927 ultimately gave up any "central" claim to these revenues.

For all its importance, the "transaction costs" of the land tax were fairly high in terms of maintaining land and tax records, collecting the tax itself (in kind or in cash), and monitoring compliance. Although land taxes could, in theory, be increased by reassessing land usage and productivity at periodic intervals, in practice the cost of conducting land surveys for this purpose was prohibitive relative to expected gains. Generally speaking, then, increases in land taxes in the warlord era were not pursued by changing base tax rates but by simply including new "add-on" fees to established tax assessments. By the end of the era, these fees often exceeded the original land tax itself. Another means of raising land tax revenues was the advance collection of land taxes for future years. This was sometimes justified by emergency situations requiring new revenues; but it often occurred when a warlord gained control over territory previously held by another warlord who had already collected, and spent, that year's tax revenues. While in theory advance collections relieved taxpayers of future obligations, in practice advance collections—in extreme cases extending more than a decade—simply became additional assessments.[4]

The traditional importance of the land tax in China as state revenue, including initial warlord regimes, has perhaps contributed to an overly "territorial" notion of the bases of warlord power, grounded on the assumption that warlords would focus on accumulating and holding land from which taxes could be extracted. Simply in terms of reducing transaction costs, though, most warlords paid more attention to garrisoning administrative nodes through which land taxes were processed than in patrolling, or fighting over, parcels of territories on which the land tax was based.

This situation can be seen in the fragmented sub-provincial "garrison area" system that developed in Sichuan Province in the warlord era. Robert Kapp's study of one major garrison area commander, Liu Xiang (who held power in eastern Sichuan from 1926 to 1937), notes that the exact number of counties in any one garrison area varied considerably over time, but long-established county borders continued to serve unchanged within garrison areas boundaries (Kapp 1974, 161). In other words, "territorial" struggles among warlords did not focus on actual acreage but on county seats that remained the administrative collection points for county taxes within established boundaries. Interestingly, in many of Sichuan's garrison areas, the garrison area commanders at the top of the provincial military "food chain" actually yielded the right to collect local land taxes to their local military subordinates to cover their own military expenses, thus mirroring to a certain degree the devolution of land tax revenues from the center to the provinces under the Nationalist government (Kapp 1974, 162). In the end, Liu Xiang, like many other major warlords, did not depend primarily on land taxes for their power. As Kapp notes, Liu Xiang's control over his garrison area ultimately depended on the more lucrative resources he gained by establishing his administrative base in the major Yangzi River port and commercial city of Chongqing in eastern Sichuan.[5]

Although the amount of land taxes collected continued to grow, over time they became less important as a major source of warlord financing. This was only possible because of the availability of larger and more easily collected revenues. Thus, by the late 1920s, land taxes only accounted for 5–10 percent of the revenues for Chen Jitang's warlord regime in Guangdong. As Alfred Lin notes, this situation was made possible by the proliferation of a large number of miscellaneous taxes, including a gambling tax, that provided 14–20 percent of Chen's revenues (Lin 2002, 189). Across China, the proliferation of such taxes emerged as a major way in which warlords met their rising costs. James Sheridan provides a list of seventy miscellaneous taxes and fees collected in Xiamen (Amoy) in 1924, including a night soil tax, a lower-class prostitute singing tax, a narcissus bulb tax, and a "superstition tax" on paper money offerings used in funerals, as well as more mundane taxes on pigs, flour, tea, cotton yarn, and street lamps (Sheridan 1966, 25).

Simply listing the diversity of taxes that were instituted in the warlord era in China may, however, again obscure the topography of warlord financing that was determined by the nature and location of goods that presented the most lucrative sources for taxation. While nearly any good or service could be a target for taxation, it was a simple matter of efficiency to focus tax collection in urban areas where concentrated populations and commercial activity guaranteed a higher yield. In this context, it is again not surprising that warlords focused their main attention "spatially" on the control of cities rather than on the countryside per se. Cities were not just appealing targets because they served as administrative centers for taxation systems that extended into the countryside but also because they were arenas for easy collection of high-yield commercial taxation. This was especially true for certain high-value products that could be taxed easily as they passed through cities along major transportation routes. One prominent example was the importance of taxes on opium, largely produced in China's southwest provinces. For warlords along shipping routes leading out of opium production areas, a simple military roadblock or a gun emplacement along a riverbank could potentially reap huge and consistent tax revenues.[6] For this reason, roads and commercial waterways acted as the main sinews connecting the urban nodes of warlord financial power.

The ability of warlords to collect such a range of taxes (and to raise rates on these taxes) was ultimately legitimized by the official positions they held. This did not mean that they were simply able to impose new taxes by fiat. One reason for seeking the authority of a public office was that it allowed the warlord to gain some degree of compliance from the population for his tax assessments—which resulted in lower transaction costs than if funds were simply collected at the point of a gun.[7] At the same time, gaining such compliance opened the way for some degree of negotiation with taxpayers, or their representatives, which could also place some limitations on the amount of taxes that could be raised. For example, Wang Zhanyuan normally sought the approval of the Hubei Provincial Assembly for tax increases. Although Wang bribed assemblymen to keep them amenable to his proposals, they retained enough autonomy if not to refuse then to renegotiate tax hikes in some cases. Other interest groups, such as chambers of commerce, could also use their influence to negotiate tax increases downward in exchange for a guarantee of smooth tax deliveries (McCord 2014b, 59–60).[8]

In the end, most successful warlords found some way to reach accommodations with merchants and other civil elites to ease their access to needed financial resources. Thus, Zhang Zuolin developed a special relationship with one member of the civil elite, Wang Yongjiang, who served as Zhang's civil governor. Wang mediated an implicit bargain between Zhang and Manchuria's business elites that, for nearly a decade, ensured that Zhang's revenue needs for his growing army would always be met, but in a way that produced the least amount of disruption of the local economy (Suleski 2002, 33–160). Robert Kapp notes that Liu Xiang initially faced some open opposition to new taxation from Chongqing's merchant community, including a merchant strike in 1929. Nonetheless, Liu worked hard to develop personal relationships with merchant leaders, seeking their advice on financial issues, and generally winning them over to help him meet his fiscal needs. Kapp suggests that the merchants' seeming submission to Liu's will was paradoxically due in part to the "investment" the merchant community made to the consolidation of Liu's position over time. Working with a known incumbent was, in the end, less harmful than the prospect of a change in military control and the warfare that would normally accompany such a transition (Kapp 1974, 157–58).

Given the existence of a tipping point where the transaction costs of raising taxes could outweigh the additional funds raised, no successful warlord relied solely on taxation. Most therefore also pursued other "special" revenues from a variety of sources. In many cases, though, it was still the warlord's official position that eased the acquisition of such revenues.

Hubei's Wang Zhanyuan again provides a good example of the pursuit of such special revenue sources. Wang was able to use his position as provincial governor to negotiate official loans, pledged against provincial properties and future tax revenues, with both foreign and domestic investors. Thus, he obtained two 1 million yuan loans from Japanese and American bankers in 1919 and 1920 respectively. Domestically, Wang also reportedly issued over 2 million yuan in bonds through the Hubei government, none of which were ever fully redeemed, to meet his military expenses. As willing lenders became increasingly difficult to find, Wang turned to more forceful means of exacting "loans" directly from chambers of commerce in the Hubei capital.

Warning that without these funds he could not guarantee the good behavior of his troops, Wang demanded first a 600,000 yuan loan from the chambers followed shortly after by another demand for an additional 2 million yuan (McCord 2014b, 60–61).

Currency manipulation was another popular means of "revenue enhancement." The location of the Hubei Mint within Wang Zhanyuan's capital essentially provided him with opportunities to increase the issue of coins and to print money to meet deficits in his military payrolls. One estimate was that banknotes worth over 90 million strings of copper cash were issued by the Hubei Mint over the course of Wang's reign. The official status of the Mint helped to slow, if not prevent, the depreciation in the value of currency Wang created. Another way Wang sought to avoid depreciation was to hide the excess issue of unbacked currency through putative "redemptions" of old banknotes where the new notes significantly exceeded the total value of the notes redeemed (McCord 2014b, 60).

Although the Hubei Mint gave Wang Zhanyuan a special resource, most warlords also worked through other official financial institutions, or even private banks, to issue supposedly state-backed currency of various types.[9] Some military commanders resorted to the issue of "promissory notes" or special "military scripts" to meet troop payrolls, requiring merchants to accept these notes as if they were actual currency. The value of these notes relied on the threats of angry soldiers, who were paid in these notes, if merchants dared to reject them. The total value of various financial instruments used to cover expenses by various warlord regimes often reached astronomical levels. Thus, Chen Jitang's government in Guangdong issued over 100 million yuan through a succession of treasury notes and public bonds from 1929 to 1936. Meanwhile, over time Liu's administration also authorized the Provincial Government Bank to issue nearly 200 million yuan in banknotes, while also borrowing over 80 million yuan directly from the bank, to cover administrative and military expenses (Lin 2002, 202–3).

In the end, there were still some limits on the extent to which warlords could simply print money to solve their fiscal problems without leading to devaluations that would decrease their utility. Kwong Chi Man (2014) has shown the extreme efforts Zhang Zuolin had to make in Manchuria to maintain the stability of the currency issued by his regime, particularly since he had to compete for public confidence with alternate Russian and Japanese currencies that circulated in his territory. Beyond the intrinsic market value of the currency issued, Kwong shows how success or failure in military ventures (often specifically pursued to acquire additional financial resources, such as Zhang's decision to extend his power over Beijing in 1926) could have an impact on civilian confidence in a warlord's currency, easing or exacerbating his fiscal problems.

Although there were many commonalities in warlord finance in early twentieth-century China, the main one being the constant drive for increased revenues to meet growing military expenses, there could also be considerable variation from one warlord to the next as they adapted to and took advantage of available resources. The competition for these resources also generated conflicts for the control of more lucrative administrative and commercial centers and transportation networks. Although the need to maintain the military foundations of warlord power underlay all such struggles, the possibility of personal enrichment was an additional factor behind the constant drive for revenue enhancement. This situation contributed to the particular "predatory" nature of warlord rule.

PREDATORY WARLORDISM

Although rarely used in Chinese warlord studies, the term *predatory rule* has been applied in many other cases to describe the nature of warlord governance. There is, however, considerable diversity of opinion on how to define this term.[10] In many cases, it seems more deployed for its evocative imagery (of warlords as predators) than as a clear analytical concept. Margaret Levi made one of the more widely cited efforts to give this concept greater clarity. She argues that "Rulers are predatory in that they always try to set the terms of trade that maximize their personal objectives, which . . . require them to maximize state revenue" (Levi 1988, 10). In attributing the aspiration to maximize revenues to all rulers, with differences in performance only resulting from various constraints such as transaction costs, Levi would seem, however, to define most governments as predatory. As such, the term loses much of its analytical or comparative value. In seeking to provide greater utility for the application of this concept to warlordism, I have argued for a more specific focus on the personal objectives of rulers in terms of their financial policies and actions, proposing that predatory rule be defined as "a form of governance whereby political position is deployed to maximize the ruler's personal power and private wealth to the detriment of the public good" (McCord 2014b, 51).

Many Chinese warlords in the early twentieth century were notable in the extent to which they used their positions to acquire considerable personal wealth, exhibiting the qualities of what might then be called predatory warlordism. According to one estimate, the wealth of the Manchurian warlord Zhang Zuolin in 1925 reached around 18 million yuan, divided between real estate holdings and cash deposits (Suleski 2002, 10). Wang Zhanyuan's wealth at the time of his departure from Hubei in 1920 was estimated at 10 million yuan (Liu 1922, 3). To put this into perspective, the entire annual official budget for the province of Hubei in this period was approximately the same amount: 10.8 million yuan (*Shibao*, August 2, 1920).

Even if numbers can usually only be estimated, the wealth achieved by many warlords was often easily observable in terms of their acquisition of land and property.[11] Even so, the specific ways in which this wealth was acquired is sometimes less easy to determine. This is partially true because many warlords made little distinction between public and private purses. For this very reason, though, it was also clear that the foundation of warlord wealth was often, if not always, initially built on the embezzlement of public funds. It was fairly common, for example, for military officers up the chain of command in both the late Qing and early Republic to withhold, and transfer into their own pockets, a portion of the pay supposedly allocated for their soldiers, or funds for unit expenses. Another method at higher command levels involved falsely reporting higher than actual troop numbers in order to pocket the pay of missing soldiers. Wang Zhanyuan turned this technique into a high art by filling up to 10 percent of the troop rosters in all units under his command with "empty names" for nonexistent soldiers. By marking these soldiers as "on assignment" to his office, Wang was able to pocket the pay for these men without raising too much attention. He also delayed troop pay so he could use payroll funds for short-term investments. Finally, he regularly embezzled funds intended for military expenses. His ability to appoint loyal followers to military and financial offices in charge of such funds allowed him to obscure the amounts that ultimately ended up in his own accounts (McCord 2014b, 62–63; Yan 1989).

Wang, who later in life often bragged about his business acumen, did not simply let these embezzled funds lie fallow. Rather, he invested them in a wide range of business opportunities, including the purchase of rental properties and the establishment of, or investment in, a wide range of industries. In many cases, the manipulation of his official position helped to increase his profits in these investments. For example, he ordered all Hubei police and military units to acquire uniforms, bedding, and leather products from companies he established to produce these goods. He was also actively involved in commerce, taking advantage of official transportation and tax waivers for the shipment of "military use" goods to increase his profits (McCord 2014b, 63–64; Zheng 1962, 256). Wang accumulated enough wealth by the time of his fall from power to invest in an even wider range of business opportunities, expanding his fortune in retirement to an estimated 40 million yuan (Jiang 1983, 27).

Wang Zhanyuan was perhaps one of the most successful of China's Republican era warlords in terms of personal wealth accumulation. But he was not alone. This can be seen in the importance of warlord capital as a major source for industrial investment in North China in this period

(Zhu 1979). Sichuan warlords likewise found ample opportunities for investment in real estate, banking, opium trafficking, and a range of other commercial activities. Their military positions were again often useful in increasing the profitability of their investments. For example, Liu Xiang invested in a river steamer to transport opium downriver, using military flags to avoid customs inspections (Kapp 1974, 159). Likewise, Chen Jitang generated enormous personal profits from a sugar monopoly created by his government in Guangdong. Reflecting the extent to which warlords could intermingle public and private purses, when Chen was forced from power in 1936, he was able to carry away 7 million yuan and nearly 4 million in Hong Kong dollars from the Guangdong Provincial Bank (Lin 2002, 201–3).

The regularity with which so many warlords parlayed military and political power into personal wealth has often led to the inclusion of predatory rule, even if not using this exact terminology, in the definition of Chinese warlordism. Nonetheless, Wang Zhanyuan's case also shows how excessive attention to personal wealth acquisition could contribute to a loss of military and civil power. Indeed, Wang's example was perhaps a cautionary tale about the trade-off between the pursuit of wealth and the maintenance of political power. Wang's personal greed played at least some role in his downfall by alienating not only public opinion (infuriated by Wang's continual demands for more financial resources) but also, and perhaps more importantly, the loyalty of this own troops, who saw Wang grow rich even as they suffered repeated delays or cuts in their pay.

Realizing this, many warlords prioritized maintaining power over personal enrichment (though clearly not ignoring how this power still guaranteed a certain level of personal wealth).[12] Concern for the maintenance of power then led many warlords to conclude that their political performance in areas other than military prowess could also be useful in sustaining their positions. This concern was evident in the varying effects of warlordism on, and of warlord attention to, the provision of public goods.

WARLORDS AND THE PROVISION OF PUBLIC GOODS

In many ways, the 1911 Revolution was the crowning moment of a reformist movement that emerged in the last decades of the Qing dynasty, the goals of which were not just political change but the transformation and strengthening of China through increased state attention to the expansion of education, the growth and reform of the national military, the development of transportation and communication systems, and the general promotion of commerce and industry. The immediate impact of the emergence of warlordism in the early Republican period, though, was a general weakening, not the increase, of state capacity in these areas, perhaps most obviously seen in a decline in the provision of public goods. The only goal that did not seem to suffer was the growth of the Chinese military, though not necessarily meeting reformist demands for increased military quality. Military expansion was in turn a major reason for the decline in other reform projects, as the funding needed for this expansion left far fewer funds for nonmilitary projects.[13]

Some warlords such as Wang Zhanyuan would argue that the main public good they provided, and which they assumed was sufficient to assure them of public support, was the use of their armies to preserve local order (Liu 1922, 2). This was an increasingly difficult position to maintain, however, in the context of continual warlord conflicts (or in Wang's case, the outbreak of violent and destructive mutinies among his own troops). Wang perhaps stood at one end of a continuum in openly resisting advice that he build additional "merit" in the eyes of the public by attention to other activities that would benefit the people's livelihood (Zheng 1962, 257). There were other warlords, however, who actively sought to gain popular support for their regimes by the provision of public goods, whether in terms of traditionally expected government services or in meeting the reformist demands of the modern era.[14] And there is at least some evidence that paying attention to such issues increased the longevity of particular warlord regimes.

One of the most prominent examples of a warlord who gained a reputation for his reform and public welfare projects was the warlord of Shanxi Province, Yan Xishan. Yan was an educated New Army officer who led Shanxi's military forces against the Qing dynasty in 1911, resulting in his appointment as military governor by Yuan Shikai in 1912, beginning a long rule over the province that lasted, with some ups and downs, until 1949. In his early years, Yan initiated many programs influenced by late Qing reform movements, including the suppression of foot-binding, the promotion of literacy classes and vocational schools for women, the establishment of a medical school, the expansion of public education (providing four years of public schooling for all children), the organization of public health campaigns, and the formation of militia to suppress banditry. To grow his province's economy, he set up chambers of commerce, expanded road systems, promoted reforestation, and established, with varying degrees of success, a variety of light industries, including flour mills, a cigarette factory, a paper mill, and a large textile mill. As a result of these efforts, Yan became known as the "Model Governor" (Gillin 1967).

Warlord promotion of various projects to improve the economies of their territories and the lives of their inhabitants picked up pace in the period of residual or party warlordism when legitimation based on adherence to

Nationalist Party principles required at least some attention to the provision of public goods or, as Alfred Lin describes it, "provincial regeneration" (Lin 2002, 177–80). Lin's studies of Chen Jitang's regime in Guangdong provide a good example of the extensive efforts undertaken toward this end by one prominent warlord. First, Chen was engaged in an extensive range of public works, including the building of over 17,000 kilometers of highways. He also contributed to the development of the province's economy with the founding of sugar and cement plants (Lin 2002, 179, 200). Finally, he took a personal interest in the provision of "social relief work," organizing a new Social Welfare Bureau to unify philanthropic activities in the province and, at least in theory, provide expanded and more efficient services. Among the projects instituted were free health clinics and public dormitories providing housing for the poor and indigent (Lin 2004).

Other examples can be found in other warlord regimes in this period. Liu Xiang's administration initiated the construction of a network of modern streets in Chongqing and established a new business district outside the original walls of the densely packed old city. He also developed partnerships with several private companies to advance the development of commerce and industry. For example, with Liu's backing, the Minsheng Company revived Chinese-owned shipping based in Chongqing, and then branched out into other activities: restoring a defunct coal company, building a railroad for coal transportation, and establishing a refrigeration plant, a shipyard, and machine shops, among other industries (Kapp 1974, 149–53). The main warlord in Hunan during the Nanjing decade, He Jian, also initiated an extensive state-building program to aid in the regeneration of his province. He was particularly dedicated to the improvement of education, overseeing the opening of over 5,000 new primary schools. He also quadrupled the number of motorized vehicle highways in the province, laid down extensive telephone and telegraph lines, and saw to the completion of the last leg of the Beijing-Canton railroad through his province. In a synopsis of his achievements published after he left office in 1937, he credited his administration with improving waterways, founding orphanages and hospitals, overseeing disaster relief, and improving local administration (McCord 2014c, 132–34).

Alfred Lin (2002, 178–79) cites a number of other studies that he argues show "genuine" efforts at provincial regeneration carried out by a large number of warlords in various areas. One cannot, however, view these efforts in purely altruistic terms. First, as Lin notes, most of these warlords saw the success of such regenerative projects as also increasing their regime stability and legitimacy by appealing to popular opinion. Second, altruism and self-interest could intermingle, particularly in cases where industrial development projects also provided opportunities for profit by warlord investors. Finally, various projects that could serve the public good in various ways were often still linked to broader revenue maximization goals.

The best example of this last point might be Liu Xiang's development of the Minsheng Company to revive Chongqing-based shipping along the Yangzi River. One of Liu's stated goals at the time was to eliminate the privileges of foreign shipping that had been established by unequal treaties with foreign powers. On one hand, he offered tax relief to the Minsheng Company to make it more competitive with foreign shipping lines; on the other hand, he used political pressure and the threat of nationalist boycotts to convince the foreign companies to relinquish their privileges. Liu's success greatly enhanced his popular status by making himself appear as a leader in an anti-imperialist shipping rights recovery movement, leading Anne Reinhardt (2008) to use this case as an example of the way that warlords, mainly known for protecting their political autonomy, could still be effective in achieving nationalist goals, in this case "decolonization on the periphery." But Liu was hardly motivated by patriotism alone. First, as an investor in the Minsheng Company, Liu had a personal stake in its success. Second, and more importantly, Reinhardt shows how Liu's initial motivation was still more derived from a desire to consolidate his ability to control revenues from shipping through Chongqing by not only monopolizing Chinese shipping but also eliminating the treaty-based tax-exempt status of foreign shipping lines (Reinhardt 2008, 263).

It is important, then, not to rely on an over simplistic understanding of warlord motivations or actions. While some warlords may have sought to use their command of military force for personal enrichment, as well as for the consolidation of political power, others may have also had genuine interests in using their power for the greater benefit of society, or at least of the people in their garrison areas. Different warlords were influenced by a confluence or a combination of motives depending on the contexts in which they operated, and their personal predilections. None of this, however, could withstand the underlying logic of warlord power. As Alfred Lin notes,

> Notwithstanding differences among warlords, no warlord could have failed to realize that the very survival of his regime depended on ready access to the mainstays of war. Thus, a warlord's primary concern was maximizing revenue to finance his war machine. Such an overriding focus undercut whatever desires a warlord might have for the betterment of society. (Lin 2002, 178)

Successful warlords were those who never forgot the priorities forced upon them by the competitive nature of warlordism, which always made revenue acquisition to maintain their armies a top priority.

THE EFFECTS OF WARLORDISM

The effects of warlordism on China, and on the Chinese economy, in the early twentieth century were wide-ranging—and largely negative. The most immediate and obvious of these negative effects was the sheer physical destruction of property and the loss of life that occurred during the incessant warfare of the warlord era. Ordinary Chinese, however, often experienced this loss of life and property not only as a by-product of the battles that raged around them but also as a result of deliberate violence by ill-disciplined troops who took advantage of the environment of war, and their access to weapons, to carry out casual looting, wholesale pillage, murder, and rape. One of the features of the warlord era, then, was the frequent occurrence of military atrocities, which in some cases could result in the destruction of entire communities. This violence was such that "military disasters" (*bingzai*) were often paired with "natural disasters" (*tianzai*) as the main afflictions suffered by the Chinese people in this era (Lary 1985, 71–82, 111; McCord 2015).

In the areas where they occurred, the baneful effects of warlord wars also reached far beyond immediate destruction of public and private property or the loss of civilian lives. Battles, or even the passing of combatant forces, interrupted agricultural cycles. Family livelihoods were disrupted as countless civilians were impressed from farms and shops to serve as bearers for armies on the move. Massive flows of refugees fleeing troop violence disrupted the economies of the communities they fled from as well as those where they sought refuge. The seizure of rail and water transport for military use, as well as the general blockage of transportation routes during military confrontations, disrupted commerce, bankrupted businesses, and created shortages of food and other necessary goods. Meanwhile, even the threat of war, let alone the outbreak of actual military conflict, created financial panics and currency instability. This was particularly true because the expanded costs of war forced participating warlords to increase their regular financial exactions. The defeat of a warlord could result in the collapse of the currency supported by his regime and defaults on the bonds and loans that had aided in the maintenance of his army. Banditry also flourished as guns discarded by defeated troops, or the incorporation of these troops themselves, increased the resources of bandit bands, even as warlords became less amenable to risking their own soldiers in bandit suppression.[15]

Beyond the direct and indirect effects of warlord conflicts, there were the more general economic consequences of warlord financing. Here, some caution against overgeneralization is perhaps due. The tendency of both contemporary and more recent scholarly accounts of Chinese warlordism to focus on its destructive economic consequences has contributed to negative assumptions about the overall weakness of the Republican economy. Contesting such assumptions, Thomas Rawski has shown that on the balance, and at the macro level, the Republican period (including the warlord era) was generally a time of trade expansion and economic growth. More controversially, he has argued that unlike normal portrayals of excessive financial exactions by warlord regimes (and the following Nationalist government), the Chinese people were relatively undertaxed in comparison to other societies in similar stages of development (Rawski 1989, xix–64). Leaving aside the question of whether a standard can be set for "over" or "under" taxation, these rosy conclusions fail to take note of the impact of warlord financing as actually experienced, albeit subjectively, by the Chinese people.

There is no question that both taxes and other financial exactions rose exponentially during the warlord era. More important, though, was the way in which an increasing proportion of state revenues collected by the warlords was dedicated to military purposes—directly as a result of the competitive military needs created by warlordism. The issue, then, is not just the economic burden imposed on the people by the warlords but the opportunity costs in terms of how the funds spent on the military might have been put to more productive use. Aggravating this questionable application of state funds was the way in which predatory warlords also drained away considerable portions of these funds by lining their own pockets. While it might be argued that corruption was a perennial problem throughout Chinese history, the power gained by military commanders over public finances during the warlord period exacerbated the negative effects of this practice.

As seen in this chapter, however, there are also paradoxes in the role that warlords played in China's economic development, which go beyond a simplistic portrayal of economic harm. For example, predatory warlords who accumulated a large amount of capital not surprisingly often ended up as capitalist investors in major industrial and commercial enterprises. Donald Gillin has argued that "[a]t least in some instances the division of China into competing warlord regimes created an environment favorable to economic growth, since in order to provide their armies with the latest weapons and other necessities warlords were compelled to build factories and otherwise develop the productive resources of their domains" (Gillin 1967, 293–94).

There is a hint here of the broader theory of how war, for all its destructive effects, has often been a force behind processes like state formation and economic development in many contexts. And not all warlords were equally predatory in their pursuit of personal wealth. As seen above, many warlords, particularly in the period of residual warlordism, also deduced that their long-term survival could be enhanced by attention to the provision of public goods, and the promotion of economic development. Certainly, the efforts of warlords such as Yan Xishan, Chen Jitang, Liu Xiang, or He Jian to strengthen the economies of their domains may still be seen as primarily driven by pragmatism—simply another transaction cost for the maintenance of their power. But variations in levels of support for such activities suggest that their motivations, while not purely altruistic, point to an internalization of the values of public service among some warlords in an age of demanding nationalism. The point is not to rehabilitate Chinese warlords as positive forces in China's modern development but to suggest that the effects of warlordism were more complicated than conventional negative portrayals would allow.

The effects of Chinese warlordism on Chinese society were not, of course, limited to financial or economic consequences. There were often also economic factors at work below the surface of what might seem primarily political or social changes. One example of this is the militarization of the elite in the Republican period as political and social power shifted increasingly into military hands. The development of the New Armies in the late Qing began a process of changing Chinese attitudes toward the status of military service, not the least because the organization of these New Armies provided attractive new career options for educated young men (Fung 1980, 62–113). This attraction only grew stronger with the even greater military expansion of the warlord era, combined with the greater ability of a military career to open a pathway toward political power, social status, and personal wealth. At a personal level, then, economic concerns certainly influenced the flow of men into military careers, even as the benefits of these careers allowed at least some warlords to become not just political leaders but also business entrepreneurs. Military officers and their families frequently emerged, both in active service and after retirement, as a distinct, and often dominating, layer of the social elite in their home communities in terms of both wealth and influence (McCord 2014a). In some cases, warlord financial policies even played a direct role in this outcome. For example, in Sichuan, increased land taxes undermined traditional landlords from the civil elite who then sold their lands to military officers who were better able to use their influence to negotiate preferential tax exemptions (Gunde 1976).

The only exception to this picture of social, political, and economic advancement for military men under warlordism might be common soldiers, who for the most part were unpaid, ill-treated, and socially disdained (Lary 1985). Even so, the steadily increasing demand for soldiers offered not just a chance at economic survival but a masculine alternative to the ideal of married life for unmarried men at the margins of society (McCord 2015, 224). Such benefits were strong enough for one local gazetteer to complain about how even farmers were abandoning their fields in enroll in the army (*Liling xian xiangtu zhi* 1920, 15–16).

In the end, it is difficult to confine an investigation of the economic consequences of warlordism to purely economic matters. Economic effects were nearly always intertwined at every level with other social and political developments. This is perhaps best shown in the way that some of the economic factors discussed here also contributed to the greater political transformations of the era. The popular conception of warlordism as it was constructed in this era was strongly grounded in a critique of its negative consequences, which often stressed the harms to the Chinese economy and the livelihood of the people. Individual differences aside, warlords as a body were generally defined as corrupt predators. Emphasis was placed on the destructiveness of warlord wars, the violence of warlord soldiers, and the burden of warlord financial exactions. Such appraisals became the building blocks for an anti-warlord political narrative, with political consequences that began with specific anti-warlord political struggles and ended with the creation of new revolutionary political movements that made anti-warlordism a main pillar of their political agendas.[16] Thus, it is important to examine not just the economic consequences of warlordism but also how perceptions of these consequences had even farther ranging effects.

CONCLUSION

The premise of this chapter is that, beyond the obvious need for control over military forces, access to economic or financial resources are essential for the emergence and survival of warlordism in any context. That also means that the specific character of warlordism in any situation will also be influenced strongly by the nature of these resources. In the case of China, one key element in the ability of emerging warlords to gain access to the funds necessary to support their military forces was the general survival of administrative systems, and their capacity for taxation, from the Qing dynasty into the Republican period. As a result, Chinese warlords did not simply emerge as "non-state" military actors filling a political vacuum; rather, they turned their efforts toward acquiring official positions that would legitimate their capture of portions of the state administrative system. Another advantage for Chinese warlords was the existence of a highly developed commercial economy. This gave them access to the resources of a sophisticated financial sector and the ability to raise additional funds through commercial taxes with only minimal additional transaction costs. These advantages were also responsible for a unique nodal structure of warlord power that emphasized the control of urban administrative and commercial centers and the transportation networks that connected them.

The diversity of warlord behaviors seen in this chapter should also caution against a common tendency to tar all warlords with the same, largely pejorative, characterizations. In the Chinese case, a popular anti-warlord narrative emerged that labeled all warlords as corrupt, conservative, and unpatriotic.

There were certainly predatory warlords like Wang Zhanyuan who turned corruption into a highly refined skill. But there were other warlords, such as the "Christian general" Feng Yuxiang, who were known for relatively upright and honest administrations.[17] Likewise, while some warlords were notable reactionaries, an early path-breaking study by Winston Hsieh showed that some could also hold relatively progressive and patriotic viewpoints (Hsieh 1962). To a certain extent, all Chinese warlords had to operate within a similar set of opportunities and constraints, but their financial policies and behaviors could also reflect personal values and strategies. Thus, while Wang Zhanyuan was particularly adverse to wasting his potential income on projects that might bring economic benefits to the people, other warlords such a Yan Xishan and Chen Jitang established their reputations (and enhanced popular support for their regimes) precisely by the promotion of such projects.

Finally, this chapter argues that it is important to understand not only the financial foundations of warlord power but also how the economic exigencies of warlordism impacted on their societies. Additional complexity is introduced by recognizing how the economic and financial decisions and policies of individual warlords could have different outcomes based on the mix of resources available to them and their own strategic calculations. Any conclusions about the economic effects of warlordism should also realize that these consequences were rarely just economic. Instead, they were often entwined in social and political conditions and could have broader results.

In the end, then, this chapter, in a very broad sense, seeks to use the case of Chinese warlordism to challenge comparative generalizations that do not provide room for the ways in which different contexts shaped the character of warlordism in different historical and locational settings. At the same time, any understanding of Chinese warlordism itself must also be able to accommodate the impact of local financial contingences and individual warlord behaviors into its conclusions.

NOTES

1. In one of the clearest expressions of this view, Lucian Pye (1971, 8) states, "With the Revolution of 1911, the destruction of the formal monolithic structure of government was complete . . . . Few formally organized groups closely related to the interests of the total society, or even of particular segments of the society, were directed to, and capable of, seeking political power to carry out specific policies. The only organizations that were in any sense able to seek political power were those in the military field . . . military commanders had control of the means of violence to achieve political and economic objectives. Political power therefore gravitated to

these men because society was devoid of other groups that could effectively contend for governmental control."

2. Winston Hsieh (1975) emphasized the importance of the survival of administrative systems in the "economics of warlordism." Robert Kapp (1974, 162–63) also noted that Sichuan "provincial militarists introduced no radical changes in local administrative practices," and that "local institutions generally followed the pattern laid out in the late Ch'ing [Qing]."

3. Among the most prominent of these warlord holdovers were the members of the Guangxi warlord clique, best studied by Lary (1974). An example of a "new" warlord was He Jian, who ruled Hunan for most of the Nanjing period (McCord 2014c).

4. By the middle of the 1930s, the land taxes in some areas of Sichuan were reportedly paid up to the 1970s and 1980s! (Kapp 1974, 156).

5. The intense competition by a succession of warlords prior to Liu Xiang's consolidation of his control over the city shows the broader recognition of the importance of Chongqing's resources. (Kapp 1974, 146–47, 153).

6. Taxes on opium were initially justified as a means of inhibiting opium trafficking. The profitability of this tax, however, led many warlords to encourage rather than discourage opium cultivation. In the end, "opium suppression" taxation was transformed into a military protection racket for the opium trade. Sichuan warlords particularly benefited from opium taxes because of their control over transportation routes for Yunnan and Guizhou opium (Kapp 1974, 157). Also see Baumler (2007, 89–110).

7. My understanding of "transaction costs" is adopted from Levi (1988, 23–28).

8. Even brothel owners and prostitutes were able to use a strike to force Wang to lower proposed increases in brothel taxes (*Shibao*, January 8 and February 12, 1920).

9. Each garrison area in Sichuan, for example, circulated its own currency (Kapp 1974, 158).

10. A good overview of varying concepts of predatory rule can be found in Alex Bavister-Gould (2011).

11. One example of such popular awareness is seen in the open criticism directed against a National Party military commander over the large boatload of building materials and goods shipped back to his family's hometown during the Northern Expedition to expand the family residence (Chen n.d., 6).

12. Even Wang Zhanyuan, who actually grew even wealthier after his fall from power, spent much of his retirement scheming for ways to regain control over his army and his original political position (McCord 2014b, 71).

13. From 1912 to 1930, 93 percent of all taxes collected in Guangdong went to pay for military expenses (Lin 2002, 189). In many areas, education was particularly hard hit. Hunan, for example, was devastated when an invading northern warlord, Zhang Jingyao, assumed the post of military governor from 1918 and proceeded to redirect most public funds for schools to pay for military expenses (Hunan shanhou xiehui 1919, 1: 301–21).

14. Pierre Fuller (2013) argues that many early warlord regimes remained fairly responsible in the coordination of traditionally expected government services, such as disaster relief.

15. A detailed discussion of the effects of war as seen in one major case can be found in Waldron (1995, 119–60)

16. Public responses to warlord exactions and military atrocities resulted in series of popular protests and specific anti-warlord movements (McCord 2001, 2005, 2014b). Waldron (1995) argues that the unprecedented scale, and consequences, of the military conflict that broke out in 1924 between the Zhili and Fengtian warlord factions (usually referred to as the Second Zhili-Fengtian War) helped to create a nationalist upsurge that opened the way for the success of the Nationalist Party in its 1926 anti-warlord Northern Expedition.

17. Even though Feng participated in an attempted Northern conquest of Hunan in 1918, the people of the town he garrisoned proposed raising a temple in his honor in gratitude for the quality of his administration (at least relative to that of other warlords) (*Shibao*, July 15, 1919).

REFERENCES

Baumler, Alan. 2007. *The Chinese and Opium under the Republic: Worse than Floods and Wild Beasts*. State University of New York Press.

Bavister-Gould, Alex. 2011. "Predatory Leaderships, Predatory Rule and Predatory States." *Concept Brief 01* (Development Leadership Program).

Chen Xiong. N.d. "Minguo shiqi caozong Qiyang xianzhengde 'yiguo sangong'" ["One Country, Three Lords" in the Manipulation of Qiyang County Government in the Republican Period]. Manuscript no. 3754, Hunan zhengzhi xieshang huiyi, wenshiban [Historical Materials Office, Hunan Political Consultative Conference].

Ch'i, Hsi-sheng. 1976. *Warlord Politics in China, 1916–1928*. Stanford, CA: Stanford University Press.

Chong, Ja Ian. 2009. "Breaking Up is Hard to Do: Foreign Intervention and the Limiting of Fragmentation in the Late Qing and Early Republic, 1893–1922." *Twentieth Century China* 34 (1): 75–98.

Fuller, Pierre. 2013. "North China Famine Revisited: Unsung Native Relief in the Warlord Era, 1920–1921." *Modern Asian Studies* 47 (3): 820–50.

Fung, Edmund S. K. 1980. *The Military Dimension of the Chinese Revolution: The New Army and Its Role in the Revolution of 1911*. Vancouver: University of British Columbia Press.

Gillin, Donald G. 1967. *Warlord: Yen Hsi-shan in Shansi Province, 1911–1949*. Princeton, NJ: Princeton University Press.

Giustozzi, Antonio. 2005. "The Debate on Warlordism: The Importance of Military Legitimacy." *Crisis States Discussion Papers* (Crisis State Development Research Centre) 13 (October).

Gunde, Richard. 1976. "Land Tax and Social Change in Sichuan, 1925–1935." *Modern China* 2 (1): 23–48.

Hsieh, Winston. 1962. "The Ideas and Ideals of a Warlords: Ch'en Chiung-ming (1878–1933)." *Papers on China* (Harvard University East Asia Research Center) 16: 198–252.

Hsieh, Winston. 1975. "The Economics of Warlordism." *Chinese Republican Studies Newsletter* 1 (1): 15–21.

Hunan shanhou xiehui [Hunan Rehabilitation Association], ed. 1919. *Xiangzai jilüe* [A Record of Hunan's Disasters]. N.p.

Jiang Yannan. 1983. "Huo-E baniande Beiyang junfa Wang Zhanyuan" [The Beiyang Warlord Who Devastated Hubei for Eight Years, Wang Zhanyuan]. *Wuhan wenshi ziliao* [Wuhan Historical Materials] 12: 22–27.

Kapp, Robert A. 1974. "Chungking as a Center of Warlord Power, 1926–1937." In *The Chinese City between Two Worlds*, edited by Mark Elvin and G. William Skinner, pp. 144–70. Stanford, CA: Stanford University Press.

Kwong, Chi Man. 2014. "Finance and the Northern Expedition: From the Northeast Asian Perspective, 1925–1928." *Modern Asian Studies* 48 (6): 1695–739.

Lary, Diana. 1974. *Region and Nation: the Kwangsi Clique in Chinese Politics, 1925–1937*. Cambridge: Cambridge University Press.

Lary, Diana. 1985. *Warlord Soldiers: Chinese Common Soldiers, 1911–1937*. Cambridge: Cambridge University Press.

Levi, Margaret. 1988. *Of Rule and Revenue*. Berkeley, CA: University of California Press. *Liling xian xiangtu zhi* [Liling County Local Gazette]. 1920.

Lin, Alfred H. Y. 2002. "Building and Funding a Warlord Regime: The Experience of Chen Jitang in Guangdong, 1929–1936." *Modern China* 28 (2): 177–212.

Lin, Alfred H. Y. 2004. "Warlord, Social Welfare and Philanthropy: The Case of Guangzhou under Chen Jitang, 1929–1936." *Modern China* 30 (2): 151–98.

Liu Cuochen. 1922. *Ezhou canji* [Hubei's Tragic Record]. N.p.

Liu, Kwang-ching. 1974. "The Limits of Regional Power in the Late Ch'ing Period: A Reappraisal." *Tsing Hua Journal of Chinese Studies* (New Series) 10 (2): 207–23.

MacKinnon, Stephen R. 1973. "The Peiyang Army, Yuan Shih-k'ai, and the Origins of Modern Chinese Warlordism." *Journal of Asian Studies* 32 (3): 405–23.

McCord, Edward A. 1993. *The Power of the Gun: The Emergence of Modern Chinese Warlordism*. Berkeley, CA: University of California Press.

McCord, Edward A. 2001. "Burn, Kill, Rape and Rob: Military Atrocities, Warlordism and Anti-Warlordism in Republican China." In *The Scars of War: The Impact of Warfare on Chinese* Society, edited by Diana Lary and Stephen MacKinnon. Vancouver: University of British Columbia Press.

McCord, Edward A. 2005. "Cries that Shake the Earth: Military Atrocities and Popular Protests in Warlord China." *Modern China* 31 (1): 3–34.

McCord, Edward A. 2014a. "Military Office and Local Elite Power: The 'Three Lords' of Qiyang County, Hunan." Chap 5 in *Military Force and Elite Power in the Formation of Modern China*, pp. 147–73. London and New York: Routledge.

McCord, Edward A. 2014b. "Predatory Warlordism: Wang Zhanyuan in Hubei." Chap 2 in *Military Force and Elite Power in the Formation of Modern China*, pp. 49–81. London and New York: Routledge, 2014.

McCord, Edward A. 2014c. "Residual Warlordism under the Nationalist Party-State: He Jian in Hunan." Chap 4 in *Military Force and Elite Power in the Formation of Modern China*, pp. 110–146. London and New York: Routledge.

McCord, Edward A. 2015. "Military Atrocities in Warlord China." In *Civil-Military Relations in Chinese History. From Ancient China to the Communist Takeover*, edited by Kai Filipiak. London and New York: Routledge.

Michael, Franz. 1949. "Military Organization and Power Structure of China During the Taiping Rebellion." *Pacific Historical Review* 18 (4): 469–83.

Pye, Lucian W. 1971. *Warlord Politics: Conflict and Coalition in the Modernization of Republican China*. New York: Praeger.

Rawski, Thomas G. 1989. *Economic Growth in Prewar China*. Berkeley, CA: University of California Press.

Reinhardt, Anne. 2008. "'Decolonization on the Periphery': Liu Xiang and Shipping Rights Recovery at Chongqing, 1926–38." *The Journal of Imperial and Commonwealth History* 36 (2): 259–74.

Sheridan, James E. 1966. *Chinese Warlord: The Career of Feng Yu-hsiang*. Stanford, CA: Stanford University Press.

Shibao [Eastern Times]. Shanghai.

Suleski, Ronald. 2002. *Civil Government in Warlord China: Tradition, Modernization, and Manchuria*. New York: Peter Lang.

van de Ven, Hans. 1996. "Public Finance and the Rise of Warlordism." *Modern Asian Studies* 30 (4): 795–827.

Yan Jing. 1989. "Wang Zhanyuan chadu Hubei gailüe" [Outline of Wang Zhanyuan's Poisoning of Hubei]. *Hubei wenshi zhiliao* [Hubei Historical Materials] 27: 56–60.

Waldron, Arthur. 1995. *From War to Nationalism: China's Turning Point, 1924–1925*. Cambridge: Cambridge University Press.

Zheng Tingxi. 1962. "Wo suo zhidao de Wang Zhanyuan" [The Wang Zhanyuan I Knew]. *Wenshi ziliao xuanji* [Selected Historical Materials] 51: 252–68.

Zhu Chunfu. 1979. "Beiyang junfa dui Tianjin jindai gongye de touzi" [Beiyang Warlord Investment in Tianjin's Modern Industry]. *Tianjin wenshi ziliao xuanji* [Selected Tianjin Historical Materials] 4: 146–62.

Part III

CONTEMPORARY WORLDS

Chapter 8

Friend, Foe, or in Between? Humanitarian Action and the Soviet–Afghan War

Jonathan Benthall

THE LEGACY OF THE SOVIET–AFGHAN WAR FOR HUMANITARIANISM

The Soviet–Afghan War (1979–89) was fought between insurgent groups known as mujahideen, who were backed by Pakistan, Saudi Arabia, and the United States, and the Democratic Republic of Afghanistan, backed by the Soviet army. The war was preceded by a coup in 1978 that left the Afghan Communist Party in power but facing vigorous opposition, till a further coup by the Soviet army the following year. A conservative estimate of the number of resulting battle deaths is 500,000 (Lacina and Gleditsch 2005: 154).

The war takes its place in history as one episode in a chain of conflicts and of faltering efforts made to alleviate the consequent suffering. International relief aid organized in Europe may be dated back to the period of the Crusades and the foundation of sovereign orders of knighthood with mixed military and "hospitaller" aims. One of the Enlightenment's innovations was that the suffering of the wounded and defeated in battle (like that of victims of "natural" disasters) no longer needed to be accepted with fatalism. Humanitarian relief, as a corollary of warfare, may be conceived as an aspect of war economics in a broad sense. Economics has the highest status among the social sciences and often aspires to occupy other domains of knowledge. By contrast, many historians and most sociocultural anthropologists reject sharp divisions between the economic, the political, the juridical, and the ideological. A concept of economics that confines itself to material resources, ignoring transactions in symbolic goods, will inevitably be one-dimensional. The various forms of merit aspired to through charitable and eirenic activities, motivating the supply of goods and services, have an economic aspect. So do governmental decisions to outlaw certain professedly charitable enterprises on political grounds, and permit others to enjoy the legal privileges of charities even when their activities are overt adjuncts to military operations.

The instrumentalization of humanitarian action either as an ally or as an enemy is extremely widespread. Non-state actors are supported by the intervention of states with money and other resources, some armed and some relying on persuasion by diplomatic or journalistic means; but national governments also criminalize aid initiatives without necessarily deferring to the brittle authority of International Humanitarian Law. At this time of writing, various interlinked conflicts in the Middle East come specially to mind. But the conjuncture during the Soviet–Afghan War—of post-colonial superpower enmity, the waning of communism, religious fundamentalism, guerrilla warfare, secret funding, manipulation of charity law, mediatization, and humanitarian entrepreneurship—was unique. This chapter will chronicle an intimate commingling of humanitarian, diplomatic, financial, and military support for the mujahideen. In the case of the U.S. administration, this mixing was extensive and sustained; in the case of Médecins Sans Frontières (MSF, aka Doctors Without Borders), it was limited to medical provision, advocacy, and mediatization—since no-one suggests that they actually permitted the smuggling of weapons. Much fruitful attention has been given in recent years to the study of humanitarianism in general (Fassin 2011; Barnett 2011; Donini 2012; Dromi 2020), and much has been written about the Soviet–Afghan War and its prolonged repercussions for Afghanistan and for the world. This chapter sets out to ask what specific takeaways can be pulled out from the story of the war for our understanding of humanitarianism and charity, and of non-state war economies. A case study from the U.S. criminal justice system will be adduced to argue that the government's clamping down on Islamic charitable activity through statutory measures during the late 1990s, and especially after 2001, exposed it to the charge of moral equivocation, and also had negative effects on a whole sector's evolution. The Islamic tradition of charity has been able to adapt and flourish elsewhere when freed from exaggerated political opposition. As for MSF, the war was the culmination of an until then largely unexamined symbiosis, which soon began to be widely questioned, between humanitarian entrepreneurship and the media.

We will begin with a flashback to 1983, evoking the debate in Western "foreign policy" circles at the height of the war. We will single out two participants in a U.S. think-tank conference, one Afghan and the other French, both of whom pressed a strong case for support of the mujahideen. We go on to trace their respective future activities during the remainder of the war years. We then consider the war's repercussions in the humanitarian sphere after the withdrawal of Soviet forces.

THE SOVIET–AFGHAN WAR VIEWED FROM CALIFORNIA IN 1983

In November 1983, some four years after the Russian invasion of Afghanistan and the installation of a pro-Soviet regime, an international conference on "Afghan Alternatives" was held at the Monterey Institute of International Studies, California, under U.S. government auspices. The thirty-five participants were mainly American or European, with a few Asians. The book based on the conference (Magnus 1985) provides insight into the state of expert debate at the height of the Soviet–Afghan War. We know now that Western support for the Afghan mujahideen provoked a blowback with immense consequences: the fomenting of violent Islamist extremism. The Iranian revolution of 1979 had come as a surprise to virtually all Western commentators. Most of the contributors to the book evinced little concern about the risks of inflaming Islamist militancy in Afghanistan. Admittedly, one think-tank director did state:

> When I hear the term *anti-Western materialism*, which has been used to describe the so-called progressive Muslims, I run for cover. . . . [R]ightly or wrongly, this has come to represent for us a code word for something that goes a good deal beyond philosophical or cultural differences. . . . I simply want to tell you that when I hear that they reject Western materialism, my question is: (1) Can we live with such a regime assuming that it comes to power? and (2) can we even collaborate with it on its way to power?

And a political scientist, reflecting particularly on the Iranian revolution, mentioned that "the Soviets apparently perceive Islamic fundamentalism in the region as no less a threat than Western influence."[1]

At the time, U.S. foreign policy was dominated by the Reagan Doctrine, the rolling back of Soviet-backed governments across the world, in opposition to the Brezhnev Doctrine, which challenged any regression toward capitalism by countries belonging to the socialist family. But the Carter Doctrine had preceded Ronald Reagan's inauguration in 1981, asserting the U.S. intention of using military force, if necessary, to defend its national interests in the Persian Gulf. Covert CIA operations in Afghanistan had begun in July 1979, under the authority of Carter's National Security Adviser, Zbigniew Brzezinski, six months before the Soviet invasion, when uprisings were already beginning to spread against the Russia-friendly regime of Nur Muhammad Taraki. (Taraki was killed in 1979 and replaced by Hafizullah Amin. In the same year, Amin was killed by Soviet forces and replaced by Babrak Karmal, who was replaced in turn by Mohammad Najibullah in 1986.) "Which was more important in world history?" Brzezinski was to ask later, in 1998, "the Taliban or the fall of the Soviet empire? A few overexcited Islamists or the liberation of central Europe and the end of the Cold War?" He even claimed to have lured the Russians into the "Afghan trap."[2] (Most historians today attribute the collapse of the Soviet empire to multiple causes.)

The contribution of two participants in the Monterey conference and publication will be analyzed here, and then related to later events in which they and their associated organizations were prominent. Coming from very different backgrounds, they were united by strong support for the mujahideen. Sabahuddin Kushkaki was an Afghan politician and journalist with Islamist sympathies. Claude Malhuret was the French president of MSF.

KUSHKAKI AND MALHURET

Sabahuddin Kushkaki, born in 1933, was the son of a well-known journalist and Islamic scholar, and had taught journalism at Kabul University. He served briefly as minister of information and culture in 1972 under a reformist government until the last king of Afghanistan, Mohammed Zahir Shah, was ousted in a coup in 1973. In 1978, after the leftist Saur Revolution, Kushkaki was imprisoned in the notorious Pul-e-Charkhi prison in Kabul, then released after two years under a surprise political amnesty, after which he fled the country.[3] In the 1985 publication, he is listed as a Fellow at the Woodrow Wilson Center for International Scholars, Smithsonian Institution. He called for more military aid for the mujahideen, and advanced a plan for withdrawal of Soviet troops, joint action by all resistance forces subscribing to Islamic, anti-atheistic principles, neighborly relations with all countries, and cooperation with all countries that had committed to opposing the Soviet invasion.[4] He died in 2000 in the United States.

Claude Malhuret, born in 1950, was director of MSF, the French (later international) humanitarian agency founded in 1971 in the aftermath of the Nigerian civil war. While qualifying as a medical doctor, he had expressed socialist and third worldist sympathies, then took part in a smallpox eradication program in India with the World Health Organization. After working with MSF medical teams in refugee camps on the Thai frontier during 1976–1977, he was elected a board member in 1978 and director in 1980, establishing a practical and financially sound basis for the organization in succession to the swashbuckling approach of one of MSF's original founders, Bernard Kouchner. Later, in 1986, Malhuret was appointed secretary of state for human rights in Jacques Chirac's center-right government. Between 1989 and 2017, he was the right-wing (Union de la droite) mayor of Vichy in southern France.

At the conference, Malhuret reported that MSF had twenty-two doctors working in Afghan provinces: "we are going everywhere we want, provided we are with the resistance organizations." He opposed current proposals for negotiation with the Soviet Union through the United Nations. Malhuret advocated a three-pronged strategy of direct aid for the mujahideen: humanitarian, military, and diplomatic. In doing so, he went beyond the established MSF policy of *témoignage*, bearing witness to inhumane behavior. As events turned out, he was to be proved correct in predicting the fall of the Soviet Empire, though he also predicted, unsuccessfully, that the then divided Afghan resistance would eventually unite.[5]

HUMANITARIAN AND MILITARY AID DURING THE SOVIET–AFGHAN WAR

The principles of neutrality and independence in humanitarian aid are always fragile. During the Vietnam War, U.S. ambassador Ellsworth Bunker warned aid staff against activities that might benefit the Viet Cong: "If you're helping the VC, that is treason, and you know the penalty for treason" (Donini 2012: 46). A journalist pointed out caustically in 1991 that the state secretariat for humanitarian action in Paris "can be seen as the after-sales service for the gun manufacturers who occupy the neighboring ministries."[6]

In late 1981, Saudi Arabia began to match the CIA dollar for dollar in the purchase of weapons for the Afghan resistance. In 1984, President Reagan signed a National Security Council directive calling for efforts to drive out the Soviet forces from Afghanistan "by all means available." Congress started to vote huge sums, and Reagan authorized the delivery of Stinger surface-to-air missiles. By 1985, annual U.S. military aid to the mujahideen, channeled through Pakistan's Inter-Services Intelligence (ISI), operating as a "government within a government," grew to $280 million, with bipartisan political support (Rasanayagam 2003: 105–6, 116). Mikhail Gorbachev was elected general secretary of the Communist Party of the Soviet Union in 1985: in February 1986, he described Afghanistan as a "bleeding wound." In February 1988, the Soviets announced that they would pull out troops after one year. The Geneva Accords were signed in April 1988. Najibullah was installed as president in 1986 and the Soviets continued to pour in weapons and funds to shore up his regime until his overthrow in 1992,[7] though in 1991 the United States and the USSR agreed to cut off aid to both sides. By this time, the country split into small fiefdoms, leading to a civil war in which Gulbuddin Hekmatyar, previously funded by the CIA, enhanced his existing notoriety for ruthlessness and religious fervor; and then to the rise of the Taliban in the mid-1990s. After the overthrow of Najibullah, American aid gradually petered out as the "freedom fighters" began to be redefined as terrorists.

The number of refugees in Pakistan rose to about 3.5 million by the end of the 1980s. As well as the UN High Commissioner for Refugees (UNHCR) and the World Food Program, some 265 NGOs were directly or indirectly involved in providing aid, first to refugees only and later through cross-border operations into Afghanistan. The Pakistan government blurred the distinction between passive refugees and armed resistance fighters, as did many NGOs, wittingly or unwittingly, so that in practice the aid efforts supported the mujahideen. As well as Muslim states, almost all the non-Muslim world, except India but including China, were hostile to the Soviet-backed Afghan regime (Baitenmann 1990).[8] The U.S. government played an important role, funding numerous Christian and secular "volags" (NGOs), advising them on their programs and mediating between them and the Pakistan government. The Soviets made some efforts to win "hearts and minds" through infrastructure projects and building schools and hospitals, while the position of women was somewhat improved in the big cities (Steele 2011: 108; Braithwaite 2011: 147–52), but the military behaved with a brutality that the mujahideen reciprocated.

The U.S. policy was to keep a low American profile, so as not to damage the credibility of the Afghan resistance as an indigenous struggle for freedom, or compromise the reputation of American-affiliated volags. A candid article in *Time* magazine in 1984 outlined the pipeline of military and communications equipment sent by the CIA to the mujahideen via Saudi Arabia. "Politically the CIA's main challenge has been to avoid linking its operation to the government of Pakistani President Zia ul-Haq," which would compromise his peace negotiations through the United Nations and might give the Soviets a pretext for moving into Pakistan's North-West Frontier Province. The CIA had also discreetly recruited about 100 Afghan refugees in Europe and the United States who "seemed thoroughly reliable and unquestionably pro-mujahidin," training them in "shipping, running travel agencies and sending large containers overseas." Land mines were sometimes sent in crates described as telephone equipment for a religious organization.[9]

The International Committee of the Red Cross, World Health Organization, and other international agencies were expelled from Afghanistan in 1979, and with one or two exceptions the humanitarian NGOs working in Pakistan made little effort to aid noncombatants living in government-controlled Afghan cities. Numerous small NGOs were founded, often working secretly and with strong support from the U.S. government, using the International Rescue Committee as an intermediary to support European NGOs in cross-border operations. There were also over seventy "advocacy NGOs" supporting the military and humanitarian operations, united by anti-communism.

Saudi Arabia responded vigorously to the political signals from Washington at the height of the war. All analysts agree that the boundaries between humanitarian assistance, military assistance and *da`wa* (Islamic missionary activity) were blurred by the Saudis. Their official humanitarian aid was first channeled through the Saudi Red Crescent and a campaign coordinated by the Popular Committee for Fundraising and its chairman Prince (later king) Salman. Allegedly (and it has not been denied), the Saudi Red Crescent was co-opted to facilitate the transport of arms within Afghanistan itself, by providing a channel of finance for various Afghan political parties. After the mid-1980s, numerous semiofficial Saudi agencies were also active. Two protagonists in the rise of global jihadism, Abdullah Azzam (1941–1989) and his onetime disciple Osama bin Laden, had temporary affiliations with Saudi charities. In 1986, an umbrella body in Peshawar (some 35 miles from the Afghan border), the Council for Islamic Coordination, was formed by the Saudi and Kuwaiti Red Crescent societies, the Muslim World League, and a number of Islamic aid agencies. Azzam was among the rotating presidents of the council, before his unexplained assassination in 1989. After the withdrawal of the Russian military from Afghanistan in 1988–1989, Pakistani and Saudi aid continued until the fall of Najibullah (Hegghammer 2007: 198) but then gradually dried up.

AFGHAN JEHAD (1987–1992)

Sabahuddin Kushkaki was appointed managing editor of a magazine, *Afghan Jehad*, which first appeared in 1987 and was published, monthly in Pashtun and Dari and quarterly in English, for years, by the Cultural Council of Afghan Resistance, based in Islamabad, Pakistan.[10] He had formerly served as a full-time consultant to the Voice of America's Dari and Pashtu broadcasts. A specimen issue dated April–June 1988 (volume 1, no. 4) was published just after the signature of the Geneva Accords in 1988 by the foreign ministers of Afghanistan, Pakistan, the Soviet Union, and the United States. The Accords called for withdrawal of all Soviet troops within nine months, noninterference in each other's affairs by Pakistan and Afghanistan, and the voluntary repatriation of Afghan refugees. It has been suggested[11] that the Ecuadorean diplomat Diego Cordovez, who as a UN under-secretary general negotiated the Accords, saw the Afghan crisis more as a proxy conflict between the superpowers than as one with local political and social origins. The mujahideen were not seriously involved in the mediation process, and were not parties to the Geneva Accords, which they refused to accept. As the April–June 1988 issue was being produced, Soviet forces were beginning to withdraw, and the UN began to raise funds for a recovery program

Figure 8.1 Front cover of Afghan Jehad: Quarterly Magazine of the Cultural Council of Afghanistan Resistance, vol. 5 no. 2, January–March 1992, published in Islamabad, Pakistan, with subsidy from the U.S. Government through the National Endowment for Democracy.

in Afghanistan and aid to the refugees. The two great powers now agreed informally to a position of "positive symmetry," whereby they reserved the right to send arms in response to shipments made by the other side.

Kushkaki now publishes similar views to those he had contributed in the Monterey meeting. He calls the Geneva Accords a "mockery"; the mujahideen "have vowed not to stop war until they dismantle the Kabul puppet regime," both through military action and through psychological warfare. Kushkaki praises those mujahideen who ignored the head of the UN monitoring team's injunction that they should refrain from attacking departing Soviet troops—"yet another proof of the partiality of UN mediators." Kushkaki rejects the Kremlin's claims to be trying to achieve a peaceful, independent, and non-aligned Afghanistan. Disdaining Najibullah's offer of a coalition with his opponents—since communists are "to the overwhelming majority of our people traitors"—Kushkaki calls for the newly formed seven-party alliance, the Islamic Unity of Afghan Mujahideen, known also as the Peshawar Seven, to form a credible interim government, and for the return of seven million refugees. The aim was to establish a "government of God" in Afghanistan, based on Shariah.[12]

In retrospect, *Afghan Jehad* was a tool of the U.S. policy of rejecting Najibullah's offer of negotiations, and thus prolonging the war after the Soviet withdrawal. The senior CIA director of operations in the area, Charles Cogan, was to admit in a 1997 interview that he now considered this to have been a mistake. The journalist Jonathan Steele comments: "Had Washington walked away after 1989, the country might have had a better chance of resolving its conflicts and starting on reconstruction" (Steele 2011: 136).

The Cultural Council of Afghan Resistance was in fact a mere shell. Neglected in standard historical coverage of the Soviet–Afghan War is the use made of the purportedly independent U.S. charity sector as a supplement to direct government funding. A number of U.S. nonprofits with tax-exempt status under the Internal Revenue Code (IRC)—technically, 501(c)(3) organizations—such as American Friends of Afghanistan were formed to channel funds through USAID and the National Endowment for Democracy (NED), itself a 501(c)(3) organization though largely government-funded. The subsidy of *Afghan Jehad* was one of these activities. Others were arranging for injured mujahideen to be flown to the United States for medical treatment, training journalists to comment favorably on the mujahideen, and publishing leaflets for religious scholars.[13]

CHARITABLE OBJECTS AND MILITARY ACTIVITIES

The U.S. law on charities derives historically from 400-year-old English common law, but fleshed out by many statutes and precedents. It is applied both at the federal level via the Internal Revenue Service (under the U.S. Treasury) and by individual states. It accepts as tax exempt a wide range of activities conducive to the public good, including religious and educational programs, and "lessening the burden of government," but excluding participation in political campaigns and substantial lobbying activities. The NED, founded in 1983 and still at the time of this writing active in many countries and funded as to 98 percent by government agencies,[14] has been criticized on various grounds, but presumably has stayed within the law. Providing medical assistance is self-evidently charitable, and training of imams and journalists can no doubt be justified as educational. However, inciting the mujahideen, as *Afghan Jehad* did, to oppose the Geneva Accords (to which the United States was a party) and to violently overthrow the Najibullah government might be accused of having stretched the definition of charity too far.

This could be a naïve conclusion, in that the boundary between charitable and noncharitable in Anglo-American law and practice is in practice more porous than might be assumed. With regard to the Red Cross and Red Crescent Movement, there is an inherent historical contradiction in that the National Societies are required to adhere to its fundamental principles, including independence and neutrality, but also to be auxiliaries to the public authorities and national armies. In the United States, the Jewish National Fund has raised no objections today when it has collected tax-exempt funds for the improvement of military installations in Israel: currently, meeting points for Israel Defense Force soldiers and their families.[15] In Britain, meanwhile, the national law of charities actually specifies:

> The armed forces exist for public defence and security. It is charitable to promote the efficiency of the armed forces of the Crown as a means of defending the country. That includes ensuring that those forces are properly trained and equipped during times of conflict. It also includes providing facilities and benefits for the armed forces.[16]

Examples of permissible charitable purposes in Britain with a military content include technical education for members of the armed services, increasing their physical fitness, supporting officers' messes, and "encouraging esprit de corps." Noraid, or Irish Northern Aid, the New York–based charity that since 1969 raised funds in the United States for Republican—that is to say, Catholic—charities in Northern Ireland, was regularly accused of spending some of the funds on weapons until the Irish Republican Army accepted the peace process in 1996.

The connection between charity and military activities is closer in the Islamic tradition. The Islamic lexical field centered on *zakat* (obligatory alms), *ṣadaqa* (optional "good works"), and *waqf* (analogous to the European charitable foundation) has overlaps with the Christian principle of "charity" but is not identical. The difference most relevant here is that one of the eight categories of permitted beneficiaries of *zakat* and *ṣadaqa* specified in the Qur'an is those "in the way of God" (*fī sabīl Allāh*), identified with jihad—the most contentious term in Islamic studies—literally "striving," but with the historically dominant meaning of "making war against outsiders." We may surmise—since there was no military structure in the years of foundational Islam—that making war came naturally to the Prophet Muhammad's tribal contemporaries, and so was taken for granted as an element in what is now called the "public good." This heritage remained vivid throughout the centuries. Liberal Muslim apologists today have revived a strain in the premodern tradition that elevated spiritual striving, the "greater jihad," above war making. A number of prominent Islamic authorities, however, laid down at the time of the Soviet–Afghan War that Muslims should help the mujahideen in any way possible, including both humanitarian (especially medical) and military means.[17]

The outcome was that, though the Euro-American concept of charity with its Christian overtones might be claimed to be at the polar opposite of military force, there was in practice no incompatibility between the U.S. policy of comprehensive support for the Afghan mujahideen, including use of the Federal system of tax exemption for nonprofits, and the Islamic principles of charitable works and jihad that Afghans, Pakistanis, and Saudis had in common. Only the Russians condemned the U.S. policies as supporting what they saw as international terrorism (Donini 2004: 121).[18] Hegghammer (2020: 198) writes of "the pan-Islamist conviction that aid and jihad are two sides of the same coin, because both are about helping fellow Muslims in need. We must also bear in mind that the Afghan jihad was a dirty war with extensive human rights abuses and neglect of the Geneva conventions on both sides of the conflict."

THE CLOUD OVER ISLAMIC CHARITIES SINCE 9/11

Among the consequences of the attacks on the United States on September 11, 2001, was a resolute campaign by the George W. Bush government to clamp down on Islamic charities, widely held to be conduits for the financing of terrorism. This may have been preceded however by a report allegedly prepared by the CIA for the State Department in 1996, completed just as the Bosnian war was winding down and focused on support for the mujahideen in Bosnia. It had concluded that of more than thirty Islamic NGOs in existence, "available information indicates that approximately one-third . . . support terrorist groups or employ individuals who are suspected of having terrorist connections."[19] At around the same time, U.S. law enforcement agencies had been investigating links between certain Islamic charities and Hamas, the militant Palestinian movement.[20] However, the suspicions against Islamic charities only became a major public issue after the 2001 attacks. Despite President Obama's speech entitled "A New Beginning" that he delivered in Cairo in 2009, U.S. governments continued with the same policies of blacklisting and criminalization.

Care for the poor and disadvantaged has been a central principle or ideal in the history of Islam. Since the 1970s, two movements—the expansion of NGOs worldwide, and the Islamic revival—combined to generate the growth of Islamic charities in the modern sense. During the Soviet–Afghan War and for some years afterward, they formed a kind of parallel humanitarian system, with minimal communication with non-Muslim aid agencies and minimal recognition in the Western media. In Britain, a combination of judicious leadership and their sympathetic encouragement by the government and its regulator, the Charity Commission, resulted since the 1980s in continuous growth of a vigorous Islamic charity sector that has won respect from the non-Muslim humanitarian mainstream. It has nonetheless endured obstruction up to the time of this writing by obstacles put in its way as a result of the "global war on terror." Led by Islamic Relief Worldwide, based in Birmingham, England (founded in 1983), the leading U.K. Muslim charities decided to endorse the principles of nondiscrimination and transparency, and to abstain from all proselytism and "reislamization" (stiffening the religiosity of Muslim populations), interpreting *zakat* and *ṣadaqa* as exclusively aimed at the relief of suffering and poverty. This has been described as a process of secularization, following the example of some major Christian agencies such as Christian Aid. But from another perspective, humanitarian values may be discerned in all religious traditions and can coexist with secular humanitarian cultures typified by Oxfam or Médecins Sans Frontières. Ethical values articulated in a theology may be likened to a system of springs that feed a river. The upstream system may be studied for its own sake—there is a voluminous literature on *zakat*—but the river as it is observed downstream has had its flow altered by rockfalls. Islamic Relief Worldwide followed a definite logic in that it brought the Islamic tradition in line with International Humanitarian Law and with widely accepted codes of conduct for NGOs (Benthall 2016).

Osama bin Laden and Abdullah Azzam cooperated to found the Office of Services to the Mujahideen (*maktab al-khidamāt*) in Peshawar in 1984. An organization known as Al-Kifah ("struggle") began fundraising in the United States two or three years later as its U.S. affiliate. Branches opened in over thirty American cities, as Muslim Americans donated millions of dollars to support the Afghan war. The Al-Kifah Refugee Center was based in Brooklyn, New York. Azzam made repeated trips to the United States and other countries, giving religious approval to the anti-Soviet military jihad in Afghanistan and recruiting hundreds of Muslim fighters (Hegghammer 2020: 258–63). Undoubtedly, these two leaders and some of their associates were committed to a strategy in which some ostensibly charitable organizations were made use of for belligerent purposes.[21]

Following the trauma inflicted on the United States by the 9/11 attacks, some influential American commentators decided to believe the worst of all Islamic charities and their supporters. However, it is likely that in some prominent cases, the problem was due less to warlike intentions at headquarters than to ramshackle administration that had given free rein to some local individuals to pursue belligerent goals (Bokhari et al. 2014; Benthall 2018). At the same time, the principle of *da`wa*, interpreted as the "comprehensive call to Islam," held sway in Saudi Arabia and among some other Sunni Muslim communities, especially those influenced by the Muslim Brothers; and this interpretation chimed with those *ulama* who taught that one of the permissible objects of *zakat* was support for anti-colonial resistance movements.

THE MUNTASSER/CARE INTERNATIONAL CASE

The criminal case against a Libyan citizen and permanent U.S. resident, owner of a chain of furniture stores in the Greater Boston area, illustrates the contradictory position in which the U.S. government found itself during the 1990s. "By 1996," writes the civil liberties litigator Harvey A. Silvergate,

> when the Taliban took over control of Afghanistan, the CIA and other orientalists in the American foreign policy establishment were recognizing that some of the American-funded Afghani mujahideen who fought the Soviets were allying with the radically conservative Taliban and turning on their erstwhile American sponsors and other Western interests. Suddenly anyone in the United States who continued to support, among others, the dead and injured fighters became suspect. (Silvergate 2011: 241)[22]

Emadeddin Muntasser served as director of the Boston branch of the Al-Kifah Refugee Center, advertised as a vehicle for the teaching of Sheikh Abdullah Azzam. In 1993, shortly after the World Trade Center bombing on February 26, newspaper articles linked the Brooklyn branch of Al-Kifah to Islamic militant groups. Muntasser dissolved the Boston branch of Al-Kifah, and he incorporated Care International in Massachusetts as a humanitarian charity,[23] with himself as president until 1996, when he resigned. Its avowed purpose was to help destitute Muslims in war-torn areas, mainly in Afghanistan and Bosnia. Its activities during its short lifetime substantially mirrored those of Al-Kifah's Boston branch, including the sale of books advocating jihad, and the publication of a newsletter entitled *Al-Hussam* ("The Sword") which included—together with religious instruction on, for instance, how to observe correctly the holy month of Ramadan—solicitation of funds to support mujahideen in Bosnia and to sponsor children whose fathers had been martyred in the cause. Azzam remained after his "martyrdom" a primary religious reference, and Care published and distributed a translation of his *Join the Caravan* (1987), which had enjoined committed Muslims to become mujahideen.

To simplify a rather complex legal case: in 2008, Muntasser was convicted in a district court in Worcester, Massachusetts, of making a false statement to the FBI during a formal interview in 2003. He disclosed then that he had traveled to Pakistan in 1994 or 1995, but denied that he had also traveled to Afghanistan and met with the Afghan politician and warlord Hekmatyar. Muntasser was sentenced to twelve months' incarceration and a fine of $10,000, but acquitted on two other counts relating to Care's application to be registered as a 501(c) (3) nonprofit: scheming to conceal material facts, and conspiracy to defraud the United States. In 2011, the U.S. Court of Appeals, First Circuit, reviewed the case and, reversing the district court's decision, found Muntasser guilty of a conspiracy. The district judge, to whom the case then reverted in 2012, decided that, though the Justice Department sought a sentence of five years in prison, it should be viewed narrowly as a tax fraud and false statement case, with no connections to terrorism. Muntasser was finally sentenced only to a further six months of home confinement.[24]

The prosecution refrained from making use of the statutes criminalizing all forms of "material support" for terrorism, which had been passed in 1994 and 1996 and strengthened in 2001 (Doyle 2010). Muntasser's defense team showed that the U.S. government had been engaged in exactly the same activities promoting jihad in Afghanistan—through such conduits as the NED and USAID—up to 1992, a year before the formation of Care. "Activities that were considered charitable in 1985, 1989, 1991, or 1992," the defense attorneys argued, "do not become non-charitable in 1993 because the identity of the donor changes, or because the United States' strategic interest in jihad has lessened"; and they specified the subsidy by the U.S. government of *Afghan Jehad* in the 1980s. The prosecution could not claim that any of Care's activities were in themselves criminal.

These are the facts of the Muntasser case, but we may speculate as to the defendant's motivation. At the final court hearing, he apologized to the court for the words he had used in promoting Care "as a young unmarried man who had no responsibilities for a family and the furniture business that he now has." He was indeed twenty-eight when he founded Care. The magazine *Al-Hussam* was published openly, with plentiful advertisements for local businesses in the Boston area. It seems likely that he was following what he took to be legitimate religious leadership, and had no reason to question the lax practices of charity regulation that prevailed in the United States at that time, owing to the nation's strong tradition of freedom of thought and association, guaranteed in the Constitution. We may further surmise that he failed until his resignation from Care in 1996 to notice the change of U.S. foreign policy after 1992.[25]

A similar asynchrony may well have affected the work and lives of some other Muslim charity organizers, both in the United States and in the Middle

East. The draconian measures taken by the United States since 2001 to criminalize and severely punish "material support" for terrorism—which can include even such projects as trying to persuade a paramilitary organization to drop its arms and embrace the political process—have come to bear hard on all international NGOs working in conflict zones, but especially on Islamic charities even when they have taken every step to comply with financial and other regulations.[26]

CLAUDE MALHURET AND MSF

In May 1979, four years before the meeting in California in which Malhuret took part as director of MSF, refugees were already flowing in large numbers into Pakistan as a result of the uprising against the Kabul regime. Malhuret sent an MSF emissary to Afghanistan and persuaded his colleagues in Paris to back a series of clandestine interventions to provide medical aid. Eventually, more than 450 doctors, nurses, and logisticians are said to have passed through the dangerous Afghan maquis during the decade of the war (Vallaeys 2004: 429–30). Juliette Fournot, locally known as Djamila, whose father had been an aid worker and who had spent her teenage years in Kabul, became the organizer of an elaborate network bringing teams and medical equipment into distant parts of Afghanistan as far as Badakhshan in the northeast, close to the Soviet border. She operated from a large rented house in Peshawar nicknamed the "White House" (Weber 1995: 269, 282–83).

At about the time of the California conference, Malhuret published a less optimistic prediction in *Foreign Affairs* as to the future of Afghanistan: "the Afghan resistance will hold out for a long time, but in the end it will probably be beaten. . . . It might not be beaten, however, if in the coming years there is a profound change in the international balance of power and in the reaction of Westerners to Soviet totalitarianism" (Malhuret 1983/1984). Fournot testified before the U.S. Congress about MSF's work, arguing that humanitarian aid should be given directly to the various resistance networks within Afghanistan, not to the political parties installed in Peshawar. Politicians and journalists in Washington expressed keen interest in MSF and offered her large grants for its work, which she refused, preferring the independence that has to this day been one of the keystones of MSF's policies (Weber 1995, 283–84; Vallaeys 2004, 443–44). As a result of two widely publicized incidents of hostage-taking, Malhuret in an article in *Le Monde* called for the evolution of international law to afford more protection for humanitarian teams and war reporters (Malhuret 1984).

In 1986, an MSF caravan—of 120 horses carrying 5 tons of medicines and 150,000 vaccines—was intercepted by mujahideen, and 10 French doctors and nurses were taken hostage; they were freed after one month (Vallaeys 2004, 450–52). In 1990, a young French logistician, Frédéric Galland, was murdered by three masked men in a small MSF hospital in eastern Afghanistan. Rony Brauman, who had been elected president of MSF in 1982 and who formed a triumvirate with Malhuret and Francis Charron during the earlier years of the decade, decided in 1990, while not directly in charge of the program, to terminate their missions to Afghanistan (Vallaeys 2004, 444).[27]

There had been long-standing debates in the Paris headquarters of MSF about the cost-effectiveness of the Afghan program. A documentary film *En Plein Air*, shot by Juliette Fournot and colleagues in 1986 and edited and released in 2006, gives the flavor of the work that she coordinated: hair-raising journeys across rocky cols, the deaths of pack animals en route, then provision of medical services in a makeshift clinic, including surgical reconstruction of a young man's seriously injured face. One of the team was Didier Lefèvre (1957–2007), a biologist with MSF who later became a photojournalist, and who co-published a three-part book *Le Photographe*. Powerfully combining his photographs with cartoons, this recorded his travels through the mountains with MSF in 1986, including a disastrous solo journey back to Pakistan as he ran out of film.[28]

MÉDECINS SANS FRONTIÈRES AND THE MEDIA

The rupture with Bernard Kouchner in 1978 was partly due to Kouchner's publicity-seeking. He endorsed what he called *la loi du tapage* (the law of hype), seeing journalists and humanitarians as locked into an inevitable if often testing partnership. Malhuret and Brauman shared Kouchner's combativeness and ambition but were disinclined to court personal publicity as opposed to a high media profile for MSF. The MSF tradition of *témoignage* underpinned their policies. But the cross-border ventures in Afghanistan—like those of two other French organizations, Médecins du Monde and Aide Médicale Internationale—were conducted with some discretion, to avoid the risks of reprisals from the Soviet military and expulsion from Pakistan.

In retrospect, Afghanistan was seen by MSF as "the theater of the craziest missions in the history of the association." "Amid the romance of running clandestine missions," writes Peter Redfield in his monograph on MSF (2013: 61), "any pretense of adherence to neutrality and discretion vanished." In Brauman's words, it was specially naïve to assume that the war would end with the departure of the Red Army: "we were thinking of peace, the refugees returning, mine-clearing, taking the hospitals in hand" (Vallaeys 2004: 397, 454).[29]

For Malhuret, the "French doctors" and Western war reporters had in common their exposure to the same dangers of kidnapping or death. The Soviet strategy of massive reprisals against the population at large "necessitates one condition, among others, to succeed: secrecy. International public opinion would never accept such oppression if it was correctly informed about it. Hence the hermetic closure of the borders to journalists as well as doctors" (Malhuret 1984).[30] One seasoned journalist offered a more jaundiced analysis:

> The only way [for Western journalists] to cover the conflict was to endure days and nights of walking along precarious mountain paths with guerrilla fighters from mujahedin safe havens in Pakistan. A few stories that appeared in Western papers via this route were careful and low-key, but many were romantic, self-promoting accounts of heroic exploits by reporters who donned a *shalwar kameez*, the long-tailed shirt, and a *pakol*, the pie-shaped Afghan woollen hat, to slip into Afghanistan alongside the men with the guns . . . . Mujahedin groups encouraged this adventure journalism, uncritical, exaggerating and occasionally dishonest. . . . Footage of mujahedin crouching behind rocks and firing weapons was often artificial since there were no Soviet or Afghan Government troops nearby. But it helped to bring support and funding from Western governments and sympathetic aid groups. (Steele 2011: 54–55)

The decade of the Soviet–Afghan War happened to coincide with a turning point in the social sciences, the "crisis of representation," under the influence of Edward Said, Roland Barthes, Michel Foucault, and John Berger, as well as some feminist writers. Criticism of the entire narrative structure of disaster relief began to be expressed within some leading NGOs. By the mid-1990s, a political economy of disaster relief was coming to be recognized: a fairly stable system whereby representations of misery from the global "South" are exported northwards, via an oligarchy of news agencies and broadcasting organizations, as consumables which are reciprocated by aid flows. The assumed heroic role of the Western aid worker came increasingly to be questioned (Benthall 1993).

It is true that Fournot in her deposition to the U.S. Congress made clear that the priority was to strengthen the capacity of her Afghan interlocutors to organize themselves in areas that the Soviets did not control (Vallaeys 2004: 445). But the cover and title of *French Doctors: La grande épopée de la médecine humanitaire* ("the great epic of humanitarian medicine") by Olivier Weber, himself a *grand reporter* for *Le Point* and ally of the mujahideen in the 1980s, suggests that in 1995, its year of publication, the heroic narrative was still dominant in some Parisian circles.[31] By 2003, when *Le Photographe* was published by Guibert, Lefèvre, and Lemercier, the tone has become ironic, even self-deprecatory.

Since then, MSF has negotiated turbulent times to become genuinely international rather than predominantly French, inspired by independence of spirit and a determination not to be co-opted by government interests. The dilemma of reconciling the ideal of neutrality with the imperative of *témoignage* continues to be debated within this unusually self-critical aid agency.[32]

CONCLUSION

The unintended long-term outcomes of Western support for militant Islam, obscured by the imperative to weaken the Soviet Union, have often been noted. Less often noticed as an indirect consequence—and here the theories of Mary Douglas on "purity and danger" can shed light (Douglas 1966)[33]—is the adoption by the U.S. executive and judiciary of draconian measures criminalizing material support for any activities deemed to be affiliated to a terrorist organization, even if these are hospitals or bakeries. It is as if the slightest pollution by an ideology opposed to U.S. policies is enough to condemn activities that would otherwise be welcomed as expressions of common humanity.[34] This policy has led to contradictions with International Humanitarian Law, which (contrary to much popular belief) has no special standing in domestic law. The guardians in the United States of the purity of charity have never accepted their share of blame for the muddying of that purity in the cause of jihad in the 1980s.

As for MSF, while it remained an essentially French institution until the early 1990s, it successfully propagated a myth of the "aristocracy of risk" in the words of Kouchner. The 1980s were the high-water mark of this theatricalization. Indeed, in retrospect—with its strongly articulated credo, its foundation myths, and its confrontation with the facts of suffering—MSF met some of the criteria for a quasi-religious movement stressing the redemptive power of saving lives and alleviating distress. Many of its middle-class young recruits seem to have undergone conversion experiences on joining it (Benthall 2008: 96–106). MSF's later leaders came to reflect on the period with wry detachment.

Looking back at the Monterey conference in 1983, one must credit the U.S. government of the day with having convened a wide variety of experts and published their exchanges. One speaker observed with prescience: "We certainly would not want to see the Afghanistan suffering today exchanged for an Afghanistan under the cloud of a civil war."[35] But the religious dimension was almost obscured by the concern to support those whom a Pakistani think-tank director called "our brave Afghan brothers, now fighting the battle of the free world."[36]

If Arnold Toynbee, author of the once-celebrated twelve-volume *A Study of History*, had not become monumentally unfashionable by the 1980s, his reflections on the much longer time-scale of the Islamist challenge to Christian and post-Christian values might have stimulated more circumspection at Monterey. "Pan-Islamism is dormant," he wrote in 1946, "yet we have to reckon with the possibility that the sleeper may awake if ever the cosmopolitan proletariat of a 'Westernized' world revolts against Western domination and cries out for anti-Western leadership" (Toynbee: 1946: 212). As the French railway sign warns, "Un train peut en cacher un autre."[37]

ACKNOWLEDGMENTS

Malik Ghachem first drew my attention to *Afghan Jehad*. Rony Brauman, Didier Fassin, Emanuel Schaeublin, and Jonathan Steele kindly commented on drafts of this chapter, but the responsibility for any errors is mine alone.

NOTES

1. Gerard C. Steibel and Marvin G. Weinbaum (Magnus 1985: 197, 115). The latter added that "[a]t least for the present, even seemingly benign Islamic fundamentalism is not likely to be welcomed in Washington."
2. Interview in *Nouvel Observateur*, January 15–21, 1998, by Vincent Javert (Cooley 2000: 20).
3. Fatima Ayub, "Not my grandfather's country; Afghanistan at the brink," *New York Times International Edition*, November 1, 2008, Opinion, p. 8. Additional information from Professor Amin Saikal, pers. comm., September 10, 2017.
4. Magnus 1985: 129–30. See also pp. 48–50, 95–97, 129–30, 141, 167–69, 183–84, 202–3, 210.
5. Magnus 1985: 101–4, 178–82.
6. "Edouard Mir" (Lanfranco Pace), *Libération*, December 20, 1991. My translation.
7. He was hanged by the Taliban in 1996.
8. This article by Helga Baitenmann is an indispensable source.
9. Pico Iyer, reported by Dean Brelis, Karachi, *Time*, June 11, 1984, pp. 38–40.
10. This is to be distinguished from *Al-Jihad*, a monthly Arabic-language magazine launched by Abdullah Azzam in 1984, which circulated to about fifty countries and ran to over a hundred issues until closing down in 1995 (Hegghammer 2020: 230).
11. By the Afghan political scientist Amin Saikal, cited in Rasanayagam 2003: 121.
12. *Afghan Jehad*, 1.4, April–June 1988, 3–6.

13. Sources include:

NED Summary, proposal for Afghanistan Democratic Education Project (6 page typescript, late 1980s, n.d.) https://nsarchive2.gwu.edu/NSAEBB/NSAEBB78/propaganda%20145.pdf. Accessed December 27, 2020.

List of four NED grants to American Friends of Afghanistan, 1990–1992, totaling $207,462, including $118,412 for *Afghan Jehad*. This list is cited in the court submission (Defendants' Motion to Dismiss and Incorporated Memorandum) referenced here in fn.24.

See also "Afghanistan Relief Committee," *Militarist Monitor*, updated December 31, 1990, https://militarist-monitor.org/afghanistan_relief_committee/. Accessed December 27, 2020.

14. Latest annual report available, for 2014; total revenue $155.6 million.

15. http://www.kkl-jnf.org/people-and-environment/community-development/soldier-family-meeting-points/. Accessed July 20, 2020.

16. Charity Commission Guidance on Charitable Purposes, https://www.gov.uk/government/publications/charitable-purposes/charitable-purposes. Accessed July 20, 2020.

17. Prominent among these was Yusuf Al-Qaradawi (Bellion-Jourdan 2003: 71).

18. We shall not add here to the extensive literature on the problem of "humanitarian intervention" by military means, designed to protect vulnerable populations, sometimes ironically rephrased as "humanitarian war."

19. Glenn Simpson, "U.S. Knew of Ties Between Terror, Charities," *Wall Street Journal*, Eastern edition, May 9, 2003. The authenticity of the document that Simpson refers to has been challenged.

20. For sharply contrasting accounts, see Burr and Collins 2006: 271–76 and de Goede 2012: 139–45.

21. Hegghammer questions as a "conspiracy theory" the allegation that the U.S. government orchestrated Azzam's tours of numerous U.S. cities, but asserts that they "happened without interference from, and largely under the radar of, domestic US authorities" (2020: 260–62, 590 n. 103).

22. It may be, however, that opposition to Shi`a Iran impelled the United States to turn a blind eye to the rise of the Sunni Taliban—funded in part from Pakistan and Saudi Arabia—until the bombings of the American embassies in Kenya and Tanzania in August 1998, when Washington demanded bin Laden's extradition by the Taliban (Saikal 2002: 25, 2004: 223).

23. No connection with the major U.S. charity CARE.

24. Lee Hammel, "6 months of home confinement added to sentence in Muslim charity tax fraud case," *Telegram and Gazette*, Worcester, May 29, 2012, http://www.telegram.com/article/20120530/NEWS/105309924. Accessed July 20, 2020.

See also U.S. District Court, District of Massachusetts, *USA v. Muhamed Mubayyid and Emadeddin Z. Muntasser*, Defendants' Motion to Dismiss and Incorporated Memorandum, October 5, 2006, https://groups.google.com/g/alt.lawyers/c/GtYFk96SEsk?pli=1. Accessed December 27, 2020; and United States Court of Appeals, First Circuit, *USA v. Mubayyid and Muntasser*, and *USA v. Al-Monla*, decided September 1, 2011, https://casetext.com/case/us-v-mubayyid-5. Accessed December 27, 2020.

See also fn.13.

25. For another analysis of the Muntasser case, stressing the anxiety that such prosecutions provoked among Muslims, see James 2019: 152–55.

26. For comprehensive coverage see the Charity and Security Network website, based in Washington, DC: https://charityandsecurity.org.

27. MSF had left an installation in northern Afghanistan in 1985 after being stigmatized as "Crusaders" by Azzam's followers (Hegghammer 2020: 190–91). It was later to return, however, through the days of civil war and Taliban rule—until withdrawal again in 2004 after the murder of five team members (Redfield 2013: 162–63).

28. This was a collaboration between Lefèvre, Emmanuel Guibert, a cartoonist, and Frédéric Lemercier, a designer (Guibert, Lefèvre, and Lemercier 2003, 2004, 2006). Translated into English as *The Photographer* (Guibert, Lèfevre, and Lemercier 2009).

29. My translation.

30. My translation.

31. The color photograph on the cover shows a handsome young white doctor with a stethoscope holding a small underfed black female child who gazes into his eyes in mute gratitude, one hand extended to touch his face.

32. Among many changes in the humanitarian environment since the 1980s, four stand out. First, it is by no means as clear as it used to be to war reporters and their managers that publicity given to suffering populations will shock the so-called International Community into humanitarian action (though underreported wars are even more catastrophic for those caught up in them). Second, violent attacks on aid workers and journalists are increasing in frequency. A third change is the dissemination of new communication technologies barely dreamt of in the 1980s, but arguably this has not changed the fundamentals of the relationship between donor countries and the global periphery. A fourth change is the increasing recognition of structural racism among aid professionals.

33. I have set out elsewhere to analyze the quest for purity in various ideologies of humanitarianism (Benthall 2016).

34. The contrast between the United States' clamping down on its Islamic charities and the softer and more flexible approach of the U.K. Charity Commission has often been noted. Malick W. Ghachem has argued that the difference is partly due to the First Amendment culture forbidding "entanglement" by the federal government with religion, whereas the British state has a tradition of involvement in religious institutions (Ghachem 2010). For a discussion see Chong 2020.

35. Marvin J. Weinbaum (Magnus 1985: 209).

36. Noor A. Husain (Magnus 1985: 194).

37. One train may hide another.

REFERENCES

Baitenmann, Helga. 1990. "NGOs and the Afghan War: The Politicization of Humanitarian Aid." *Third World Quarterly* 12, no. 1 (January): 62–85.

Barnett, Michael. 2011. *Empire of Humanity: A History of Humanitarianism*. Ithaca: Cornell University Press.

Bellion-Jourdan, Jérôme. 2003. "Helping the 'Brothers'." In *The Charitable Crescent: Politics of Aid in the Muslim World*, edited by Jonathan Benthall and Jérôme Bellion-Jourdan. London: I.B. Tauris.

Benthall, Jonathan. 1993. *Disasters, Relief and the Media*. London: I.B. Tauris (New edition 2009, Wantage: S. Kingston).

Benthall, Jonathan. 2008. *Returning to Religion: Why a Secular Age is Haunted by Faith*. London: I.B. Tauris.

Benthall, Jonathan. 2016. "Puripetal Force in the Charitable Field." In *Islamic Charities and Islamic Humanism in Troubled Times*. Manchester: Manchester University Press.

Benthall, Jonathan. 2018. "The Rise and Decline of Saudi Overseas Humanitarian Charities." CIRS Occasional Paper no. 20, Doha: Center for International and Regional Studies. https://repository.library.georgetown.edu/bitstream/handle/10822/1051628/CIRSOccasionalPaper20JonathanBenthall2018.pdf?sequence=1&isAllowed=y.

Braithwaite, Rodric. 2011. *Afghantsy: The Russians in Afghanistan 1979–89*. London: Profile Books.

Burr, J. Millard and Robert O. Collins. 2006. *Alms for Jihad: Charity and Terrorism in the Muslim World*. Cambridge: Cambridge University Press.

Chong, Agnes. 2020. "(Self-)Regulation of Muslim Charitable Sectors in the US and the UK in the Post-9/11 Era." *Journal of Muslim Philanthropy and Civil Society* 4, no. 1: 1–26.

Cooley, John K. 2000. *Unholy Wars: Afghanistan, America and International Terrorism*. London: Pluto Press.

Donini, Antonio. 2004. "Principles, Politics, and Pragmatism in the International Response to the Afghan Crisis." In *Nation-building Unraveled? Aid, Peace and Justice in Afghanistan*, edited by Antonio Donini, Norah Niland, and Karin Wermester, 117–42. Bloomfield: Kumarian Press.

Donini, Antonio, ed. 2012. *The Golden Fleece: Manipulation and Independence in Humanitarian Action*. Sterling, VA: Kumarian Press.

Douglas, Mary. 1966. *Purity and Danger: An Analysis of Concepts of Pollution and Taboo*. London: Routledge.

Doyle, Charles. 2010. "Terrorist Material Support: An Overview of U.S.C. [United States Code] 2339A and 2339B." Congressional Research Service. http://fas.org/sgp/crs/natsec/R41333.pdf.

Dromi, Shai M. 2020. *Above the Fray: The Red Cross and the Making of the Humanitarian NGO Sector*. Chicago: Chicago University Press.

Fassin, Didier. 2012. *Humanitarian Reason: A Moral History of the Present*. Berkeley: University of California Press.

Ghachem, Malick W. 2009–2010. "Of 'Scalpels' and 'Sledgehammers': Comparing British and American Approaches to Muslim Charities Since 9/11." *UCLA Journal of Near Eastern and Islamic Law* IX, no. 1: 25–66.

De Goede, Marieke. 2012. *Speculative Security: The Politics of Pursuing Terrorist Monies*. Minneapolis: University of Minnesota Press.

Guibert, Emmanuel, Didier Lefèvre and Frédéric Lemercier. 2003. *Le Photographe. Tome 1*. Marcinelle: Editions Dupuis.

Guibert, Emmanuel, Didier Lefèvre and Frédéric Lemercier. 2004. *Le Photographe. Tome 2*. Marcinelle: Editions Dupuis.

Guibert, Emmanuel, Didier Lefèvre and Frédéric Lemercier. 2006. *Le Photographe. Tome 3*. Marcinelle: Editions Dupuis.

Guibert, Emmanuel, Didier Lefèvre and Frédéric Lemercier. 2009. *The Photographer*. New York: First Second.

Hegghammer, Thomas. 2007. "Violent Islamism in Saudi Arabia, 1979–2006: The Power and Perils of Pan-Islamic Nationalism." Doctoral diss. Institut d'Études Politiques de Paris.

Hegghammer, Thomas. 2020. *The Caravan: Abdallah Azzam and the Rise of Global Jihad*. Cambridge: Cambridge University Press.

James, Erica Caple. 2019. "Policing Philanthropy and Criminalizing Charity in the 'War on Terror.'" In *Governing Gifts: Faith, Charity, and the Security State*, edited by Erica Caple James. Santa Fe: School for Advanced Research Press.

Lacina, Bethany and Nils Peter Gleditsch. 2005. "Monitoring Trends in Global Combat: A New Dataset of Battle Deaths." *European Journal of Population* 21, no. 2–3 (June): 145–66.

Magnus, Ralph H., ed. 1985. *Afghan Alternatives: Issues, Options, and Policies*. New Brunswick: Transaction Books.

Malhuret, Claude. 1983/84. "Report from Afghanistan." *Foreign Affairs*, Winter.

Malhuret, Claude. 1984. "Le droit de secourir et de témoigner." *Le Monde*, September 26.

Rasanayagam, Angelo. 2003. *Afghanistan: A Modern History*. London: I.B.Tauris.

Redfield, Peter. 2013. *Life in Crisis: The Ethical Journey of Doctors Without Borders*. Berkeley: University of California Press.

Saikal, Amin. 2002. "Afghanistan, Terrorism, and American and Australian Responses." *Australian Journal of International Affairs* 56, no. 1: 23–30.

Saikal, Amin. 2004. *Modern Afghanistan: A History of Struggle and Survival*. London: I.B. Tauris.

Silvergate, Harvey A. 2011. *Three Felonies a Day: How the Feds Target the Innocent*. New York: Encounter Books.

Steele, Jonathan. 2011. *Ghosts of Afghanistan: The Haunted Battleground*. London: Portobello.

Toynbee, Arnold J. 1946. *Civilization on Trial*. London: Oxford University Press.

Vallaeys, Anne. 2004. *Médecins Sans Frontières: La biographie*. Paris: Fayard.

Weber, Olivier. 1995. *French doctors: La grande épopée de la médecine humanitaire*. Paris: France Loisirs.

Chapter 9

War Economy, Warlordism, and Social Class Formation in South Sudan

Clémence Pinaud

In December 2013, two years after its independence, South Sudan plunged back into civil war. This was its third since the independence of Sudan in 1956. The country had gone through a first civil war intensifying in the early 1960s until 1972. Yet its longest civil war was its second, lasting for twenty-two years from 1983 to 2005. Khartoum, dominated by the pro-*shari'a* law National Islamic Front (NIF) and then National Congress Party (NCP), violently tried to assert power by fighting with and fighting through various rebel groups in the South. In 2005, a peace agreement between the government of Sudan and the Southern rebels of the Sudan People's Liberation Movement/Army (SPLM/A) ended Africa's longest war. The Comprehensive Peace Agreement (CPA) promoted the SPLM/A to the position of representative of the Southerners and de facto ruler of the now semi-autonomous South. From rebels, the SPLA and other factions' officers became statesmen. In 2011, the South gained independence through a referendum, and the statesmen officially emancipated themselves from Khartoum's tutelage for good.

The SPLM/A, founded in 1983, and supported by communist Ethiopia, was initially of Marxist-Leninist inclination. In its 1983 manifesto, it insisted that it was unlike the compromised Southern bourgeoisie who sold the Southern autonomy to Khartoum after the 1972 Addis Ababa Agreement ending the first civil war. The SPLM/A would fight for a "New Sudan" with equality secured for all, regardless of the color of their skin, their religion, or their geographic origin. No non-"Arab" would be considered a second-class citizen anymore under SPLA rule. Yet, by the end of the second civil war and the 2005 peace agreement, the SPLA had designed its own system of social oppression by constituting itself as a dominant class in areas under its control (Nyaba 1997, 33, 38–39, 49, 53; *Horn of Africa* 1985; Woodward 1990,

162; Johnson 2011, 63–64, 127; "Food and Power in Sudan: A Critique of Humanitarianism" 1997, 65; Pinaud 2015).

This chapter explains how the SPLA's control of the war economy and the rise of warlords resulted in the formation of its own military aristocracy and in the making of social classes. This led to the subjugation of civilians in a system of domination that borrowed elements from both the feudal and slavery systems,[1] and I focus here on the feudal elements. Along the making of social classes, control over the war economy also marked the advent of a proto-state. Wartime South Sudan displayed processes very reminiscent of what Charles Tilly and Marc Bloch had observed in early modern Europe—namely the making of a military aristocracy, and the organization of a war economy that resulted in social differentiation and state-building (Tilly 1985, 1992; Bloch 1989). At the same time, the South Sudanese case showed that such processes in a twentieth-century African civil war could not be adequately understood without considering international factors promoting the rise of these warlords to the category of so-called warlord democrats (or statesmen) after the war.[2]

This chapter investigates the sociopolitical processes occurring in the context of a war economy. It is based on field research conducted in various locations across South Sudan between 2009 and 2017. Even if only a few interviews are cited here, mostly from the towns of Rumbek, Juba, Bentiu, and Aweil, the conclusions are based on corpus of over 500 interviews with both female and male fighters, ordinary civilians, aid workers, local politicians, international diplomats and aid workers, on the second and the third civil wars and the interwar period. I also build my analysis on previous publications on the making of a military aristocracy and military kinship ties in South Sudan's second civil war (Pinaud 2014, 2016).

I first analyze why the SPLA was mostly not depicted in international policy and academic circles as a "greedy" armed group during the second civil war (1983–2005) before turning to the making of its military aristocracy and dominant class through the war economy. I then address the creation of a lower stratum—intermediaries, or middle-class—of indebted followers through the patronage of marriage, and how this played out in the aftermath of the second civil war. Finally, I address the specific example of SPLA warlord Paul Malong.

THE WAY WE SEE THE SPLA

The academic literature on South Sudan's past civil war has highlighted the importance of the war economy in sustaining all the warring parties (Johnson 2007, 92–93; Nyaba 1997, 129; El-Batahani, Elbadawi, and Gadir Ali 2005,

193; De Waal 2014; Keen 2008; Walraet 2008a, 2008b; Duffield 2001, 154). Yet the SPLA was never popularly considered on par with other African armed groups notorious for their economic activities, such as Sierra Leone's RUF or Angola's UNITA, both involved in the diamond trade. Douglas Johnson, one of the most reputed historians on South Sudan, noted that the war in Sudan was not like Angola's, where both government and rebels had access to their own exportable mineral resources, or like Sierra Leone's where the government, rebels, and individuals each had equal access to a highly exportable resource like diamonds (Johnson 2007, 154–55). It was inferred that because the SPLA did not have access to oil resources—like Khartoum did—or, supposedly, diamonds—the armed group's emphasis was less on illicit trade than the RUF or UNITA, and this located the SPLA in a different category of the armed group.

This analysis was popular given the general state of the field of inquiry on armed groups. For example, political scientist Jeremy Weinstein, in his study on insurgent violence, distinguished between the ideologically motivated "activist" groups operating in resource-poor contexts, and having to strike bargains with the local populations (following Maoist teachings), and those other "opportunistic" armed groups that were motivated by resource extraction, and much less in need of popular support. Weinstein argued that opportunism made a group more likely to violate human rights because it was less interested in controlling violence (Weinstein 2007, 9–10). Weinstein, who followed in the footsteps of political scientists in the late 1990s–early 2000s carrying out research for the World Bank (such as Paul Collier) and subscribing to the thesis that armed actors were motivated by "greed" rather than "grievances" and driven by the opportunity to rebel depending on their environment,[3] did not specifically study South Sudan. But if one applied Weinstein and other Collier followers' analysis to South Sudan, rebel leader John Garang and his SPLA would allegedly fit into the "grievances" camp (with strong ideological polarization between North and South Sudan), rather than into the "greed" camp (even if Collier's followers argued that a number of environmental factors still played a part in explaining why people go to war). Despite acknowledging the SPLA's predatory behavior, Collier's followers argued that the SPLA "fixed" its predatory ways through the development of its administration,[4] when in fact and as this chapter shows, the exact opposite occurred.

Still according to these authors, South Sudan was indeed characterized by a myriad of splintering armed groups who were "greedy." They subscribed to SPLA leader John Garang's rhetoric and quoted him multiple times as saying that in the South, it "pays to rebel" (El-Batahani, Elbadawi, and Gadir Ali 2005, 193, 212). This implied that the SPLA was different. The SPLA was the armed group fitting best into the "grievances/ideological" category, mostly because it kept the same leadership throughout the twenty-two-year-long war. It also retained the same name, unlike the other armed groups. This gave it a semblance of political consistency, even though Marxist-Leninist ideology never took hold of its recruits and was largely abandoned after its 1991 split. This image of political consistency, added to the advantage of not being "Islamist"—unlike its northern adversary—but secular, and with Christian affinities attracting international sympathy, implied that the SPLA was a "good"—or at least "better"—armed actor.

But the SPLA complicated the distinction between ideologically and politically motivated armed actors on the one hand, and "opportunistic" armed groups on the other, not least because it committed gross human rights violations. Such distinction omitted other factors such as the war's length (twenty-two years), geographical variations in violence and in command and control over troops, international politics dictating varying support to the SPLA throughout the war, and politics within the SPLA, especially surrounding the 1991 split of the armed group. All in all, the SPLA's motives were neither solely ideological nor just "opportunistic." They varied with time and with the composition of the rank and file, and depended on individual commanders, most of whom enriched themselves. Recruitment also determined the SPLA's attitude toward civilians and the leadership's motivation to enforce discipline, and its ability to do so. Finally, the SPLA was involved in mining both gold and diamonds, and it had devised a transportation system and trade networks. So it did capture lootable and exportable resources, and it transported them and other comparatively less "exportable" resources such as looted cattle and teak, in lorries to neighboring countries, using roads renovated by relief agencies.

In fact, the SPLA displayed its versatility in the ways it adapted to local contexts wherever its troops were stationed throughout twenty-two years of armed struggle. As a result, its war economy revolved around diverse commodities. From its presence in the Ethiopian refugee camps at the inception of its struggle to the end of the civil war in 2005, the SPLA traded commodities it looted and/or taxed off civilians, including cattle, relief items, food aid, civilians' crops and other belongings (from clothing to kitchen utensils), natural resources including minerals such as gold and diamonds, but also teak and marijuana.[5]

Therefore, the idea of the SPLA fitting one category of armed groups ("greedy") or the other ("ideological/political") was largely disconnected from reality on the ground. The idea was in fact mostly informed by politics. Evidently, until December 2013 and the new civil war, the SPLA was perceived as a "political" movement because it fit with U.S. foreign policy goals, as I explain later. After 2014, tongues loosened up as the new state plunged back into war, which made it somewhat permissible at first, and then commonplace, to describe the elite as inherently "greedy," corrupt, and violent—therefore without "politics," or "ideology." Since 2014, little attention has been paid to "politics." As of 2018, the political scene of South Sudan is often described in policy circles as "greedy," with all rebels taking up arms to loot and/or bargain for political and military positions, not because they follow their own political agendas. We have fully tipped over to the other side of the coin—violent greed.[6]

Back in the 1980s and 1990s, the perception of the SPLA as "ideological/political" rather than "greedy" was partly informed by the way the SPLA presented itself. In this regard, Will Reno's analysis of how armed groups adapt their political strategies toward outsiders is highly relevant. Paradoxically, while the "greed" (or "criminal conspiracy") narrative gained traction in the late 1990s, the SPLA seemed largely impermeable to it and managed to uphold what Reno, writing about the depiction of wars in Liberia, Angola, and Namibia, called a "war of liberation narrative" (Reno 2005, 1800). The SPLA portrayed itself with a strong ideology of national liberation with Marxist-Leninist rhetoric, against the exploitative regime in Khartoum. Before 1991, the SPLA adopted a predatory behavior that was somewhat kept in check by the fact that it was not split in different factions yet. But it was supported by communist Ethiopia and therefore denigrated by the United States, who initially backed Khartoum against the Southern rebels. In 1991, the collapse of the Soviet block and the fall of the Ethiopian Derg ended a much-needed line of military supplies to the SPLA. It also coincided with the split of the rebel group into various factions, which heralded a new phase of increased asset-stripping raids, violence, and predation in the South. Garang's admission that "in the South, it pays to rebel" was meant to explain southern factionalism and defuse criticism about the SPLA itself, supposedly different from the rest of the "greedy" factions. Explaining the mushrooming of rival factions by greed also deflected criticism about the SPLA's own internal governance issues. But this did not mean the SPLA was not exploitative either, as I show later.

All in all, after 1991, "greed" could be seen as much more prominent a feature of the civil war. Resource capture was practiced by more actors, in more disorganized and violent fashion. Of course, the SPLA's image of a "political" rather than "greedy" armed group was not just informed by the way the SPLA wanted to present itself. It needed purchase, and it catered to the way outsiders—especially Americans—wanted to see it. From 1991 to 1994, considering the collapse of the Soviet block, and Khartoum's ties with the Muslim Brotherhood and al-Qaeda, the United States progressively changed its stance toward the South and especially the SPLA (Johnson 2007, 80; Patey 2010, 630).

It found a perfect interlocutor in John Garang, the Dinka SPLA leader who had studied in Iowa for a PhD in agricultural economics, and who was a very gifted orator when it came to convincing different audiences of different goals. Some of his political adversaries pointed out he was inconsistent, but to his interlocutors in Washington, DC, he was an authoritative politician who managed to stay on top of a large rebel formation for twenty-two years, until his death in 2005 in a helicopter crash. Garang was particularly adept at persuading his Western foreign friends (especially Americans) of the South's political potential for steering regime change in Khartoum, from an Islamist state sponsoring terrorism to a Western-allied (and particularly U.S.-allied) secular state. In response to the West's concerns about the SPLA human rights record and institutional strength, Garang ushered what looked like a reform in 1994, through the SPLM/A National Convention. This reform meant to build the SPLA administration. International aid in the form of support to institutional building to the Southern rebels was hoped, as liberal peacemaking thinking had it (spearheaded by institutions such as the World Bank), to steer the South toward democratic development (Young 2019, 7). In an opening speech to National Convention in 1994, SPLA commander Yussif Kuwa described the pre-1994 period as "childhood," and what was coming as "manhood" with "responsibility, seriousness and accountability" (Rolandsen 2005, 112).

But predation and lack of accountability continued, unabated. The few critical voices arising from human rights organizations denouncing the SPLA's exploitative patterns that continued after 1994 were mostly ignored. De Waal called the international community's attitude toward relief diversion "functional ignorance" in one of his reports (De Waal 1995, 7). All in all, as international aid to the region increased by the mid-1990s, the SPLA rebels were perceived as mostly "good" rebels.

Yet, institutional building in SPLA-controlled areas only routinized predation, and increased the enrichment of commanders. Therefore, the most efficient at predation it got, the more support the SPLA received. A former Dinka child soldier attested: "The 1994 civilian administration was a good way for the SPLA to continue these (extractive) practices on a larger scale: that's when the system of rationed contribution was set up and looting increased, being systematized" (Former SPLA child soldier 2014).

Many ordinary civilians felt that by the end of the war "most SPLA commanders had gone out to Australia and other places. They were gone out of the frontlines. Very few people in the SPLA were there for political reasons. Most of them were criminals" (Member of civil society 12 2014). In other words, there was little doubt to ordinary civilians that the SPLA commanders were "greedy" rather than "political" by the time they got promoted as future leaders of the semi-autonomous region in 2005. But the international community supported the SPLA rather than any other armed group in South Sudan. The same civilian explained the stakes for the United States, Norway, and the United Kingdom, members of the so-called Troika: "For the international community if the SPLA was defeated, South Sudan was over . . . . The Comprehensive Peace Agreement was imposed from outside" (Member of civil society 12 2014).

Western advocacy circles cared more about how "bad" Khartoum was to the Southerners—especially the Dinka—than about how extractive the SPLA acted in the South—especially toward the non-Dinka. The irony was that the Southern rebels were reenacting, in their predatory behavior, century-old patterns of extractive relationship between North and South.

Slavery laid the historical foundation for the predominantly Dinka SPLA's ethnically exclusionary predation in areas under its control. Indeed, the very mode of production through which the predominantly Dinka SPLA elite accumulated wealth, especially at the expense of other ethnic groups, was rooted in the Sudanese history of slavery: in a mode of production that was inherently racist. Even if forced labor in SPLA-held areas was not slavery, it certainly was reminiscent of its economy. The SPLA also used its court system to force civilians with a prison sentence to work in its farms/mines and earmarked some of the production for the division commanders, much like it used court fines to collect cattle. This was again a remnant of the organization of slavery. SPLA-run farms were reminiscent of the system of the *zarai'b*—especially prevalent in Bahr El Ghazal during the nineteenth century. There, female slaves were forced to cultivate too. Besides, because the SPLA was mostly Dinka but controlled non-Dinka areas (such as Equatoria) that were key to its war economy, forced labor became ethnically ranked in those areas as well. Forced labor, ethnic ranking in access to military training, and ethnic discrimination in access to positions of resource control to the detriment of the few non-Dinka officers, meant that ethnic ranking and dominant-class formation resting on predation thus converged. On the whole, this SPLA-dominant class had very few ethnic outsiders (Pinaud 2021).

But only a few authors focused on describing the processes of violent exploitation and resource accumulation by the SPLA.[7] The "functional ignorance" of the international community—diplomats and aid workers—seemed to permeate academic writings on the SPLA. This meant that little was written on the social implications of predation, which I now turn to. Yet predation and its long-term effects were highly relevant: they structured society during the war, and for decades to come. In contributing to the making of social classes, predation also structured the fabric of military power.

THE DOMINANT CLASS AS AN ARISTOCRACY

Throughout the war, the SPLA became the vehicle for resource accumulation. The armed group despoiled civilians' resources, and funnelled them into "forced markets" just like the pro-government militias and army did in areas under Khartoum's control.[8] SPLA cadres constituted themselves into a military aristocracy, a dominant class (Pinaud 2014). In analyzing this dominant class, I follow Larry Diamond's definition of a "category encompassing those who have similar economic motivation because they have similar economic opportunities, even if class consciousness, class solidarity, or class action do not exist. A class may be considered socially dominant if it owns or controls the most productive assets, appropriates the bulk of the most valued consumption opportunities, and commands a sufficient monopoly over the means of coercion and legitimation to sustain politically this cumulative socio-economic pre-eminence." With "high degrees of class consciousness and social coherence—constituting in the Marxian sense a 'class-for-itself,'" a dominant class will consolidate, particularly through the transmission of its status to next generations (Diamond 1987, 569).

When applying this definition to South Sudan, it emerges that wartime predation—and not political corruption, as advanced by Diamond and others—initiated a process of dominant-class formation.[9] Under these circumstances, the guerilla group—not the political party—was the instrument of the rise of a military aristocracy and of its lower strata. This military aristocracy was a dominant class, not a nobility. "Not every dominant class is a nobility," as stressed by Marc Bloch in his examination of feudal society (Bloch 1989, II:2). Bloch, even as he observed that the word *noble* was used in ninth-century western Europe to denote both distinction of birth and the measure of wealth, indicated that what *made* a nobility was the recognition of both social privileges and hereditary succession by law—the existence of a social pedigree. Therefore, the nobility popularly associated with the Ancien Régime appeared relatively late in western Europe in the twelfth century, taking shape in the thirteenth century along with the demise of vassalage (Bloch 1989, II:2, 4–5).

Yet the word *noble* was already by then used loosely for men who gained prominence in society in the midst of a government breakdown and the need for protection. The vassals' role as arms retainers made them look like an aristocracy. In sum, nobility as a legal class did not exist yet, but this social class of nobles did. Bloch noted that "it was principally by the nature of its wealth, by its exercise of authority, and by its social habits that this group was defined" (Bloch 1989, II: 7). Some of these lords were self-made men. They derived their wealth from various means including land, tolls, markets fees, fines. The common denominator was some form of exploitation—wealth acquired on the labor of another man. Exploitation was justified by the idea that the noble could only dedicate time to his own function, that of a warrior.

War-torn South Sudan shared many characteristics with the feudal societies described by Bloch (Bloch 1989, II: 167). Organized forced labor, the primacy of kinship ties, the existence of a warrior class, ties of dependency from the top to the bottom of the social scale between the warlords and their vassals, as well as state weakness, were key features in South Sudan that were reminiscent of feudal societies, in addition to features it inherited from slavery. Besides, the so-called western European "nobles" who predated the thirteenth century were also the subordinates to superior lords. In South Sudan, even warlords had to account to higher lords—in the SPLA, to leader John Garang. They were vassals who also thought of themselves as fulfilling their function of warrior. That function was the highest, and with the SPLA officers thinking of themselves as "the best," the dominant class acted like an aristocracy.[10]

Similarly, to Bloch's "nobles," war provided these men with the opportunity to change their socioeconomic standing and sustain their new ascendency. This applied to the highest levels, including two key SPLA figures, the SPLA leader John Garang, and his second in command and future president, Salva Kiir. A former SPLA commander recalled that before the war "Salva and Garang were very poor, even if Salva's father was a spear-master. Salva and Garang enriched themselves to death during the war" (Former SPLA commander 2014).[11] This leaves little doubt about the centrality of the war in these men's social trajectory. Yet, the SPLA cadres still came from diverse social backgrounds.

Some were from chiefly descent, and were selected precisely because of that social capital. They were rewarded with high-ranking positions for promoting recruitment into the SPLA early on in the war using the chiefs and their social capital. Others were military career officers from the Sudanese Armed Forces (like John Garang, Salva Kiir, or Kerubino Kuanyin) and played an instrumental role in starting the SPLA. One did not exclude the other—as Salva Kiir combined both a chiefly heritage and a military career. Finally, another category of cadres fits much more than the category of self-made men who emerged through this war. "Some people from the cattle camps made it into the SPLA top leadership," explained a Dinka civilian. "Peter Gadet, for example. Paul Malong, who was not educated. He didn't even get primary school education. Paul Malong used to assist as a non-trained nurse in Aweil. Those who joined in the bush and were good, made it to seniority" (Member of civil society 6 2014). This last type of warriors would especially invest in long-term kinship expansion strategies.

CLASS CONSCIOUSNESS, INTERESTS, AND THE HYPER-CONCENTRATION OF WEALTH

In spite of the warriors' various social backgrounds, the new military aristocracy acquired an overarching class consciousness. It displayed it in ways of living and in taste—all elements of "social distinction." These were all the more observable in the post-2005 era when this dominant class consolidated itself through access to oil money. As I explained elsewhere, the dominant class displayed similar taste in dining, cars, and housing (Pinaud 2014). But the SPLA aristocrats already acted, in a Marxist sense, as a "class for itself" during the war. They especially demonstrated their consciousness when defending their class interests. They violently controlled markets, for example, banning civilians from trading their own cattle, forcing civilians to cultivate their farms and to mine for gold, and controlling the price of the commodities extracted through forced labor (Walraet 2008b, 2008a; Pinaud 2021).

A former SPLA child soldier described how: "The SPLA dominated the gold trade and prevented people from mining from the rivers. Regional governor and commanders were involved. Kuol Manyang was commander in Kapoeta. Certain people became rich, in gold, teak, cattle" (Former SPLA child soldier 2014). Another civilian confirmed that "relatives of SPLA big people managed the extraction of the gold," which already suggested an attempt to pass on privileges to other generations. "Junior officers got gold and gave it to big officers and got their share. The gold was sold to Kenya and even outside Africa. They traded it for luxurious goods—Hummers and cars and houses in Nairobi, Uganda. They bought new houses" (Member of civil society 9 2017). The trades of various commodities, such as gold, cattle, and relief items, were all intertwined, and the commanders became savvy businessmen. Speaking of Louis Lobong, a key SPLA figure in Kapoeta (Eastern Equatoria) at the time, a former SPLA soldier explained how he "made a lot of money": "he sold relief food and used that money to buy gold and resell it in Uganda and Kenya" (sixty-year-old displaced man from Ikotos 2017).

This emerging dominant class made sure to yield a considerable surplus value in all its economic ventures. "The commanders in Bahr El Ghazal had a lot of cattle," continued the former child soldier. "Some of the cattle (maybe ¼ or more) could stay in the hands of the commanders and not ever reach the movement or soldiers. The same went for what was collected as rations. The commanders were involved in trades a lot: they took the vehicles captured from the government and sold them in Uganda" (Former SPLA child soldier 2014).

It is more accurate to analyze the aristocrats' strategies in defending their class interests and in consolidating their status, as a form of wealth "hyper-concentration."[12] Speaking of increased inequalities between this dominant warrior class and the rest of its soldiers and despoiled civilians does not suffice to describe this process of wealth accumulation and distribution. Wealth was concentrated at the top by the shrewd commanders, in the SPLA but also in rival factions. A Nuer civilian remembered how in Unity state, "the commanders got taxation money—they were the richest, 99% of the money got to them" (Member of civil society 10 2016). Of course, as I show later, the warrior aristocracy was careful to trickle down some of its wealth to soldiers in order to cement their allegiance and create a lower stratum. But the aristocrats were first and foremost focused on securing their own ascendency.

SECURING LONG-TERM DOMINANCE THROUGH LARGE-SCALE POLYGAMY

In accumulating and concentrating wealth—especially in cattle—the military aristocrats used the surplus value they derived from controlling the war economy and usurping civilians' resources toward establishing long-term social dominance. "What do you do when you have cattle?" asked a Nuer parliamentarian. "You marry!" (Political Representative 4 2014). The military aristocrats dominated the marriage market that rested on a system of bridewealth exchange, often paid in cattle. In addition to investing newly acquired wealth into foreign bank accounts, as well as new business companies, they reinvested their new wealth into "people" via bridewealth payment.[13] Practicing large-scale polygamy, they considerably expanded their kinship networks, and their capital in the long run. More women begat more children and future bridewealth, therefore more wealth in cattle.

These strategies contributed to shape a patrimonial capitalist system: where capital is owned through wealth inherited by rentiers, and status is consolidated through marriage.[14] Again, domination of the marriage market and polygamy by "big men" were also reminiscent of systems of slavery (Cooper 1979, 117; Strobel 1979, 48; Robertson and Klein 1983, 6, 9; Lovejoy 1983).

The Dinka SPLA commander Paul Malong, in the Bahr El Ghazal region, was certainly the most well-known case of large-scale polygamy in the SPLA. The exact number of Malong's wives remained debated, and oscillated between forty and ninety (Member of civil society 8 2015; Member of civil society 6 2014; Member of civil society 13 2014). Ordinary people estimated Malong's close relatives numbered between 300 and 500 after the war (Member of civil society 8 2015; Member of civil society 9 2017; Member of civil society 23 2014). Of course, they also created a mythology around Malong's persona. Some considered he had built an "empire" through large-scale polygamy (Member of civil society 8 2015). Others contended that after the war, "Malong had ostriches at home and so his 500 children travelled on ostriches in the compound. He had 100 wives in the compound" (Member of civil society 9 2017).

But there were other lower-level and lesser-known cases of SPLA commanders practicing large-scale polygamy as well. "The Governor of Lakes state in 1972 is a good example," explained a former SPLA commander. "In 1983 he joined the SPLA and he became a division commander and accumulated a lot of wealth. He has 14 wives and many houses in Juba, Lakes and upstate Lakes. He eloped most of his wives, paid less than 20 cattle and that's it. The women decided to join him, and there was no competition because he was a commander" (Former SPLA commander 2014).

Besides, both the SPLA aristocrats' large-scale polygamy and their patronage of soldiers' marriages were mirrored in areas controlled by other rival Nuer military factions. "The practices of bridewealth payment in both SPLA and SPLA-Nasir (a Nuer faction) were similar," explained Nuer civilians. "What was done here, was done there" (Three members of civil society 1 2015). And Nuer commanders were just as polygamous as the Dinka: "John Koang, Bol Kong, Peter Gadet, Paulino Matiep (Nuer commanders) accumulated many wives who joined them and had their bridewealth paid for later—the parents were proud to have their daughters marry a commander" (Former SPLA commander 2014). The cases of Paulino Matiep and Peter Gadet, both Nuer, are most illustrious. "Matiep had the most wives, but still not as much as Paul Malong," explained a Nuer civilian. "Peter Gadet had many wives as well. He married mostly from the Nuer—from Lankien, Akobo, Mayom, etc. He always married on the way, wherever he passed by" (Member of civil society 2 2015). Nuer civilians estimated that "Peter Gadet has about 150 boys from 80 wives: he still continues to marry. Everywhere you go, you marry, you get a wife, and then another, etc. Gadet mentioned 150 boys because it means they will carry his name" (Member of civil society 20 2016). All in all, people disagreed over who had the most wives—Malong, Matiep, or Gadet. But this was mere bickering.

In hyper-concentrating wealth and women through their control of the marriage market, both the Dinka and Nuer military aristocrats transformed the economy and society. Large-scale polygamy was traditionally practiced by men of chiefly lineage. But large-scale polygamy became the norm rather than the exception for high-ranking officers in this dominant class. They used it as a tool of social distinction. Control over women provided long-term control over future and cumulative wealth, since women "produced" both immediate and future bridewealth through reproduction. This new dominant class contributed to increase bridewealth prices and to commodify women in the long run. It continued to use marriage as a tool of social differentiation, domination, and class consolidation after the war. "Raising bridewealth prices enables the elite to ban out people with low income," explained a former high-ranking Dinka SPLA officer turned government official after 2005 (High-ranking Government Official 1 2014). "A girl is like a cloth in the market," said a Dinka cattle-keeper. "I love you but I know I have nothing. And I compete with the big politicians on high prices of dowry . . . . High prices practiced by the elite are meant to discourage poor people to marry into the elite" (Cattle-keeper 2014). By banning ordinary civilians from entering its class by seizing and concentrating both their resources and securing privileged access to their women, the dominant class defended its class interests. It secured long-term wealth but also devised extreme and long-term inequalities.

In this patrimonial capitalist system, where wealth was hyper-concentrated, the only way to achieve social mobility for the non-aristocrats was through marriage. "Parents gave their daughter for promotion," explained a Nuer civilian. "If your daughter has been married by a big person, you can do whatever you want, you can be protected" (Member of civil society 20 2016). "Political marriage was a way to get a promotion in the SPLA," corroborated a former Dinka SPLA officer. This would continue "after the war," he added: "it became a way into government jobs" (Former SPLA Lieutenant Colonel 2014).

The expansion of immediate kinship networks via large-scale polygamy not only secured the social reproduction of the aristocracy, and some ordinary civilians' social climbing and protection. It also mounted the aristocrats' military and political power. Indeed, if families marrying "big persons"—or big men—could be "protected," the flip side for them was that "if someone mistreats Peter Gadet you have to go and defend him," explained a Nuer civilian (Member of civil society 20 2016). Large-scale polygamy also defused potential opposition. Referring to Paul Malong, who married from different counties in Northern Bahr El Ghazal, a civilian explained

> After all, Malik Abdel Aziz, the King of Saudi Arabia, united the Arab tribes by marrying from different tribes. Malong married in 4 different communities—all of them from Northern Bahr El Ghazal. This is a very strategic plan! because you can't fight with the husband of your sister. And he used to pay so many cows! (Member of civil society 13 2014)

Peter Gadet, the Nuer commander mentioned earlier, did exactly the same: "Gadet married from Bul Nuer and other counties and other states: even 2 to 3 wives from Jonglei (Bor), 4 wives from Leer, and even from Mayendit" (Member of civil society 20 2016).

Of course, neither Malong, Matiep, nor Gadet fathered all of their children. This was not the point. Prolonging their name and expanding their power was at stake, not securing a supply of women for sex. Accordingly, they delegated to their soldiers the task of impregnating their wives with their second child and onwards, just like other Nuer and Dinka "big men" had in the past—for example, nineteenth-century Nuer prophet Deng Laka (Johnson 1994, 126). "For Paul Malong, the first children were his, the rest were (born) because his followers impregnated his wives . . . he married from different sections . . . . So he built a wide network of connections" (Two members of civil society 1 2015). Similarly, "Gadet has about 80 wives. He doesn't know who impregnated which one. He just birthed the first boy, the rest doesn't matter," explained a Nuer civilian. "Even his soldiers can impregnate them, so long as the child is named after him, he doesn't care" (Member of civil society 20 2016). Numerous children guaranteed long-lasting military manpower and control over the future state's institutions and military apparatus. Consequently, the aristocrats placed their children at every echelon of the new state after 2005. For example, "most of Matiep's children joined the SPLA," said a Nuer civilian (Member of civil society 25 2016).

BUILDING MILITARY KINSHIP TIES AND LOWER STRATA

Yet, looking back, not all SPLA commanders followed the same strategies in consolidating their status of dominant social class. Speaking of this practice of large-scale polygamy, a former SPLA commander explained: "That's what happened for most commanders, except the educated ones such as Pagan Amum, Piang Deng, Guer Chang, Oyii Deng Ajak, who did not invest their wealth in wives but in offshore accounts" (Former SPLA commander 2014).

These "educated ones" chose a type of reinvestment that was essentially financial, and not kinship-related, and as such military. Given how politics are played in South Sudan out of the barrel of a gun, this was not a strategic decision: "What's valuable in our country is cattle," explained a Dinka civilian. "Cattle is very important. If you have money, you're not respected. Those who have cattle are the most respected" (Cattle keeper 2014). The reason was simple: wealth in cattle meant wealth in people, and the circle of people—and military power—expanded.

Indeed, this warrior-dominant class also cared about cementing its base outside of its immediate kinship circle. The military commanders redistributed part of their captured wealth to their followers, in gifts of bridewealth and wives. Assuaging tensions arising from stark inequalities on the marriage market was a military necessity for the SPLA to continue to function as a rebel army. These ties reinforced military cohesion within the rebel army, as other soldiers also participated in the payment of their brother-in-arms' bridewealth price. But bridewealth payment was also a strategy for the commanders, especially after 1991 and increased predation, to cultivate their own personal base. Again, SPLA and Nuer factions' commanders practiced the same patronage of their soldiers' marriage, as Nuer civilians in Unity state recalled how Gadet "paid for the dowry of his bodyguards or close friends" (Member of civil society 20 2016).

Through gifts of bridewealth to their soldiers, commanders substituted themselves for their soldiers' fathers (Pinaud 2016). They expanded their military kinship ties and, therefore, their military base. They weaved ties and social contracts that were both reminiscent of the feudal ties between lords and vassals described by Bloch, and broadly illustrative of Marcel Mauss's analysis of the social contracts and potlatch as affairs involving feelings too (Mauss 2011, 18). Through such practices, the SPLA commanders created lower strata. These lower strata enjoyed some, on a much lower scale, of the military aristocracy's privileges. Soldiers of the lower strata had several wives, and they were above ordinary civilians. A civilian explained, ten years after the war ended, how in Northern Bahr El Ghazal, "many of Paul Malong's followers have become rich now—like Garang Garang, special guard and then tax collector in Warawar, who brought taxes at the state houses. He's from Aweil east" (Member of civil society 13 2014).

Malong's power epicenter continued to be grounded upcountry in Northern Bahr El Ghazal for years. Unlike many military aristocrats, he spent the postwar period of 2005–2013 mostly in his home state as governor. This explains why it was so easy for him to levy manpower in his home area to form Dinka militias who would play an instrumental role in the new civil war of December 2013.

The other military aristocrats had settled in the country's capital with the 2005 peace agreement. The agreement granted the SPLM/A the political leadership in the South, and ushered in a period of institutional building that concentrated on the capital Juba. The lower strata created during the war through gifts of wives and bridewealth provided the military aristocracy with an entourage. The warlords were "courticized" around the president's house in Juba. From "warriors," they turned "courtiers," in a process reminiscent of Europe's from the eleventh to the eighteenth century (Elias 2008). "After 2005, when the commanders came to Juba, each of them had a house and a commando—especially the big bosses, like Salva, Wani Igga, Wani Konga, Ismail Kony, and Paulino Matiep," explained a Nuer parliamentarian (Political representative 4 2014). "These people retained their own soldiers and supported them to get married, even after 2005," he added. The lower strata thus became part of the warrior's "courts": they were "courticized" too. As such, their main function was to socially—and no longer militarily—demonstrate the ascendency of the dominant class in the capital Juba. They were mostly seen as "hanging out" in their warrior's compounds, at big hotels and at restaurants by the Nile, parading in new large shiny vehicles, driving well above the speed limit around Juba, and stopping traffic and roughing up civilians who had not immediately interrupted their activities as a sign of deference and submission.

Some of the courticized warriors—those who were not formally educated and had especially benefited from the war's social elevator by amassing cattle and people, such as Matiep—continued to cement their social ascendency by paying for their followers' marriages. For others who were left in the countryside, like Malong, consolidating their social dominance outside Juba's scrutiny was even easier (and Matiep died of illness in 2012). Of this type of warriors, the Nuer parliamentarian said: "In the villages, in Bor or in Bahr El Ghazal, they have so many cattle kept by their soldiers. Huge camps belong to one person" (Political representative 4 2014). Therefore, some warlords never became fully courticized, and the patronage of marriage did not rescind.

Everything could have remained the same indefinitely in Juba, with Nuer and Dinka warrior-dominant classes and their courts aggregating in Juba in a typical process of "elite fusion."[15] But these ethnic dominant classes that had come to coexist in Juba during the CPA period continued to compete. The SPLA Dinka dominant class won this competition. President Salva Kiir's faction sidelined other Dinka competitors from the deceased SPLA leader John Garang's faction and other ethnic competitors. This propelled ethnic ranking within the state.

Meanwhile, some warlords retained their base upcountry, continued to amass wealth and wealth in people, and were therefore never fully courticized. The dominant class was never fully coalesced. This made the strength and reach of the state largely dependent on the bargains it could strike with these warriors. This meant that some of these warlords became particularly influential in the process of state-building post-2005. The most notable was Paul Malong, a close ally to President Salva Kiir.

Shortly after the eruption of the third civil war in December 2013, Malong was promoted to the position of SPLA chief of staff. His promotion to "warlord-in-chief" was both a reward for his instrumental support to President Kiir and an attempt by Kiir to reign him in. Pushed out of his position as SPLA chief of staff in 2017, Malong reverted to the status of a rebel. He was not able to fully return to his status of warlord, since he sought to devise a rebellion from outside the country. Yet the case of Paul Malong illustrated the rise of a feudal-type warlord through the war economy, parallel to the rise of a proto-state, and participant to the making of an ethnic dominant class. Such warrior, although turned statesman, but never fully "courticized," could easily challenge the state again if he was not successfully marginalized by the center.

CONCLUSION

All in all, the case in South Sudan shows us the long-lasting sociopolitical implications of a war economy. The South Sudanese case illustrates how a rebel group—and not the political party, as commonly accepted by scholars of African politics—started a process of social class formation that went hand-in-hand with an exercise of proto-state-building and the development of a patrimonial capitalist system. This process of social class formation was marked by ethnically exclusive extractive violence and sexual violence. The hyper-concentration of wealth by the dominant class in the making was achieved through the exploitation of ordinary civilians, particularly ordinary women. They were commodified in this process of wealth accumulation, and turned into capital.[16]

Social class formation in SPLA areas was similar to that of other factions' Nuer areas. What made the process even more striking in SPLA areas, and arguably particularly influential after 2005 when SPLA rebels became statesmen, was that from the mid-1990s onward, the organization of the war economy in SPLA areas went hand-in-hand with the building of a predatory state supported by the international community.

In 2005, the CPA comforted the SPLA's position and consolidated the social processes at play during the war. Wealth continued to be concentrated, and civilians continued to experience violence. But the Nuer and Dinka ethnic dominant classes who came to fusion in Juba after 2005 never fully aggregated. This was largely due to a process of ethnic ranking in the new state driven by the Dinka faction behind Salva Kiir, which played a key role in the resumption of war in December 2013.

NOTES

1. Elements of the colonial system persisted as well. Feudalism was based on land tenure (fiefs or administrative units) ruled by lords invested with political power to the service of a military oligarchy, and slavery was founded on the exchange and commodification of people, both of which—land and people—were forms of capital (in the case of people, "slave capital"). Different definitions of feudalism and how they could apply to Africa exist. I borrow from Marc Bloch, Max Weber, and Joseph Strayer. See Goody 1963, 3; Bloch 1989, II:167. On the relationship between capitalism and slavery, see Piketty 2014, 46.

2. I borrow the term of *warlord democrat* from Anders Themnér (Themnér 2017).

3. For a summary of Collier's approach and of the debate between the two camps, see Keen 2012.

4. See the way the SPLA political project and the way it garnered support amongst non-Dinka is described in El-Batahani, Elbadawi, and Gadir Ali 2005, 200, 203, 204.

5. For a more in-depth exploration of these SPLA trades and networks, see Pinaud 2021.

6. *The Guardian* became quite adept at framing the conflict in such terms. For example, an article read: "Largely lacking any ideological basis, South Sudan's

conflicts have become a carousel of violence pitting rival elites from different tribes and political groupings against each other as they compete for power" (Beaumont 2018).

7. Most notably Alex De Waal, Anne Walraet, and Zachariah Mampilly.

8. The concept of "forced market" was forged by David Keen to understand famine in northern Bahr El Ghazal, whose beneficiaries were above all the army, the merchants, and elements of the Baqqara (Keen 2008, 109–11).

9. Larry Diamond recognized political corruption as being the "primary mechanism of dominant-class formation" (Diamond 1987, 579).

10. See for the links between aristocracy and nobility, Morsel 2004, 7.

11. All interviews are anonymized to protect the identity of the respondents who gave informed consent to be interviewed.

12. I borrow from Piketty's observations of wealth hyperconcentration from the Ancien Régime to the First World War in Europe. See Piketty 2014, 348–50.

13. The concept of "wealth in people" as used by Bledsoe (Bledsoe 1976).

14. See on the topic of patrimonial capitalism, particularly in nineteenth-century France and United States, Piketty 2014, 84, 115, 241.

15. Richard Sklar defined the fusion of elites as "a critical process in dominant-class formation. It identifies diverse elites (. . .) that represent various kinds and sources of power. Yet they identify with one another more firmly and in more ways than they do with their respective institutional bases or organisational activities. They appear to unite and act in concert—consciously so—on the basis of their common interest in social control, and this may be identified as the wellspring of class formation" (Sklar 1979, 538).

16. I use Thomas Piketty's definition of capital: "all forms of wealth that individuals (or groups of individuals) can own and that can be transferred or traded through the market on a permanent basis." In Piketty's definition, only in slavery can people be considered "capital" (Piketty 2014, 46). Slavery is exceptional in the sense that it is tied both to labor and to the absolute lack of choice on the slave's part (Lovejoy 1983, 4–5).

REFERENCES

Beaumont, Peter. 2018. "Born out of Brutality, South Sudan, the World's Youngest State, Drowns in Murder, Rape and Arson." *The Guardian*, June 24, 2018. https://www.theguardian.com/global-development/2018/jun/24/south-sudan-civil-war-refugees-families-flee-murder-rape-arson-nyal-global-development.

Bledsoe, Caroline. 1976. "Women's Marital Strategies among the Kpelle of Liberia." *Journal of Anthropological Research* 32 (4): 372–89.

Bloch, Marc. 1989. *Feudal Society: Social Classes and Political Organisation*. 3rd ed. Vol. II. London: Routledge.

Cooper, Frederick. 1979. "The Problem of Slavery in African Studies." *The Journal of African History* 20, no. 1: 103–25.

Diamond, Larry. 1987. "Class Formation in the Swollen African State." *The Journal of Modern African Studies* 25, no. 4: 567–96.
Duffield, Mark R. 2001. *Global Governance and the New Wars: The Merging of Development and Security*. Zed Books.
El-Batahani, Atta, Ibrahim A. Elbadawi, and Ali Abdel Gadir Ali. 2005. "Sudan's Civil War. Why Has It Prevailed for So Long?" In *Understanding Civil War: Evidence and Analysis, Vol. 1—Africa*, edited by Nicholas Sambanis and Paul Collier, 193–219. Washington, DC: The World Bank.
Elias, Norbert. 2008. "The Courtization of the Warriors." In *Early Modern Europe: Issues and Interpretations*, edited by James B. Collins and Karen L. Taylor, 385–97. Wiley-Blackwell Publishing Ltd.
"Food and Power in Sudan: A Critique of Humanitarianism." 1997. African Rights.
Goody, Jack. 1963. "Feudalism in Africa?" *Journal of African History* 4, no. 1: 1–18.
Horn of Africa. 1985. "Stated Position of the Rebels. Background and Manifesto of the Sudan People's Liberation Movement (SPLM)." 1985.
Johnson, Douglas H. 1994. *Nuer Prophets: A History of Prophecy from the Upper Nile in the Nineteenth and Twentieth Centuries*. Oxford: Clarendon Press.
———. 2007. *The Root Causes of Sudan's Civil Wars*. 2nd ed. Bloomington, IN: Indiana University Press.
———. 2011. "Twentieth-Century Civil Wars." In *The Sudan Handbook*, edited by John Ryle, Willis, Justin, Suliman Baldo, and Jok, Jok Madut, 122–32. New York: James Currey.
Keen, David. 2008. *The Benefits of Famine: A Political Economy of Famine and Relief in Southwestern Sudan, 1983–1989*. 2nd ed. Oxford: James Currey.
———. 2012. "Greed and Grievance in Civil War." *International Affairs* 88, no. 4: 757–77.
Lovejoy, Paul E. 1983. *Transformations in Slavery. A History of Slavery in Africa*. 1st ed. Cambridge: Cambridge University Press.
Mauss, Marcel. 2011. *The Gift: Forms and Functions of Exchange in Archaic Societies*. Eastford, CT: Martino Fine Books.
Morsel, Joseph. 2004. *L'Aristocratie Medievale. La domination sociale en Occident (Ve-XVe siècle)*. Histoire. Paris: Armand Colin.
Nyaba, Peter Adwok. 1997. *Politics of Liberation in South Sudan: An Insider's View*. Kampala: Fountain Publishers.
Patey, Luke A. 2010. "Crude Days Ahead? Oil and the Resource Curse in Sudan." *African Affairs* 109, no. 437: 617–36.
Piketty, Thomas. 2014. *Capital in the Twenty-First Century*. Cambridge, MA: Belknap Press of Harvard University Press.
Pinaud, Clémence. 2014. "South Sudan: Civil War, Predation and the Making of a Military Aristocracy." *African Affairs* 113, no. 451: 192–211.
———. 2015. "We Are Trained to Be Married!" Elite Formation and Ideology in the "Girls' Battalion" of the Sudan People's Liberation Army. *Journal of Eastern African Studies*, no. 9:3: 375–93.
———. 2016. "Military Kinship, Inc.: Patronage, Inter-Ethnic Marriages and Social Classes in South Sudan." *Review of African Political Economy*, June.

———. 2021. *War and Genocide in South Sudan.* Ithaca, NY: Cornell University Press.

Reno, William. 2005. "Lost in Transitions: Civil War Termination in Sub-Saharan Africa." *The American Historical Review* 120, no. 5: 1798–810.

Robertson, Claire C., and Martin Klein. 1983. *Women and Slavery in Africa.* Madison: University of Wisconsin Press.

Rolandsen, Øystein H. 2005. *Guerrilla Government: Political Changes in the Southern Sudan during the 1990s*. Uppsala: Nordic Africa Institute.

Sklar, Richard L. 1979. "The Nature of Class Domination in Africa." *The Journal of Modern African Studies* 17, no. 4: 531–52.

Strobel, Margaret. 1979. *Muslim Women in Mombasa 1890–1975*. New Haven, CT: Yale University Press.

Themnér, Anders. 2017. *Warlord Democrats in Africa Ex-Military Leaders and Electoral Politics*. Zed Books.

Tilly, Charles. 1985. "War Making and State Making as Organized Crime." In *Bringing the State Back In*, edited by Peter Evans, Dietrich Rueschemeyer, and Theda Skocpol. Cambridge: Cambridge University Press.

———. 1992. *Coercion, Capital, and European States, AD 990–1992*. 2nd ed. Cambridge: Blackwell.

De Waal, Alex. 1995. "Imposing Empowerment? Aid and Civil Institutions in Southern Sudan." African Rights.

———. 2014. "When Kleptocracy Becomes Insolvent: Brute Causes Of The Civil War In South Sudan." *African Affairs*, no. 113/452: 347–69.

Walraet, Anne. 2008a. "Governance, Violence and the Struggle for Economic Regulation in South Sudan: The Case of Budi County (Eastern Equatoria)." *Afrika Focus* 21, no. 2: 53–70.

———. 2008b. "Violence et Géographie du Pouvoir et de l'Enrichissement dans la Zone Frontière de Chukudum (Sud Soudan)." *Politique africaine* N° 111, no. 3: 90–109.

Weinstein, Jeremy M. 2007. *Inside Rebellion. The Politics of Insurgent Violence.* Cambridge: Cambridge University Press.

Woodward, Peter. 1990. *Sudan, 1898–1989: The Unstable State*. Boulder, CO: Lynne Rienner Publishers Inc.

Young, John. 2019. *South Sudan's Civil War. Violence, Insurgency and Failed Peacemaking*. London: Zed Books Ltd.

Chapter 10

Resource Wars, Oil, and the Islamic State

Philippe Le Billon

Natural resources have long attracted attention in the study of conflicts and war economies. This chapter reviews interpretations of so-called resource wars and contemporary debates about the significance of natural resources in "non-state" war economies. Dominated by sociobiological and geopolitical explanations of struggles over resources, these debates have recently benefited from more thorough empirical testing and critical perspectives. If conventional geopolitics point at major geographical factors and long-term historical patterns, critical geopolitics perspectives emphasize the framing of geographical "facts" and biased representations of "resources wars." While quantitative studies find broad patterns between resource and conflicts, political ecology perspectives emphasize their contingency and the value of local historical context within resource-based political economies. If defense studies have long emphasized the strategic dimensions of resources, including for the conduct of warfare, more recent perspectives have emphasized the impacts of resource wealth on conflict likelihood and the importance of resources as a source of funding for both state and non-state armed groups. By the turn of the century, the narrative of greedy warlords motivated by resource loot came to dominate the study of "resource wars," with the idea that war was a means of enrichment, rather than resources being mobilized to sustain politically motivated armed struggles. In addition, conflicts in "resource-rich" countries frequently came to be interpreted as the deadly outcome of a "resource curse." This chapter revisits some of the key arguments around resources wars, then turns to the specific dimensions associated with "non-state" actors, and finally examines the case of relationships between oil, conflicts, and the Islamic State in Iraq and Syria.

RESOURCE WAR STUDIES

Scholarly enquiries about resources and early warfare in pre-agricultural societies have largely focused on the role of material self-interest, the forms of conflict, the organization and the sedentarization of social groups, as well as the relative availability, density, and predictability of resources (Ember and Ember 1992; Kelly 2000). Ethnographic, archaeological, as well as evolutionary and comparative social ecology studies associate early warfare with the territorial control of abundant resources (mostly food) and uncertainty about resource access. The transition to agriculture and exploitation of resources that reshaped relations between human groups and with the "natural world" are often understood as one of the main factors in the frequency of warfare. Contrary to neo-Malthusian narratives associating conflicts with scarce resources (Le Billon 2015a), evidence points that resource abundance and higher population densities would bring about territorialization processes involving conflicts over trespass or intrusion. In contrast, areas with scarce resources and low population densities would see mutually beneficial cooperation rather than conflicts.

In common with the classical period, contemporary Western geopolitical perspectives on resources have been dominated by the equation of trade, war, and power (Findlay and O'Rourke 2007). Beyond gold-focused conquest, colonial plantation economies of tropical slave-produced commodities became the core of Western imperial extension. The importance of resource flows for industrialization and militarization—most notably coal, iron, and later oil—reinforced an ideology of resource competition among European powers, found notably in the flurry of studies over access to raw materials distribution during the first half of the twentieth century, and especially between the two World Wars (Westing 1988). The growing assertiveness of Third World states during the 1960s–1970s transformed the political landscape of sovereignty over natural resources and provided a (new) twist on ideologies of "resource wars," with, for example, some Arab states leveraging their oil production in the form of an export embargo against some pro-Israeli states. By the 1970s, broader geopolitical conceptualizations of security-incorporated issues such as population growth, environmental degradation, and social inequalities in poor countries. The ensuing concept of "environmental security" came about to reflect ideas of global interdependence, illustrated through the debates on environmental "limits to growth," political instability supposedly caused by environmental scarcity in the South, and more recently the consequences of climate change. The concept, however, represented for some a skewed and controversial "securitization" of environmental issues, calling for "military" and "international development" solutions, and constructing biased identities and narratives of endangerment in the Anthropocene that often blamed the poor (Dalby 2009). With the end of the Cold War, a view emerged that violent scrambles for resources among state and non-state armed groups were a major feature of contemporary conflicts, particularly given the decline of foreign-state sponsorship and ideology (Weinstein 2006; Le Billon 2013). The idea of economically driven wars in which looting and other forms of illicit economic gains rose to prominence (Keen 1997), both as an enabling factor within a rebellion feasibility framework, or as a motivational factor in the "greed versus grievances" framework (Collier and Hoeffler 1998). Concerns over the supply of strategic raw materials, but also agricultural land, increased in the context of rising commodity prices during the first decade of the twenty-first century, and as China challenged U.S. hegemony and multiplied overseas investments (Le Billon and Cervantes 2009). Many accounts of "resource wars" thus became associated with a combination of rapidly increasing demand for raw materials, growing resource shortages, and contested resource ownership (Klare 2008).

Mainstream accounts of "resource wars" have thus relied on two often-intertwined explanations. The first set of explanations identifies resources as crucial factors for the conduct of warfare itself and the prospect of victory. In this perspective, resources achieve a "strategic" status through their material properties, but also the financial opportunities associated with their exploitation and control. The second casts resources as a motivational factor for armed conflicts. Raiding, looting, pillaging, grabbing, capturing, annexing, and conquering all carry a sense of violent dispossession and appropriation of resources. Such motivational dimension can be mistaken for the consequences of social behavior during or after the conflict; state-led military annexation and house looting by individual soldiers being both violent dispossession, but differing in scale, intentionality, means, and outcomes. While resource "looting" may frequently happen, this does not automatically explain the conflict *in itself* (as a motivational or conditional factor, notably for its onset). Rather than being a motivating cause of the conflict, resource looting can be seen as an expression of the opportunities arising from conflict and its modus operandi. These two main explanations—often merged in conceptions of resources as loot or military means—continue to dominate much of the media, policy, and scholarly literature on resources and human conflicts. Such perspectives are most notably alive in conventional geopolitical perspectives defining "resource wars" as armed conflicts revolving around the control of "critical" or "lucrative" raw materials, which in turn give way to a narrow and militaristic notion of "resource security." These interpretive frameworks have been particulary prevalent for conflicts in Africa (especially West and Central Africa, see, for example, "The Enough Project") and in the Middle East. These perspectives have contributed to popular geopolitics already portraying war-affected regions through their resources (e.g., Angola,

DR Congo, or the "oil-rich Mideast," see Le Billon 1999; Le Billon and Shykora 2020). They have also contributed to reproducing relatively simplistic narratives facilitating the work of journalists and advocacy organizations (e.g., greed-driven warlords), the apparent "action-ability" of policy options (e.g., commodity sanctions), and linkages with the audience's consumerism and predominant economic mindset (see Le Billon 2006; Autesserre 2012).

Summing up the main theoretical perspectives on resources and wars, Benedikt Korf (2011) identifies four main perspectives. Perspectives drawing from Hobbesian arguments conceptualize resource conflicts as rational individualism in the absence of authority. Neo-Malthusian perspectives combine Hobbesian arguments with the anxieties of seeing "modern" progress and demographic growth (e.g., "surplus population," "youth bulge") overtake nature's pace and resulting in scarcity-induced resource conflicts. Utilitarian perspectives deriving in part from rational choice arguments suggest that opportunities associated with resources—such as the financial benefits of resource loot—affect conflict feasibility or shape "resource supply security" approaches. Building on Schmitt, a final set of perspectives suggest that historically complex identity narratives become in part reified through resource conflicts, which therefore should not be seen in isolation from their broader historical context. Overall, critical perspectives point out that most accounts of "resource wars" tend to simplify the causes of war, pathologize conflicts, politically delegitimate rebellion, criminalize small-scale resource exploitation and livelihood coping mechanisms (Lahiri-Dutt 2006; Le Billon 2013). Rather than questioning the dominant modes of production that gave way to conflicts involving resources, such accounts of "resource wars" tend to prioritize corporate-led economic growth over local livelihoods and environmental practices, reflecting broader interests associated with capitalist modes of production and wealth distribution. As a result, many "post-conflict" policy framing and "reconstruction" practices reproduce previous exploitative production models, facilitate "white-collar" crime such as corruption and tax evasion, securitize resource sectors through repressive forms of resource enclosures, and increase socioeconomic inequalities (Le Billon and Levin 2009; Pugh et al. 2016; Le Billon 2014, 2018).

Studies seeking to provide more nuanced and historically grounded analyses have emphasized the complex power relations around natural resources, understanding violence "as a site-specific phenomenon rooted in local histories and social relations yet connected to larger processes of material transformation and power relations" (Peluso and Watts 2001, 5; Springer and Le Billon 2016). Political ecology approaches to "resources wars" have notably made several contributions (Le Billon 2015a). First, by reconceptualizing scarcity, abundance, and dependence both historically and spatially, notably by focusing on the influence of social identities and uneven power relations on resource rights, and by demonstrating how violence—as an ongoing process involving symbolic, structural, and direct dimensions—reshapes conditions of access and control over resources, as well as the distribution of impacts from resource exploitation (Martinez-Alier 2003). Second, by questioning not only at which location but also at what scales are conflicts occurring, and recognizing the chronic and multi-scalar character of many resource-related conflicts (Watts 2004). Third, by engaging with the material and the discursive dimensions of ecological processes and resource sectors, thereby enabling an analysis sensitive to the interplay of evolving biophysical process and historically contingent mechanisms producing quasi-hegemonic truth discourses. These "regimes of truth" sustain and seek to legitimate often environmentally unsustainable and socially regressive resource-based processes of capitalist accumulation. Fourth, by accounting for a broader range of violence than geopolitical and political perspectives, thereby understanding different types of conflicts and multiple forms of violence. Fifth, by recognizing resources as material objects influencing socio-material practices, and as social subjects endowed with a set of character(istics) through "spokespersons" such as campaigners, local communities or resource companies granting them a "voice"; this combination of material enablement and social voice constitutes a form of (indirect) agency—as recognized in the concept of the "actant" coming from an Actor-Network Theory perspective (see Latour 1987). Sixth, by broadening the range of connections and actors involved, political ecology approaches allow for some degree of accountability beyond the immediate perpetrators of physical violence. Connections between resources and various forms of violence, in this regard, not only include commodification processes (i.e., how "things"—or people—become resources or commodities defined by their use and exchange values), but also fetishization ones (i.e., how imaginative aspects of resource production and consumption affect power relations and associated forms of violence).

To sum up, academic perspectives on resources and conflicts, and more specifically on resources and war economies are diverse yet broadly fall within two main categories. A mostly positivist one associates conflicts related to resources with rational competitive behavior linked with the economic or subsistence value of resources: people driven by need or greed fight over resources. A more post-structuralist category associates conflicts with historically contingent material and discursive practices shaping conflictual social relations over resources. While the first one often tends to depoliticize "resource conflicts," the second one seeks to repoliticize them. As discussed below, such relative (de)politicization is particularly important with regard to non-state war economies, as state and corporate actors generally seek to delegitimize non-state armed groups.

RESOURCES, NON-STATE ARMED GROUPS, AND WAR ECONOMIES

The conventional geopolitics literature on resource wars has mostly focused on state actors and the risk of inter-state wars, with non-state armed groups being generally considered as proxy forces. In contrast, "greed wars" or "warlords" narratives have specifically examined non-state armed groups (NSAGs), with for example that argument that some NSAGs pragmatic focus on the territorial control of resource-rich areas and key transportation routes but are not interested in formally establishing states as this would result in fewer relative rewards and bring on more costly responsibilities (see Reno 1999). Some of the main statistical findings in this regard have emphasized the role that resources can play, first in prolonging hostilities as continued plunder would take priority over ending conflict through military victory or negotiations and assuming state responsibilities, second in incentivizing recruitment among materially motivated individuals, and third in lowering economic dependence on local populations and thus aggravating human rights abuses against civilians (Weinstein 2006). Studies of the level of resource extraction by rebel groups have also suggested that NSAGs intensify resource extraction when they are actively competing with government authorities or other groups to establish their authority over a given territory (Haass 2020).

Studies on resources and non-state war economies over the past two decades have brought several insights (Le Billon 2001, 2013; Ross 2004; Walsh et al. 2018). The first is to demonstrate the broad range of resources involved, from narcotics to gemstones but also wildlife products, the diverse methods of access to funding, from direct exploitation to extortion and the tapping of royalty revenues allocated to municipal budgets, as well as the many relations involved, including the mobilization of a labor force or cooperation with organized crime (Nordstrom 2004; Laudati 2013). Furthermore, while many of these studies understandably focus on resources, they can do so at the risk of overstating the relative significance of resources, both in terms of the revenues generated and the impacts associated with resources (Autesserre 2012), as well as some of the ideological motivations that could push NSAGs to tax populations even in the presence of valuable resource (Revkin 2020).

The second is to point at the effects of resource-based economies on NSAGs, in terms of funding, recruitment, behavior toward civilians, longevity, and conflict outcome (Weinstein 2006). Many of these effects relate to the material and social conditions within local resource areas, but also the broader political economy of the resources and social relations tied to resource exploitation. Civil wars involving oil, for example, are more likely to be prolonged and severe if oil fields are within the conflict zone as rebel roots and presence in disputed oil fields offer both funding and legitimating narratives for (secessionist) insurgents (Lujala 2010). Conflicts also tend to last longer when NSAGs are able to derive revenue from the smuggling of resources, but not from extortion targeting resource extraction (Conrad et al. 2019). More broadly, resources can also affect the territorial discourses and practices of NSAGs, with resource wealth motivating rebel territorialization, but also drawing greater counterinsurgency efforts.

The third is to highlight frequent links between non-state and state armed groups for the sake of ensuring resource flows within the country and the broader region (Reno 1999). Even if central state authorities officially seek to curtail access to resources and associated financial flows, linkages are very frequent as a result of corruption or co-optation of individual officials or organizations (from high-level political corruption over resource contracts to petty bribe payments at checkpoints), as extortion payments to NSAGs are made by state authorized resource companies, or by local government authorities (e.g., municipalities), as processes of desertion, rebellion, reintegration through which NSAGs move in and out of the status of state (affiliated) armed group, notably through bidding processes, as the need to maintain food or fuel supplies to combat units or civilian populations requires accommodation between contending parties, and as businesses seek to profit from, and arrange for resource smuggling and illicit financial flows.

The fourth is that resource-related wartime and peacetime economies often blend. Temporally, some of the networks involved in the extraction and trading of "conflict commodities" were established during peacetime, while some of the wartime networks can survive the transition to peace. Geographically, areas along the commodity chain are frequently under different levels of hostilities, so that while the point of resource extraction may be a disputed territory under NSAG control, the point of export may be firmly under the control of the government and not affected by hostilities. Monetarily, the fungibility of resources often allows for a laundering of "conflict resources," so that a "blood tainted" mineral may pass as a legitimate one further down the value chain. Legally, contractual agreements either passed prior to, or during the war, as well as related resource production and trading activities can often survive, as companies seek to adapt to the wartime circumstances and seek security agreements with NSAGs. Institutionally, equity stakes and other forms of interest in resource projects are often allocated to former senior rebel commanders, including through ministerial portfolio distribution following peace agreements. Ethically, widespread postwar "white-collar crime" takes place, including resource-related corruption, fraud, nepotism, money-laundering, land/resource dispossession such as resource-based economic activities of paramilitary groups (Le Billon 2018). Financially, budgetary allocations by government and non-state groups can maintain a "warlike" budget following peace negotiations, including clandestine financial flows and a disproportionate allocation of payroll to (former) soldiers, in effect protracting the war economy into peacetime. Politically, resource-based transactions, including the redistribution of proceeds, are constitutive of both wartime and "post-conflict" political relations. As such, resource sectors and former rebels should only be considered through the lens of criminality, but be accounted for as political agents, including through the effects of "corrupt" practices (Reno 2008, 2009).

The fifth contribution is to highlight the broad range of actors involved in resource-based war economies, including local civilian populations and regional migrants involved in resource production/extraction; businesses funding these activities and trading resources both domestically and internationally; large companies transforming and distributing these resources; international organizations operating in conflict-affected countries; consumers purchasing resources; and regulators throughout the commodity chain. Not all of these actors are aware of their role in a "war economy," and even if so, they may not decide to address this contribution unless forced or incentivized to do so as a result of sanctions, certification schemes, or reputational risks (Sarfaty 2015).

Finally, some of the studies on the role of resources in non-state war economies have contributed to nuancing the experience of local populations in relation to NSAGs, in contrast to "greed war" narratives either ignoring their involvement and the potential benefits derived from resource-based war economies, or focusing on some of the worst cases of human rights abuses (e.g., forced labor). Participation in resource economies during period of recurring hostilities is often risky and indeed rife with human rights abuses. Yet, such participation offers a means of survival and even successful entrepreneurship as the conditions of access to resources, and competitiveness among resource purchasers, can at times be more "open" than during periods of stable political order, effective enforcement of resource management regulations, and market monopolies (Chingono 2000). Violence against civilians by armed groups will in part depend on the conditions of access to, and control of, labor, as well as the level of acceptance of the armed groups among civilians and livelihood opportunities; with armed groups at times having to create incentives to attract workforce and investments. The exploitation or regulation of resources by non-state armed groups can also relatively improve the living conditions of local populations, including through resources being made available to local populations and resource revenues sustaining welfare and public services, thereby reinforcing the groups' relative legitimacy and consolidating their "proto-state" (Podder 2013; Bojicic-Dzelilovic and Turkmani 2018).

This brief overview points to several important points for the study of the war economies of NSAGs. As discussed below, resources need to be given attention, but their relative significance should not lead to oversimplifying narratives. Although mostly financial, the significance of resources goes beyond monetary aspects, and includes livelihoods, control of territories, and a complex network of participants. Political dimensions also need to be given attention, in contrast with much of the literature emphasizing greed or scarcity as driving factors. This, in short, calls for a re-politicization of war economies, yet one that is not naïve enough to fail considering the economic incentives of many of the actors involved in resource-based war economies. The case of the Islamic State in Iraq and Syria is exemplary in this respect. Despite the strong ideological dimensions of the armed group, and its strongly stated desire and many practices demonstrating its commitment to create a state, many of the discursive and material engagement with oil-related issues connected with ISIS were dealt with through a depoliticizing lens. Such depoliticization was in part necessary to address several tensions, including the historical motive of Western presence in the region, the role of oil-rich governments and individuals in the conflicts, the ideological discourse of ISIS and its resonance with some of the earlier criticism by bin Laden and al-Qaeda of the corrupt and highly unequal regional political economy of oil, and the complex interplay of allies and enemies in oil smuggling networks.

RECONSIDERING "MIDEAST OIL WARS": THE CASE OF THE ISLAMIC STATE IN IRAQ AND SYRIA

On February 15, 2003, millions of people gathered in hundreds of cities around the world to oppose a U.S. and British-led military invasion of Iraq. Among their main slogans was "no more blood for oil." War, early critics argued, would bring a U.S.-compliant regime and open up Iraq's massive oil wealth to U.S. and British companies: the world's fifth largest oil reserves at 140 billion barrels, and potentially among the most profitable given their relatively low technical production costs (Le Billon and El Khatib 2004). Six years after the fall of Baghdad to U.S. troops in April 2003, American and British oil companies were indeed signing major oil exploitation contracts in Iraq for increasing the production of three "super-giant" Iraqi oil fields—Rumaila, West Qurna, and Majnoon—while junior oil companies had already taken the opportunity of investing in the Kurdistan Region of Iraq at the invitation of its largely autonomous Regional Government. Concern for a U.S. "oil grab" was also broadly shared within Iraq, where oil nationalization in the 1960s remained widely perceived as a proud historical achievement and a guarantee of future sovereignty.

A foreign takeover of Iraq's oil wealth and the application of neoliberal policies—premised on the failure of statist policies, the inefficiency and corruption of the public sector, and the need for foreign capital—were at the core of the contested politics of Iraq's oil wealth (Le Billon 2005; Mahdi 2007; Muttit 2011). But contestations extend well beyond the role of BP, Exxon, Shell, or Occidental, and whether the U.S. invasion was indeed an "oil grab." Iraq's vast oil wealth is unevenly distributed across Iraq's territory, and as sectarian tensions grew in prominence, so did the politics of revenue distribution between the different regions. The contested politics of oil are often seen through a simplistic and dangerous narrative associating the largest oil reserves with Shiite areas of southern Iraq, and to a lesser extent in the borderlands of the Kurdish region, raising concern that Shiites and Kurds would benefit from Iraq's dismemberment at the expense of the Sunnis (Le Billon 2015b). Discontent rose among Sunni populations against the inept, corrupt, and increasingly sectarian rule of the Shiite central government under Prime Minister Al Maliki from 2006 to 2014. As institutional avenues for greater federalism were denied, Iraq did become de facto increasingly "dismembered," with the central government losing control of much of the western provinces of Anbar and Nineveh to Sunni militias and al-Qaeda outfits. The conflicts eventually merged with Syria's civil war against the regime of Bashar al-Assad through the emergence of the Islamic State in Iraq and Syria (ISIS/ISIL/IS/Daech) as al-Zarqawi's al-Qaeda in Iraq took control of Raqqa from Jihadi group Al Nusra. The rise of ISIS increased international attention to the civil war in Syria and its causes, including themes around climate change-related conflicts, thereby contributing to a dangerous narrative linking fossil fuels, carbon emissions, droughts, refugee populations, and terrorism (see Selby et al. 2017).

Although al-Qaeda had by now become a more visibly "oil-funded" terrorist organized in an "oil cursed" country, some of the arguments about yet another "oil war" in the Middle East proved more difficult to promote than usual in the face of ISIS' strong ideology and its attempts at creating a state rather than profiteering from the war (see Le Billon 2020). As discussed below, ISIS thus represents an important case for the study of oil-related conflicts and war economies. The following section first briefly describes ISIS' oil economy and then discusses the relevance of major mechanisms potentially linking oil and armed conflicts.

ISIS' OIL ECONOMY

Active in Iraq since at least August 2003, five months after the U.S. invasion of Iraq, al-Qaeda in Iraq (AQI) begun to regularly access oil revenues by 2006 as it increased its presence on the ground and announced its transformation into the

Islamic State of Iraq (Hamdan 2016). Drawn most notably from the smuggling of oil products out of the Bayji refinery located half-way between Baghdad and Mosul, these revenues were notably used to seek a consolidation of ISIS' presence in Sunni Arab governorates. The US "surge" and "Awakening movement" launched in 2007 undermined AQI's operations, but by 2012 AQI was gaining more widespread support as Sunni protests against Maliki's government become more vocal. That same year, ISI officially declared the formation of the Islamic State of Iraq and Syria through a takeover of Jabhat al-Nusra l'Ahl as Sham, against the will of the local commander. This move greatly increased access to oil when ISIS seized several of the main Syrian oil fields near Deir ez-Zor in 2014. At its apex in late 2014 and early 2015, ISIS controlled about 100,000 km^2 territories within Iraq and Syria, including oil and gas fields, pipelines, tankers routes, and refineries (see Engel 2015; Solomon et al. 2015).

ISIS' "wartime" oil and gas sector represented an attempt to centralize the control of oil flows and revenues while enrolling a vast and diverse array of private entrepreneurs as well as some Syrian government power utilities (Almohamad and Dittmann 2016; Center for the Analysis of Terrorism 2016). For this, ISIS built previously developed fields and infrastructure, extensive preexisting oil "smuggling" networks establishing during previous hostilities and the UN sanctions regime, a militarized control of oil and gas regions, and both local and regional markets for crude oil, liquid fuels, and natural gas. Having peaked in June 2014 with a production of about 70,000 barrels per day, sold at a discounted price of around $30 per barrel (compared to $110/bbl international spot for Brent/WTI average at times), ISIS' production then declined until its shutdown in late 2017 (Philips 2014; Do et al. 2018).

ISIS' loss of Mosul, Raqqa, and finally Deir ez-Zor in late 2017 confined much of ISIS to remote rural insurgency in western Syria, and terrorist attacks. ISIS' "oil era" in the region thus lasted for about four years with a peak in late 2014, followed by a gradual decline until it reached an end by mid-2017. Not only did the volume of oil under production under ISIS control declined during that period, but oil prices at least on external markets had been comparatively much lower with collapse of global oil prices in 2014. This was compounded by rising production costs and growing inefficiencies within the sector as infrastructures were progressively destroyed and replaced by makeshift installations such as micro-scale refineries, yet partially counterbalanced in terms of revenues by higher local prices due to relative ffuel scarcity. As discussed below, oil was overall an important component of ISIS' "rebel economy" yet in more diverse and financially limited ways than often portrayed.

ISIS's oil "war economy" required handling some major issues (Enders 2012; Solomon et al. 2015; Almohamad and Dittmann 2016). First, it entailed taking control of oil fields from incumbent armed groups, including through turf wars with local "oil mafia" and arrangements with local tribes, rebuilding and adapting to aerial bombing, and defending key infrastructures from a takeover by ground troops, especially from Kurdish and later on Iraqi federal forces, but also Syrian government forces. Several key fields and infrastructures repeatedly changed hands, thus requiring the recurrent allocation of fighters to relatively vulnerable assets. Second, ISIS' oil economy required the organization of production, refining and transportation flows, including the recruitment of staff, supply of spare parts, refining, trucking, and distribution network through ISIS owned and private fleets, but also crucially through Syrian government pipelines and power plants. Third, ISIS had to manage the oil sector, including oil prices, with the diverging aims of increasing revenues while maintaining prices low enough for the population (and export markets), but with sufficient profit incentives for private sector involvement in a context of increased risk and low international prices. Fourth, ISIS had to address corruption and fraud within the oil sector, including risks of corruption, nepotism, and embezzlement within its own administration (e.g., favoritism toward some private oil traders), as well as cases of fraud on the part of traders and the need to bribe officials to access foreign markets. Finally, there were significant socio-environmental impacts of the reshaping of the Syrian oil economy in the context of the war on ISIS as the unavailability or destruction of larger-scale refineries had led to the multiplication of artisanal refineries with high environmental and health impacts.

Oil production in Syria and Iraq under ISIS control accounted for about 50,000 barrels per day (bpd) in the second half of 2014, and around 62,000 bpd in 2015. This compared to about 4 million bpd for Iraqi-controlled government fields, 0.5 million bpd for Iraqi Kurds (KRG), 15,000 bpd for Syrian Kurds, and 10,000 bpd for the Syrian government in Damascus in mid-2016 (Almohamad and Dittmann 2016). Estimates of ISIS oil revenues have varied widely over the previous two years, ranging from $300,000 to $3 million per day. About 80 percent of oil revenues collected at the production stage comes from the two fields of Tanak and Omar in Deir ez-Zor Governorate in eastern Syria, which were operated by the Al Furat Petroleum Company (AFPC), a Shell-led consortium founded in 1985 including the Syrian Petroleum Company (SPC) and Bergomo (a joint venture between the Oil and Natural Gas Corporation of India and the China National Petroleum Corporation).[1] AFPC was put under sanctions by the EU in December 2011, leading Shell to leave Syria, but with little consequences for the company as its production share was only about 13,000 bpd.

Having already lost control of most of the governorate's countryside, the Assad government lost control of these oil and gas fields to rebel groups and local tribe militias in November 2012. Infighting and ad hoc arrangements then took place between different rebel groups, many of them national army defectors and militia from local tribes seeking to secure their own fuel supplies and generate some revenues. Local tribal leaders generally claimed oil fields within their territory (*wajeh*), sending militias to control individual wellheads, drill into pipelines for bunkering, and trying to find staff and equipment to maintain production. Oil was sold to local traders, sometimes for as low as $5 per barrel, while natural gas was shipped to government power plant to generate electricity, and much of the liquid petroleum gas was given as "protection money" to al-Qaeda-affiliated Jabhat Al Nusra, reported to be the most powerful rebel group in the area at the time (Abdul-Ahad 2013). This period was reported as marked by lawlessness and violent competition between more ideologically driven rebel groups, including ISIS, and "oil thieves" or local warlords seeking to control oil fields, to tax road transportation and escort oil truckers, and to directly engage in smuggling. Some official rebel commanders denounced the effects of this new entitlement over oil wealth, with one arguing by May 2013 that "[i]t is all selfishness. The revolution vanished in Deir al-Zor since we tasted the oil, it is a curse," with another adding that "[t]he rebels do not want to clash with anyone right now. It is a tribal province and anything could backfire against the rebels—who themselves are sons of tribes" (Karouny 2013).

This early period saw little effort on the part of foreign powers to intervene. Having imposed an import embargo on Syrian crude in September 2011, the EU selectively lifted it in April 2013 by allowing EU importers to buy crude if authorized by the Syrian National Coalition (SNC) in order for the EU-recognized group "to take advantage of the oil and gas reserves under its control" (Pawlak and Croft 2015). Yet the SNC controlled very few oil fields, many of which were instead under the control of tribal militias and "oil thieves" with no affiliation with the SNC and who had no financial interest to give a cut to the SNC unless higher prices for oil could be obtained through such legalized channels.

By November 2013, al Nusra was reported to have taken more direct control of much of the oil fields in the province (Enders 2012; Al Jazeera 2013), while government troops continued to hold major parts of the provincial capital city. Seemingly losing ground at the time, ISIS launched a series of offensives against competing rebel groups and local tribes starting with a briefly successful operation to capture the al-Jafra oil field and Koniko gas factory on March 27–29, 2014. ISIS was then able to control and hold the towns of Markadah, Albu Kamal (on the border with Iraq), the al-Kharrat terminal, and most of the northern part of the province. Reinforced by troops and weapons seized after the fall of Mosul on June 10–11, 2014, ISIS took control of nearly all of the province, with al Nusra militants relinquishing the control of oil fields, including al-Omar, sometimes without any fight. Several armed factions also pledged alliance to ISIS, significantly bolstering the movement. Beyond fighting and military intimidation, these territorial gains had also been facilitated through politically weakening tribal groups, notably by co-opting "young tribal leaders by offering to share oil and smuggling revenues and promising them positions of authority currently held by their elders" (Weiss and Hassan 2016). Already legitimated among some of the population through their participation in the fight against Assad, some of these young leaders became the new relay for ISIS.[2]

ISIS did face resistance from some tribal groups, and was reported to have perpetrated a series of massacres against members of the Shaitat tribe—which had opposed it and reportedly controlled about twenty-one oil wells (Abdallah 2015). In one of its videos, ISIS explained that it had to fight against "oil thieves," whose financial interests were threatened by the group. By the end of August 2014, ISIS seemed firmly in control of all oil fields in Deir ez-Zor but for a few minor fields south of the Euphrates controlled by the government. ISIS then extended its control toward the oil fields of al-Hasaka Province, located to the north and closer to Kurdish/YPG-controlled areas. ISIS was able to add about 20,000 barrels per day of oil production through capturing some of the most province's southern oil fields (e.g., Margada, Al Jubaissah, Gouna, Tishreen, and Al Hol fields), several of which were lost in early 2016. Within Iraq, ISIS took he the Baiji refinery during the second half of 2014, seized relatively minor oil fields, and established control over smuggling routes to Jordan.

ISIS sold a large part of the oil it controlled directly to traders coming to the fields. Those, in turn, sold it to mostly small private refiners, which had the advantage of increasing civilian presence (and thus limiting air strikes, at least from a U.S.-led coalition seeking to avoid civilian deaths) and tapping into existing and new private entrepreneurship while reducing the need for ISIS to use its own recruits. Refiners then sold part of their refined products to the ISIS administration. ISIS did maintain some tanker trucks, refineries, and gas stations, and it taxed the sale of oil at local markets ($0.67/barrel). Yet, it was generally reported to be almost "completely disengaged from the trade" of oil across Syria and Iraq (Solomon et al. 2015). In May 2015, the U.S. military raided the compound of ISIS' Deir ez-Zor oil manager Ben Awn al-Murad al Tunisi ("Abu Sayyaf"), killing him and seizing much information on his running of the oil sector in eastern Syria (Faucon and Coker 2016). With better knowledge of the working of the sector, the U.S. bombed facilities at the al-Omar oil fields in October 2015. Many ISIS-controlled oil fields facilities as well as truck tankers and refineries were targeted by both U.S.-led and Russian air forces. For a senior state department, the goal was literally to bomb ISIS' oil sector into backwardness, "Google Earth is my friend sometimes, and you can see across territories that a year ago was just flat desert or flat open area and now [following bombardment] is hundreds if not thousands of small pits, stills [used to refine crude oil]. And part of that is moving the [ISIS oil] operation from a 20th-to-21st century operation to a 17th century operation."[3]

Bombings increased reliance on makeshift refineries—small kilns heating crude oil and cooling petrol vapors through iron pipes sunk in small water-cooled ponds. This highly decentralized system possibly reduced rents for militias, increased local employment, but had major negative health and environmental impacts. As succinctly put by a twenty-six-year-old graduate from al-Furat University in Deir ez-Zor who had already been for a year and a half at one of the many makeshift oil refineries around Tall Alu, "We only earn $15 a day but get cancer for free" (Bader 2014). This reshaping of the oil sector, and in particular the multiplication of micro-scale refining not only meant that oil was more complicated for ISIS to manage and control, but that it also gave rise to an independent (under)class of petty entrepreneurs who were often disgruntled at ISIS. As forcefully explained by a makeshift refinery owner,

> I cover my face [not only because of oil fumes, but also] because of the armed mercenaries [Islamic rebels]. They can just take you and behead you. They accuse people of being regime's Shahiba, Kurdish YPG, or whatever. They have brought nothing else other than destruction. They behead people like if they behead chickens. Islamic state or whatever. God shall not help them. We have nothing that they could come for here. People are starving to death here. . . . They do not let the people live alone. This is a failed revolution. It should no longer be called a revolution. It is robbery, larceny and burglary . . . . This is not life we are living. Why do we have to decay this way? (Ahmad 2015)

Further to the north in Kurdish-controlled areas, the YPG had set margins in the refining business so as to ensure that much of the activity went to Arab entrepreneurs and remained profitable, thereby providing a way to "buying their loyalty" (Bader 2014).

Like many other armed groups, ISIS had also made arrangements with many actors within the region in order to enable financial and resource flows. ISIS regularly dealt with the regime in Damascus to deliver oil and gas supplies, notably to power plants, thereby ensuring the provision of energy to key population areas (Kenar and Soylu 2016). As the engineer in charge of the main gas-processing plant near Deir ez-Zor explained in mid-2013 while al-Nusra was still in charge of most oil and gas fields, "the regime [in Damascus] wants production regardless of who is in control. I pump gas to the government and give the LPG gas to the terrorists" (Abdul-Ahad 2013). Arrangements were also made to facilitate shipments in the region, including Turkey and Kurdish areas in Iraq, which mobilized extensive smuggling networks.

Oil smuggling builds upon trading patterns dating back to at least the Mandate period when local entrepreneurs and members from cross-border communities sought to evade newly established international boundaries and high tariffs (Herbert 2014). Goods included commercial products, livestock, as well as hashish and opium. Syrian state complicity into smuggling increased during its twenty-nine-year occupation of Lebanon, and again during the 1990s to help Iraq bypass UN sanctions, especially with regard to oil exports and weapons imports, which proved very lucrative for the government. By late 2011, border control by the Syrian government started collapsing, especially along the Turkish border with rebel forces and criminal gangs benefiting from smuggling incomes, including human trafficking, and easier access to goods and weapons. Oil smuggling intensified and shifted to mostly crude oil exports rather than simply cheaper refined products. In late 2013, some former Syrian fighters who had taken refuge in Turkey got involved in smuggling, an activity that long predated the civil war in Syria. As one of them argued (cited in Giglio 2014), "You can't really say that we are smuggling oil, because we take permission from the Turkish side and the Syrian side . . . . But since it's under the table, we call it smuggling." In contrast, getting permission from ISIS generally meant pledging allegiance, and exclusively working under the rules of the organization, with ISIS killing smugglers secretly continuing activities on their own (Giglio 2014).

Looking more broadly at the effects of oil on governance, Weiss and Hassan (2016) suggest that "ISIS has wedded its authoritarian governance to a remarkably successful war economy," distributing oil revenues to towns under its control to provide services. ISIS was also reported to fix the price of refined products, making it (at least initially) more reliable and affordable for local populations to purchase, and in particular for farmers to run their tractors and pumps, thereby improving local agricultural production, but only for Sunni Arab farmers as others either fled or were expelled and their lands seized and rented (Callimachi 2018). The economic effect of the airstrikes on ISIS oil revenues is not obvious, since prices increased as production declined due to a closed market effect. While production was down by an estimated 30 percent, prices doubled, suggesting a possible increase of 40 percent in revenues for ISIS, though much of this could be accounted for traders and refiners absorbing the costs of staff killed, assets destroyed, and higher inefficiencies in the supply chain. Moreover, strikes on oil infrastructure meant that both higher prices and supply constraints affecting civilian populations could be blamed on the United States and Russia, rather than on the inability of ISIS to deliver fuel (Lister 2014). Anecdotally, some ISIS members seem to have personally benefited, notably by purchasing diesel fuel at one-sixth of the price for civilians and then running lucrative electricity provision businesses. By mid-2017, with its territorial losses rapidly increasing, ISIS focused on drawing out as much revenues from oil fields it still controlled and finding ways to transfer convertible currency abroad for future actions (Solomon and Mhidi 2017). By October 2017, ISIS tribal fighters were reported to have handed Syria's largest oil field, al-Omar, to the U.S.-backed and Kurdish-led Syrian Democratic Forces, in advance of the Syrian government (Aboufadel 2017; Barnard 2017). This move was notably described by Iranian media as part of a wider U.S. strategy of resource control in the region (Webb 2018). Similarly, U.S. media reported on the profit-sharing arrangements made between the Syrian regime and Russian companies for oil and gas fields seized from ISIS using contract soldiers (Kramer 2017).

ISIS AND OIL-RELATED CONFLICT MECHANISMS

The case of ISIS can inform studies of oil-related conflicts. Building on the literature on conflicts and natural resources (Ross 2004; Humphreys 2006; Le Billon 2013), and specifically oil (Colgan 2013), we briefly sum up findings relating to key mechanisms identified as linking oil and armed conflicts, for both state and non-state armed groups (see table 10.1).[4]

Resource Wars

As mentioned above, both the U.S. and British governments had concerns over access to Iraqi oil fields in case UN sanctions were to be lifted with Saddam Hussein still in power. Yet the U.S. invasion of Iraq could not be resumed to an "oil war" (Meierding 2016), from which ISIS would have emerged. With regard to ISIS, the militant group did integrate the oil sector into its short-term tactics and long-term strategic objectives. Yet, ISIS did not seek to establish a caliphate in order to reap the rewards of a petrostate. Its discourses point to a vision that does not mobilize the tropes of oil-funded modernization espoused by many of the previous regional rulers (from the Shah of Iran to Saddam Hussein and monarchs of Sunni emirates). Although some testimonies pointed at the relative luxury in which some ISIS elite members lived (Townsend 2014), the movement seems to have been guided by a strong integrity agenda and ascetic values.

Petro-Aggression

Given its revolutionary agenda, access to greater oil wealth would have likely led ISIS to pursue its expansionist agenda over the region, at least for Sunni areas. ISIS' initial expansion in 2014, however, did not initially rely on oil revenues, although it did contribute to consolidating its territorial rule

Table 10.1 Main Mechanisms Associating Oil and Armed Conflicts

Mechanisms	*Description*	*Findings*
Resource war	Oil reserves (or perceived oil reserves) raise the payoff to territorial conquest.	Yes, especially from the perspective of a large regional caliphate, but not from the perspective of a Sunni Arab area straddling the relatively oil-poor Syrian-Iraqi border region.
Petro-aggression	Oil reduces the domestic accountability of petrostate leaders, lowering the risks of instigating wars.	Yes, but there was little accountability toward the population and brutality of the movement also ensured war spoils and payment of taxes across many sectors.
Petro-insurgency	Oil income provides finances for (foreign) non-state actors to wage war.	Yes, but to a lesser extent than generally argued. Initial territorial gains were made without major oil revenues. Indirect oil income gained through foreign sponsors.
Greedy rebels	Armed groups instrumentalize the armed conflict for financial gains, either (a) independently from the state, (b) through capturing the state, or (c) through a seceding state.	Yes, through the creation of a seceding state, but not from an ideological perspective and general practices within the movement.
Oil-related grievances	Inequalities in oil revenue distribution and socio-environmental impacts motivate armed conflict.	Yes, to some extent in relation to Shiite-dominated federal government in Iraq, and to Western oil interests in the region.
Weak state	Oil wealth and dependence undermines the need for strong institutions, weakens the taxation-representation nexus, and increases economic shocks and corruption.	Yes, with regard to the Iraqi state, but not in the case of Syria. Oil wealth did not reduce ISIS' extreme form of authoritarianism and intrusive bureaucracies.
Sparse trade network	Oil wealth reduces economic diversification, trade and regional interdependence, thereby increasing conflict risk.	Yes, in the case of Iraq it was aggravated by a decade of economic sanctions, less so in the case of Syria. ISIS maintained some trade, but mostly through smuggling which itself generated conflicts.
Externalization of civil wars in petro-states	Oil creates conditions for civil war, which then leads to foreign intervention, externalization, or spillover.	To some extent in the case of Iraq as Sunni Arab populations lost out of regime change, but even less so in the case Syria.

Mechanisms	*Description*	*Findings*
Transit route	States' efforts to secure transit routes for oil create a security dilemma that produces or exacerbates conflict.	Possibly, over Iran-Iraq-Syria-Lebanon pipeline route versus Qatar-Saudi Arabia-Jordan-Syria-Turkey route.
Obstacle to multilateralism	Importers' efforts to curry favor with petrostate prevent multilateral cooperation on security issues.	Not in the case of ISIS.

Sources: Humphreys 2006; Colgan 2013; author.

in 2015. Furthermore, indirect petro-aggression may have been at work as wealthy donors from the Arabian Peninsula came to support the revolutionary movement.

Petro-Insurgency

As explained above, this mechanism was involved very much at work, although its relative significance was often overstated.[5] Overall, oil revenues played a significant role in sustaining ISIS' war economy and providing leverage over regional groups in need of fuel for nearly four years. Yet, as a *New York Times* investigation into ISIS' finance concluded, a key success of the militants was "their diversified revenue stream. The group drew its income from so many strands of the economy that airstrikes alone were not enough to cripple it" (Callimachi 2018). Given the size of the population under control and the scope of military operations, oil was perhaps more necessary as a source of energy than as a source of finance. If the end of oil revenues largely coincided with the defeat of ISIS's territorial project, this had more to do with the military action of the U.S.-led coalition, including Kurdish and Iraqi federal forces, than simply the lack of access oil.

Greedy Rebels

As mentioned above, greed seems to have been a limited motivation for the movement in general, and for militants in particular. Although salaries and advantages such as free housing and access to loot attracted some militants, many were ideologically driven.[6] Some degree of support among local residents was also obtained through the redistribution of land and assets violently seized from non-Sunni Arabs populations, but fear toward the movement remained.

Oil-Related Grievances

Oil has been a major dimension of Iraq's domestic and international politics. Most grievances are directed at the unequal distribution of rents and jobs, rather than at the socio-environmental impacts of oil exploitation. These grievances are largely the result of clientelism and corruption, but also the unwillingness or inability of the federal government to fully implement constitutional rules of revenue distribution (Le Billon 2015b). Still, it is very unlikely that a Sunni caliphate straddling the Iraq-Syria border would have yielded more revenues to local populations. As such, ISIS did not seek to address grievances associated with oil revenues.

Weak State

The weakness of Iraqi, and to a lesser degree Syrian institutions, has been noted. There is limited evidence that this is a direct result of oil wealth, however. ISIS did take advantage of the weakness of these institutions, especially with regard to those of the security apparatus and also more broadly those of the public service. The lack of channels of influence over federal governance and, in some domains, over provincial management also promoted some degree of support for a Sunni insurrection. Yet this weakness had more to do with the strain of sanctions against the regime of Saddam Hussein, the de-Baathization of the civil service that following the U.S.-led invasion, and the neglect of Sunni areas by the mostly Shiite government in Baghdad (partly the result of insurgency), than directly to Iraq's petro-dependence at the time of ISIS's rise.

Sparse Trade Network

Iraq was doubly affected by a high economic dependence on oil exports and trade sanctions. As a result, its economy was not as diversified as it could have been considering its population size as well as educational and income levels, although sanctions unintendedly incentivized domestic production of goods and services. Furthermore, much of the remaining trade networks involved smuggling or corrupt practices. Similarly, ISIS territories were largely insulated from international trade networks, other than those organized through smuggling, as well as collusion, cooperation or co-optation with local tribal militias and other armed groups (Heras et al. 2017). Rather than entice a rapprochement, many ISIS trade networks attracted military attacks by third parties and mutual accusations of complicity with terrorism, in part with the objective of delegitimizing adversaries. Most notably, the U.S. government blamed the Assad regime (and Iran) for trading with

ISIS, the Russian authorities blamed NATO-member Turkey, while Turkey blamed Russia, and Arab newspapers blamed Israel (Tahroor 2015). Political overtones were particularly blatant when the Russian government very publicly accused Turkey of direct involvement in oil smuggling, including by business interests close to Turkish president Erdogan, two weeks after the Turkey air force had downed a Russian bomber-jet along the Syrian-Turkish border.

Transit Routes

ISIS has been portrayed as a Western/Saudi-Emirati proxy in war against the Assad regime as part of a competition between a Western-backed gas pipeline from Bahrain and Qatar having to pass through Syria, and an Iranian-backed gas pipeline (Engel 2015). Though possibly part of broader motives of opposition to the Syrian regime, the argument does not stand on its own. Having represented ISIS and the context of civil war in the region as the result of oil-motivated interventions to achieve regime change, commentators have notably hypothesized that "[a]n unintended consequence of the Saudi attempts to overthrow the government of Syria, may be the overthrow of the government of Saudi Arabia with its own medicine. Should ISIS be pushed into Saudi Arabia, expect oil prices to surge" (Austin 2016).

Obstacle to Multilateralism

Although oil probably further consolidated ISIS' strategy of non-engagement with the "international community," it seems clear that this would not have been the case even without oil. Not only did ISIS have a deep distrust of other governments (and in its millenarian vision hoped to bring them down to establish Islamic rule), but it was internationally dealt with as a terrorist group and much was done to not recognize ISIS as a potential state.

DISCUSSION

ISIS has generally not been portrayed as a "greedy" organization seeking to control oil for the sake of enriching its members, but rather as one seeking to access oil to secure a state (the caliphate). Oil has been seen as central to the finances and strategies of ISIS, with for example reports that the organization would have in part refocused its territorial strategy from northern Syria to Eastern Syria and the bordering regions of Iraq in order to control oil revenues—though other factors such as control of the major city of Mosul and territorial integration of Sunni areas in Iraq were also (if not more) important factors, and the taxation of populations under its control was widespread, even in oil-rich areas (Revkin 2020).

The U.S.-led war on ISIS oil sought in this respect not only to prevent ISIS from consolidating its finances and perhaps most importantly, from the perspective of the United States, to undermine ISIS' "stateness." As explained by Amos Hochstein, State Department's Special Envoy for International Energy Affairs (cited in, Van Heuvelen 2015), "*They want to be seen as a state* . . . So they need energy, not just for profits but also for symbolizing the difference between them and other terrorist organizations—that they control territory and provide electricity and fuel. That's also a vulnerability in their operation."

This deliberate use of oil-targeting to deny ISIS its potential status as a state, and confine it to that of a terrorist organization, was part of a broad consensus among Western politicians, analysts, and commentators, while attempts to undermine "rebel" governance also extended to the military campaigns of the Assad regime against other rebel groups (see Martínez and Eng 2018). Relatively few studies seriously examined the "stateness" of ISIS, including its sophisticated bureaucratic apparatus (Benraad 2014), despite the importance of the shift and even schism the prioritization of this goal—enshrined in the very name of the organization—represented for the Jihadist movement (Shapiro et al. 2015; see also Al Ahram 2017).

As discussed above, instead of an oil-rich ISIS-ruled caliphate, what emerged was the challenging reality of squeezing out usable fuel and cash from a difficult context. ISIS controlled territories with oil fields, but many of these were already quite depleted and aging, requiring more complex techniques and recurrent investments. Operations also needed technical staff, and ISIS faced difficulties in (forcedly) recruiting former state-oil company and foreign employees. Key oil staff were targeted for assassination, including by the United States, which dispatched on the ground special ops troops to eliminate key militants and collect intelligence. To export oil outside its territory, ISIS was initially able to tap into long-established oil trading and smuggling networks. Yet, these came under growing military pressure as the means of production, refining, and transportation were progressively degraded, notably through aerial bombardments, leading ISIS and entrepreneurs to adjust to through stealth and makeshift innovation.

ISIS not only generated revenues from oil, but as mentioned above, also used oil for tactical and political purposes, in effect constructing a series of highly politicized oil markets including among its own units, civilian populations in ISIS strongholds (in both Syria and Iraq), in areas controlled by Bashar and by other rebel groups, as well as in neighboring countries. Despite its prominence within ISIS finances, oil revenues remain relatively low, notably because of the relative paucity of oil fields within ISIS-controlled parts of Syria and Iraq. As summed by a U.S. Mideast analyst, by taking on the

Table 10.2 Categorization of "Non-state Armed Groups," Oil Sector Activities and Key Relations

Categories	*Terrorist*	*Insurgent*	*Warlord*	*Proto-state*	*Near-state*
Territorial control	Absent	Temporary and heavily disputed	Peripheral and chronically disputed	Strong but challenged and unrecognized	Strong and partially recognized
Relations with oil companies	Sabotage, killings, kidnapping, extortion	Bunkering, extortion, sabotage, kidnapping	Extortion, bunkering, informal contracting with companies	Production, international contracting of experts and smuggling	Production, international contracting with oil majors and traders
Oil take	<10%	10%	20%	30%	50%
Relations with host populations	Negligible as members often have clandestine lives	Minimal and temporary services, occasionally predatory	Limited services, basic taxation often resembling predation	Essential services (food, fuel, health, "justice"), tax system in place	Full-fledged services, extensive tax system in place
Examples	AQIM	ELN	MEND	ISIS (2014–2015)	KRG (pre–2003)

Source: Author.

challenge of becoming a new territorial entity with responsibility over about 8 million people, ISIS had "gone from being the world's richest terrorist organization to the world's poorest state" (Johnson 2014). By early 2016, despite repeated air strikes and lower international oil prices, ISIS was earning an estimated $1–1.5 million per day through field-level oil sales. While still accounting about a quarter of ISIS total revenues, this amount represented only about $60 per year and per person in its overall area of control.

ISIS did rapidly move up from an insurgent to a proto-state status (see Lia 2015), and was able to operate and control the vast majority of oil fields in northeastern Syria and taxing most aspects of the oil commodity chain (see table 10.2). Yet ISIS was only able to attract individual experts rather than full-fledged companies to develop its oil sector. It also became increasingly restrained in its export options as well as its refining capacity for local consumption as a result of the sharp decline in international oil prices, destruction of tankers and key infrastructures, as well as the loss of oil fields to Kurdish and Iraqi government forces. ISIS' daily oil revenues peaked in late 2014 and came to increasingly resemble a coping economy working under severe geological, economic, and military constraints. By October 2017, ISIS had lost all its strongholds and its last major oil fields in Deir ez-Zor, leaving the remnants of the group to focus instead on attacks against government pipelines. In this regard, the U.S. strategy of bombing ISIS' oil sector was somewhat effective, but the losses of oil revenues were the result of broader military pressure and the loss of trade routes to Kurdish forces. Overall, the case of ISIS confirmed many of the mechanisms generally identified as linking oil and war, yet most did not play the dominant role that oil was often given in some of the descriptions of the militant group and the war more broadly.

CONCLUSION

Many studies of resources and conflicts are moving beyond simplistic conceptions of resource scarcity, abundance, and dependence. Rather, they consider how uneven resource entitlements and patterns of resource exploitation and consumption reflect and exacerbate the antagonizing effects of wars, as well as inform the types of violence reshaping conditions of access and control over resources. This suggests mixed methods, including historical and political economy analyses, as well as field-based studies of narratives and power relations around resources, including various forms of violence (Le Billon and Duffy 2018).

This brief study of the case of ISIS demonstrates the variety of "oil wars" narratives at play, the wide array of actors and processes involved, from outright massacres to various forms of accommodation based on the necessity to generate (or curtail) energy and financial flows in order to maintain, establish, or deny "stateness." As such, this study helps nuance some of the now-classic narratives of "rebel economies" as the result of greedy thugs battling over resource spoils, and questions some of the simplistic answers that these often call for. This study also points to the complexity of mechanisms involved. Among the ten mechanisms examined, nine were relevant, but their applicability required caveats and nuances. Perhaps most importantly, when considering the war economies of non-state actors, this study draws attention to the effects of war economy narratives and their associated counterinsurgency practices. Arguably, narratives of an oil-fuelled ISIS helped to depoliticize the group, by associating it with images of greedy criminals and oil-funded despots. Yet at the same time, counterinsurgency practices, and most notably the sustained bombing of oil assets sought to prevent ISIS from becoming a state. As such, ISIS' association with oil enabled both a further criminalization of the group and its purposeful depoliticization. From this perspective, ISIS' oil territories, and more broadly its war economy, constituted both an asset and a liability. As an asset, oil and the control of a large economy enabled it to further pursue its attempt to establish a de facto state. As a liability, oil created vulnerabilities for its financial system and exposed it to further delegitimization. Still, in this regard, ISIS' main liability was the brutal repression that it exercised in very public ways against those it considered as "nonbelievers."

The broad conclusion of this chapter for the study of resources in non-state armed groups' war economies is that resources can contribute to shaping the representations and practices of non-state armed groups as well as those of their allies and opponents. High-value resources such as oil will often taint the (perceived) motives of belligerents, guide their strategic and tactical approaches, and influence their capabilities and behaviors. Yet, to avoid raw material fetishism and other forms of oversimplification and overstatement about resources, it is crucial that studies carefully examine the diverse mechanisms potentially at work, and contextualize current resource-related hostilities within multi-scalar and historical perspectives. Interpreting conflicts through the lens of resource-related factors requires a nuanced and grounded approach sensitive to the multiplicity of agendas as well as the many motivations and materialities at work. This undoubtedly constitutes a challenging task, especially when field investigations are particularly risky, with information being derived from remote sensing and a limited range of informants.

NOTES

1. Prior to the Syrian civil war, production for these fields was reported at 75,000 bpd and 50,000 bpd, respectively, and are now assessed at 11,500 bpd and 7,500 bpd

(Shellme n.d.). AFPC's fields production peaked in 1990 at 400,000 barrels, and were described by AFPC as "mostly in a very mature stage of development, with some 88% of the 2400 mln bbl that is expected to be recoverable, 'the easy oil', already produced in the last 20 years . . . . Extraction of the remaining 300 mln bbl will take place over the next 20+ years or so, with production levels expected to decline to 50,000 b/d by 2014" (AFPC n.d.).

2. See "Except for those who repent" video, initially posted but since removed from (YouTube 2015).

3. See "Background Briefing on ISIL and Oil" (U.S. State Department 2015). By March 2016, Operation Inherent Resolve had damaged/destroyed 1,272 oil infrastructure targets (out of a total of 22,779 targets).

4. For an overview of oil-related factors and processes that actually prevent armed conflicts, such as the diplomatic and military support by the home countries of oil companies present in a country at risk of war (see Basedau and Lay 2009).

5. For a former chair of the FBI's Joint Terrorism Task Force and liaison with the Iraqi National Police, one has to "think of ISIS as an oil cartel . . . . In the end, money is the governing rationale. The religious ideology is a tool that inspires its soldiers to give their lives for an oil cartel" (cited in Kennedy 2016). In a more nuanced way, and closer to the role of oil in the running the movement and interpersonal relations, a Kurdish commander denounced attacks by al-Nusra and ISIS on Kurdish villages in Hasaka Province for aiming at lucrative oil fields and border crossings, and argued that such moves were "not a political issue. There are divisions even between these rebel units over oil" (Reuters 2013).

6. As a foreign female supporter wrote in an email back home, "I have an apartment that is fully furnished . . . . I pay no rent nor even electricity or water lol. It's the good life!!!" (Callimachi 2018).

REFERENCES

Abdallah, Wissam. 2015. "Tribal Disputes Heat Up in Syrian Desert." *Al Monitor*, July 8, 2015. http://www.al-monitor.com/pulse/politics/2015/07/syria-desert-tribes-division-oil-geography.html#

Abdul-Ahad, Gaith. 2013. "Syria's Oilfields Create Surreal Battle Lines Amid Chaos and Tribal Loyalties." *The Guardian*, June 25, 2013. http://www.theguardian.com/world/2013/jun/25/syria-oil-assad-rebels-tribes-activists-20131123151912731899.html

Aboufadel, Leith. 2017. "ISIS Tribal Fighters Defect and Hand Over Al-Omar Oil Fields to US-Backed Forces." *Al Masdar News,* October 22, 2017. https://www.almasdarnews.com/article/exclusive-isis-tribal-fighters-defect-hand-al-omar-oil-fields-us-backed-forces/

AFPC, n.d. Al Furat Petroleum Company. http://www.afpc.sy/Default_e.aspx accessed on May 13, 2016.

Ahmad, Rozh. 2015. "Crude Living on Oil in Syria." YouTube, August 2015. https://www.youtube.com/watch?v=w3Z97TksiZk

Al Ahram, Ariel. I. 2017. "Territory, Sovereignty, and New Statehood in the Middle East and North Africa." *The Middle East Journal* 71, no. 3: 345–62.

Al Jazeera. 2013. "Rebels Take Largest Syria Oilfield: Activists." November 23, 2013. https://www.aljazeera.com/news/2013/11/23/rebels-take-largest-syria-oilfield-activists

Almohamad, Hussein, and Andreas Dittmann. 2016. "Oil in Syria between Terrorism and Dictatorship." *Social Sciences* 5, no. 2: 20.

Austin, Steve. 2014. "Oil Prices and the Syrian Civil War." *Oil-Price.net*, November 21, 2014. http://www.oil-price.net/en/articles/oil-prices-and-syrian-civil-war.php

Autesserre, Séverine. 2012. "Dangerous Tales: Dominant Narratives on the Congo and their Unintended Consequences." *African Affairs* 111, no. 443: 202–22.

Bader, Martin. 2014. "Life Inside Syria's Makeshift Oil Refineries." *Middle East Eye*, December 10, 2014. http://www.middleeasteye.net/in-depth/features/life-inside-syrias-makeshift-oil-refineries-617075533#sthash.bFRrHtQJ.dpuf

Barnard, Anne. 2017. "US-backed Fighters Take Largest Syrian Oil Field from ISIS." *The New York Times*, October 22, 2017. https://www.nytimes.com/2017/10/22/world/middleeast/syria-isis-oil.html

Basedau, Matthias, and Jann Lay. 2009. "Resource Curse or Rentier Peace? The Ambiguous Effects of Oil Wealth and Oil Dependence on Violent Conflict." *Journal of Peace Research* 46, no. 6: 757–76.

Benraad, Myriam. 2014 "L'Etat Islamique: Anatomie d'une Machine Infernale." *Revue Internationale et Strategique* 4: 28–37.

Bojicic-Dzelilovic, Vesna, and Rim Turkmani. 2018. "War Economy, Governance and Security in Syria's Opposition-Controlled Areas." *Stability: International Journal of Security and Development* 7, no. 1: 1–17.

Callimachi, Rukmini. 2018. "The ISIS Files." *The New York Times*, April 4, 2018. https://www.nytimes.com/interactive/2018/04/04/world/middleeast/isis-documents-mosul-iraq.html

Center for the Analysis of Terrorism. 2016. *ISIS Financing: 2015*. http://cat-int.org/wp-content/uploads/2016/06/ISIS-Financing-2015-Report.pdf

Chingono, Mark. 2000. "Mozambique: War, Economic Change, and Development in Manica Province, 1982–1992." In *War and Underdevelopment: Volume II: Country Experiences*, edited by Frances Stewart and Valpy Fitzgerald, 89–118. Oxford University Press.

Colgan, Jeff D. 2013. "Fueling the Fire: Pathways from Oil to War." *International Security* 38, no. 2: 147–80.

Collier, Paul, and Anke Hoeffler. 1998. "On Economic Causes of Civil War." *Oxford Economic Papers* 50, no. 4: 563–73.

Conrad, Justin M., Kevin T. Greene, James Igoe Walsh, and Beth Elise Whitaker. 2019. "Rebel Natural Resource Exploitation and Conflict Duration." *Journal of Conflict Resolution* 63, no. 3: 591–616.

Dalby, Simon. 2009. *Security and Environmental Change*. Polity.

Do, Quy-Toan, Jacob N. Shapiro, Christopher D. Elvidge, Mohamed Abdel-Jelil, Daniel P. Ahn, Kimberly Baugh, Jamie Hansen-Lewis, Mikhail Zhizhin, and Morgan D. Bazilian. 2018. "Terrorism, Geopolitics, and Oil Security: Using Remote Sensing to Estimate Oil Production of the Islamic State." *Energy Research & Social Science* 44: 411–18.

Ember, Carol R. and Melvin Ember. 1992. "Resource Unpredictability, Mistrust, and War: A Cross-Cultural Study." *Journal of Conflict Resolution* 36, no. 2: 242–62.

Enders, David. 2012. "With Syria's Eastern Oilfields in Rebel Hands, a Brisk Business in Pirated Crude Grows." *Miami Herald*, November 21, 2012. http://www.miamiherald.com/latest-news/article1944774.html#.UK2EQyfeCqY.twitter#storylink=cpy

Engel, P. 2015. "This Detailed Syria Map Shows What Territory ISIS is Truly Fighting for." *Business Insider*, June 30, 2015. http://www.businessinsider.com/map-of-syria-shows-what-isis-is-truly-fighting-for-2015-6

Faucon, Benoit and Margaret Coker. 2016. "The Rise and Deadly Fall of Islamic State's Oil Tycoon." *Wall Street Journal*, April 24, 2016. http://www.wsj.com/articles/the-rise-and-deadly-fall-of-islamic-states-oil-tycoon-1461522313

Findlay, Ronald and Kevin H. O'Rourke. 2009. *Power and Plenty: Trade, War, and the World Economy in the Second Millennium.* Princeton University Press.

Giglio, Mike. 2014. "This is How ISIS Smuggles Oil." *BuzzFeed News*, November 3, 2014. https://www.buzzfeed.com/mikegiglio/this-is-how-isis-smuggles-oil?utm_term=.gml1qBzwgM#.oeGQxvBgLr

Haass, Felix. 2020. "Insurgency and Ivory: The Territorial Origins of Illicit Resource Extraction in Civil Conflicts." *Comparative Political Studies*. https://doi.org/10.1177/0010414020957682

Hamdan, Ali N. 2016. "Breaker of Barriers? Notes on the Geopolitics of the Islamic State in Iraq and Sham." *Geopolitics* 21, no. 3: 605–27.

Heras, Nicolas, Bassam Barabandi and Nidal Betare. 2017. "Deir Azzour Tribal Map Project." *Center for a New American Security*. https://www.cnas.org/publications/reports/deir-azzour-tribal-mapping-project

Herbert, Matt. 2014. "Partisans, Profiteers, and Criminals: Syria's Illicit Economy." *Fletcher Forum of International Affairs* 38, no. 1: 69–86.

Humphreys, Macartan. 2006. "Natural Resources, Conflict, and Conflict Resolution: Uncovering the Mechanisms." *Journal of Conflict Resolution* 49, no. 4: 508–37.

Johnson, Keith. 2014. "The Islamic State is the Newest Petrostate." *Foreign Policy*, July 28, 2014. http://foreignpolicy.com/2014/07/28/the-islamic-state-is-the-newest-petrostate/

Karouny, Mariam. 2013. "Insight: In Eastern Syria Oil Smugglers Benefit from Chaos." *Reuters*, May 10, 2013. http://www.reuters.com/article/us-syria-crisis-oil-tribes-insight-idUSBRE94905Y20130510

Keen, David. 1997. "A Rational Kind of Madness." *Oxford Development Studies* 25 (1): 67–75.

Kelly, Raymond C. 2000. *Warless Societies and the Origin of War*. University of Michigan Press.

Kenar, Ceren and Ragip Soylu. 2016. "Why are Russian Engineers Working at an Islamic State-Controlled Gas Plant in Syria?" *Foreign Policy*, February 9, 2016. http://foreignpolicy.com/2016/02/09/why-are-russian-engineers-working-at-an-islamic-state-controlled-gas-plant-in-syria/

Kennedy, Robert F. Jr. 2016. "Syria: Another Pipeline War." *Ecowatch.com*, February 25, 2016. https://www.ecowatch.com/syria-another-pipeline-war-1882180532.html

Klare, Michael. 2008. *Rising Powers, Shrinking Planet: The New Geopolitics of Energy*. New York: Metropolitan Books.

Korf, Benedikt. 2011. "Resources, Violence and the Telluric Geographies of Small Wars." *Progress in Human Geography* 35, no. 6: 733–56.

Kramer, Andrew E. 2017. "Russia Deploys a Potent Weapon in Syria: The Profit Motive." *The New York Times*, July 5, 2017. https://www.nytimes.com/2017/07/05/world/middleeast/russia-syria-oil-isis.html

Lahiri-Dutt, Kuntala. 2006. "'May God Give Us Chaos, so that We Can Plunder': A Critique of 'Resource Curse' and Conflict Theories." *Development* 49, no. 3: 14–21.

Latour, Bruno.1987. *Science in Action: How to Follow Scientists and Engineers Through Society*. Milton Keynes: Open University Press.

Laudati, Ann. 2013. "Beyond Minerals: Broadening 'Economies of Violence' in Eastern Democratic Republic of Congo." *Review of African Political Economy* 40, no. 135: 32–50.

Lister, Charles. 2014. "Cutting off ISIS' Cash Flow." *Brookings*, October 24, 2014. http://www.brookings.edu/blogs/markaz/posts/2014/10/24-lister-cutting-off-isis-jabhat-al-nusra-cash-flow

Le Billon, Philippe. 1999. "A Land Cursed by its Wealth? Angola's War Economy." *WIDER*. 10.22004/ag.econ.295366

———. 2001. "The Political Ecology of War: Natural Resources and Armed Conflicts." *Political Geography* 20, no. 5: 561–84.

———. 2005. "Corruption, Reconstruction and Oil Governance in Iraq." *Third World Quarterly* 26, no. 4: 679–98.

———. 2006. "Fatal Transactions: Conflict Diamonds and the (Anti) Terrorist Consumer." *Antipode* 38, no. 4: 778–801.

———. 2013. *Wars of Plunders: Conflicts, Profits and the Politics of Resources*. Oxford: Oxford University Press.

———. 2014. "Natural Resource and Corruption in Post-War Transitions: Matters of Trust." *Third World Quarterly* 35, no. 5: 770–786.

———. 2015a. "Environmental Conflict." in *Handbook of Political Ecology*, edited by Perreault, Tom, Gavin Bridge, and James McCarthy, 598–608. Routledge.

———. 2015b. "Oil, Secession and the Future of Iraqi Federalism." *Middle East Policy* 22, no. 1: 68–76.

———. 2018. "Peacebuilding and White-Collar Crime in Post-War Natural Resource Sectors." *Third World Thematics: A TWQ Journal* 3, no. 1: 80–97.

———. 2020. "Oil and the Islamic State: Revisiting 'Resource Wars' Arguments in Light of ISIS Operations and State-Making Attempts." *Studies in Conflict and Terrorism*.

Le Billon, Philippe, and Alejandro Cervantes. 2009. “Oil Prices, Scarcity, and Geographies of War.” *Annals of the American Association of Geographers* 99, no. 5: 836–44.

Le Billon, Philippe, and Rosaleen V. Duffy. 2018. “Conflict Ecologies: Connecting Political Ecology and Peace and Conflict Studies.” *Journal of Political Ecology* 25, no. 1: 239–60.

Le Billon, Philippe and Fouad El Khatib. 2004. “From Free Oil to ‘Freedom Oil’: Terrorism, War and US Geopolitics in the Persian Gulf.” *Geopolitics* 9, no. 1: 109–37.

Le Billon, Philippe and Estelle Levin. 2009. “Building Peace with Conflict Diamonds? Merging Security and Development in Sierra Leone.” *Development and Change* 40, no. 4: 693–715.

Le Billon, Philippe and Lauren Shykora. 2020. “Conflicts, Commodities and the Environmental Geopolitics of Supply Chains.” In *A Research Agenda for Environmental Geopolitics*, edited by Shannon O’Lear, 59–73. Edward Elgar Publishing.

Lia, Brynjar. 2015. “Understanding Jihadi Proto-States.” *Perspectives on Terrorism* 9, no. 4: 31–41.

Lujala, Päivi. 2010. “The Spoils of Nature: Armed Civil Conflict and Rebel Access to Natural Resources.” *Journal of Peace Research* 47, no. 1: 15–28.

Mahdi, Kamil. 2007. “Neoliberalism, Conflict and an Oil Economy: The Case of Iraq.” *Arab Studies Quarterly* 29, no. 1: 1–20.

Martinez-Alier, Joan. 2003. *The Environmentalism of the Poor: A Study of Ecological Conflicts and Valuation*. Edward Elgar.

Martínez, José Ciro, and Brent Eng. 2018. “Stifling Stateness: The Assad Regime’s Campaign Against Rebel Governance.” *Security Dialogue* 49, no. 4: 235–53.

Meierding, Emily. 2016. “Dismantling the Oil Wars Myth.” *Security Studies* 25, no. 2: 258–88.

Muttitt, G. 2011. *Fuel on the Fire: Oil and Politics in Occupied Iraq*. Random House.

Nordstrom, Carolyn. 2004. *Shadows of War: Violence, Power, and International Profiteering in the Twenty-First Century*. University of California Press.

Pawlak, Justina and Adrian Croft. 2013. “EU Governments Ease Syria Sanctions on Oil to Help Rebels.” *Reuters*, April 22, 2013. http://uk.reuters.com/article/uk-syria-crisis-eu-idUKBRE93L14M20130422

Peluso, Nancy L., and Michael Watts. 2001. *Violent Environments*. Ithaca NY: Cornell University Press.

Philips, Matthew. 2014. “Islamic State Loses Its Oil Business.” *Bloomberg*, October 14, 2014. https://www.bloomberg.com/news/articles/2014-10-14/u-dot-s-dot-airstrikes-cut-islamic-state-oil-production-by-70-percent

Podder, Sukanya. 2013. “Non-State Armed Groups and Stability: Reconsidering Legitimacy and Inclusion.” *Contemporary Security Policy* 34, no. 1: 16–39.

Pugh, Michael, Neil Cooper and Mandy Turner, eds. 2016. *Whose Peace? Critical Perspectives on the Political Economy of Peacebuilding*. Springer.

Reno, William. 1999. *Warlord Politics and African States*. Boulder, CO: Lynne Rienner.

Reno, William. 2008. "Anti-corruption Efforts in Liberia: Are they Aimed at the Right Targets?" *International Peacekeeping* 15, no. 3: 387–404.

Reno, William. 2009. "Understanding Criminality in West African Conflicts." *International Peacekeeping* 16, no. 1: 47–61.

Reuters. 2013. "Dozens of Syrian Rebels and Kurds Killed in Clashes." *Reuters,* September 12, 2013. http://www.syriahr.com/en/2013/09/12/3746

Revkin, Mara R. 2020. "What Explains Taxation by Resource-rich Rebels? Evidence from the Islamic State in Syria." *The Journal of Politics* 82, no. 2: 757–64.

Ross, Michael L. 2004. "What Do We Know about Natural Resources and Civil War?" *Journal of Peace Research* 41, no. 3: 337–56.

Sarfaty, Galit A. 2015. "Shining Light on Global Supply Chains." *Harvard International Law Journal* 56, no. 2: 419.

Selby, Jan, Omar Dahi, Christiane Fröhlich, and Mike Hulme. 2017. "Climate Change and the Syrian Civil War Revisited." *Political Geography* 60: 232–44.

Shapiro, Jeremy, William McCants, Martin S. Indyk, and Shadi Hamid. 2015. "ISIS and the Unbearable Stateness of Being." *Brookings Institution,* September 25, 2015. https://www.brookings.edu/blog/order-from-chaos/2015/09/25/isis-and-the-unbearable-stateness-of-being/

Shellme. n.d. "Shell—A New Era for Shell in Syria." Accessed July 2, 2014. http://www.shell-me.com/shell-a-new-era-for-shell-in-syria/

Solomon, Erika, Guy Chazan, and Sam Jones. 2015. "Isis Inc: How Oil Fuels the Jihadi Terrorists." *Financial Times*, October 14, 2015. https://www.ft.com/content/b8234932-719b-11e5-ad6d-f4ed76f0900a

Solomon, Erika and Ahmad Mhidi. 2017. "Isis Finds Escape Route for the Profits of War." *Financial Times*, August 23, 2017. https://www.ft.com/content/b2f616d4-8656-11e7-8bb1-5ba57d47eff7

Springer, Simon, and Philippe Le Billon. 2016. "Violence and Space: An Introduction to the Geographies of Violence." *Political Geography* 52: 1–3.

Tharoor, Ishaan. 2015. "Russia and Turkey Accuse Each Other of Buying Oil from the Islamic State." *Washington Post*, December 2, 2015. https://www.washingtonpost.com/news/worldviews/wp/2015/12/02/russia-and-turkey-accuse-each-other-of-buying-oil-from-the-islamic-state/

Townsend, Mark. 2014. "Inside the Islamic State's Capital: Red Bull-Drinking Jihadists, Hungry Civilians, Crucifixions and Air Strikes." *The Guardian*, November 30, 2014. https://www.theguardian.com/world/2014/nov/30/raqqa-isis-capital-crucifixions-civilians-suffer-jihadis-red-bull

U.S. State Department. 2015. "Background Briefing on ISIL and Oil." Special Briefing, Office of the Spokesperson, Senior State Department Official, Washington, DC, December 4, 2015. https://2009-2017.state.gov/r/pa/prs/ps/2015/12/250383.htm

Van Heuleven, Ben. 2015. "Armed with Intel, U.S. Strikes Curtail IS Oil Sector." *Iraq Oil Report*, December 28, 2015. http://www.iraqoilreport.com/news/armed-intel-u-s-strikes-curtail-oil-sector-17473/

Walsh, James Igoe, Justin M. Conrad, Beth Elise Whitaker, and Katelin M. Hudak. 2018. "Funding Rebellion: The Rebel Contraband Dataset." *Journal of Peace Research* 55, no. 5: 699–707. DOI: 10.1177/0022343317740621

Watts, Michael, 2004. "Resource Curse? Governmentality, Oil and Power in the Niger Delta, Nigeria." *Geopolitics* 9, no. 1: 50–80.

Webb, Whitney. 2018. "How the US Occupied the 30% of Syria Containing Most of its Oil, Water and Gas." *The Iranian*, April 17, 2018. https://iranian.com/2018/04/17/us-occupied-30-syria-containing-oil-water-gas/

Weinstein, Jeremy M. 2006. *Inside Rebellion: The Politics of Insurgent Violence*. Cambridge University Press.

Weiss, Michael and Hassan Hassan. 2016. *ISIS: Inside the Army of Terror*. Simon and Schuster.

Westing, Arthur, ed. 1988. *Global Resources and International Conflict: Environmental Factors in Strategy Policy and Action*. Oxford: Oxford University Press.

You Tube. 2015. "IS Video 'Except for Those Who Repent' Talks About The Al-Shaitat Tribe Rebellion and its Aftermath." https://www.youtube.com/watch?v=Ue_u2GRXE2I#t=569

Conclusion

New Perspectives on Warring Societies

Nicola Di Cosmo, Didier Fassin,
and Clémence Pinaud

Non-state war economies have been an object of major concern for international politics as well as the matter of much debate among experts in recent decades. In this volume, we have sought to address this concern and revisit this debate. We have done so by critically evaluating past contributions and expanding our understanding of these economies from an interdisciplinary perspective. On the one hand, we have reviewed past theories on war economies—from explanations of conflict in terms of "greed" versus "grievances" to economic understandings of war, and to theories of state formation based on war economy—aiming to illustrate various shortcomings, in particular to separate state from non-state actors, and to assume that state and non-state war economies are fundamentally different, as discussed by Didier Fassin. On the other hand, we have expanded the range of cases and the scope of activities that a theory of non-state war economy should consider and thus have provided a wider empirical basis on which to develop our critical approaches, as argued by Christopher Cramer.

While war economy is far from being a zero-sum game, it is often involved with social and political functions beyond wealth accumulation. Most of the authors point out that wars are structurally transformative, not merely destructive. They allow for the performance of new statehood, and for processes of social differentiation that shape new societies. Sometimes, they can become an inconvenience, and Philippe Le Billon shows that it is the case for the Islamic State's reliance on oil. "Greed," often assumed to be the main driver of non-state war economies, is thus a limited and inadequate analytical category. The same can be said for the notion of "resource wars" since resources can turn out to be burdensome. There is no set trajectory for the use of resources or for the political outcomes of war economies. The main challenge becomes, then, to realign general assumptions with empirical cases that illustrate both the specificity and the variety of the phenomenon, using theoretical keys that draw from multiple disciplines.

Several essays engaged with the theories of historian Charles Tilly ("war makes state") and economist Mancur Olson (the "stationary bandit"). In doing so, they appraised these theories' applicability, but also furthered our understanding of war economy-driven state-making processes. They questioned the idea that war makes states. William Caferro challenges the applicability of Tilly's theory, by inviting readers to consider other polities-in-the-making than classical states, such as city-states. Edward McCord's study of Chinese warlords demonstrates that warlords are not always strictly separate from the state, and they do not always attempt to establish separate independent states. Cramer proposes a third way to think of war economies, which is neither state-making nor state-destruction. Going beyond economic instrumentalism, particularly Olson's oft-cited view that taxation is mostly an economic tool that allows state-building, Nicola Di Cosmo and Zachariah Mampilly underscore the political and symbolic functions of fiscal policies in making the state. Di Cosmo argues that taxes led to state formation and to the introduction of a new class of people into the state machinery, which often created political tensions. Mampilly contends that rebel taxation was a lot more than a protection racket or a criminal activity: rebel taxation was a technology of governance with political and social valence, which, in building political legitimacy, actually outdid its fiscal and economic value.

Wars, therefore, fulfill important functions, and indeed enemies can have a social utility to the extent that wars satisfy important political and economic goals in a situation of crisis. In some cases, they can be absolutely necessary for a polity to survive, even though war may create chronic instability. The problem, then, is how to survive the various transformations associated with, and propelled by, the necessity of war and reacquire a situation of peace that transforms the former tensions onto a new order. Non-state war economies are, in this interpretation, a fundamental step to achieve a new economic order. Di Cosmo shows that competition for resources drove the creation of new political orders by unifying polities. Caferro affirms that the wealth accumulated by non-state actors, that is, the condottieri, in service of the state greatly influenced the cultural developments of the Renaissance—not the state. McCord depicts how some warlords had a positive impact in developing the economy, despite their overall negative impact on Chinese society. Clémence Pinaud establishes how control over the war economy participated to a new process of social class formation in South Sudan.

Viewing war as transformative—and in fact, creative—while accepting that different motivations drive different actors means and of course not minimizing the human costs of the war implies to let go of rational choice theory, which assumes that all actors want to maximize their gains. A change of optics in this regard is doubtless needed for a critical evaluation of contemporary international approaches to peace and reconstruction, since it questions the relevance of costly preventative approaches propelled by international bodies influenced by this camp, that is, the proponents of "greed" rather than "grievances," as Cramer points out.

More generally, and significantly, we demonstrate and illustrate the substantial similarities existing in the war economy patterns observed across space and time, even if their political outcomes remain unpredictable. The forms of war economy from the nomadic steppe empires resemble that of South Sudan's armed groups, ranging from raiding, tribute, trade, and taxes. Private military entrepreneurs, that is, mercenaries, also resemble one another, from Renaissance Italy to contemporary Afghanistan. Processes of social differentiation also echo one another, from early twentieth-century China to late twentieth-century South Sudan.

Yet, differences emerge with the introduction of international aid and the growing inter-connectedness between different types of state and non-state war economies. Both Gilles Carbonnier and Jonathan Benthall show how humanitarianism has become part and parcel of contemporary war economies. Humanitarianism in the Southern Hemisphere is highly connected to Western government and intergovernmental bodies. But even then, the introduction of humanitarian economies, and the connectedness between different economies across the world, heighten social processes that were already observed before. Where foreign interests correspond with those of wealth accumulators, humanitarian aid accelerates social differentiation.

The real novelty, as stated by Fassin, may lie in the introduction of a global moral economy of war with its norms, values, and even affects: of what is legitimate and what is not, of what is wrong and what is right, which has an incidence on the war economy itself. But our case studies show how this moral economy is challenged by the political economies of war. Le Billon notes how resources contribute to shape the representations and practices of most actors involved in warfare. McCord concurs in showing how the nature of resources shapes the specific character of warlordism, contesting the simplistic and negative conventional views of warlords' motivations, and seeking out the politics in the formation of the anti-warlord narrative. Mampilly also criticizes the perceptions of rebellion as a source of threat and of rebel taxation as a criminal activity.

Collectively, the chapters included in this volume show how ideology drives perceptions of legitimacy, and as such how ideology prompts the relegation of some activities to the realm of criminality or even terrorism. Benthall illustrates how the U.S. administration changed its perception of charities (especially Islamic ones) in Afghanistan in the mid-1990s, not based on their activities but on an ideological shift considering Islamism as the new pollution after communism. The same shift is noted by Pinaud in South Sudan, where the SPLA became an armed group the United States supported once its communist backer (Ethiopia) fell through in 1991, and its northern foe (the National Islamic Front) became viewed as a state sponsor of terrorism. Alternatively, through the Islamic State's management of oil resources, Le Billon analyzes how these resources participated in shaping the representations and practices of non-state armed groups as well as those of their allies and opponents.

Questioning of moral representations illustrates the necessity to think beyond several types of dichotomy. One must surpass the division between state and non-state actors, and not just in terms of other types of polities (such as city-states): the lines between civil and external (or inter-state) war, between civilians and combatants, or between war and peace, can also become blurry. Yet it does not mean, as Fassin points out, that one should forget the state entirely—indeed, it is never far. Instead, several authors show that modern war economies are above all networks that involve both states and non-state actors. Non-state war economies, as per Carbonnier's analysis, are a complex set of networks that involve rebel groups that take hostages, states, international aid organizations, and international insurance companies. Cramer notes the economic connections between Western countries and war-torn countries, and the globalization of war economies to the extent that they have become part of the world economy. As a matter of fact, both state and non-state war economies share similar features: the violent control over the market (to the detriment of free competition), the production of war rents, the lack of transparency and accountability, and a transformational impact over society and the economy.

In sum, over roughly the last forty years, inequality has increased almost everywhere, albeit at different speeds. Non-state war economies, connected to various state actors, are inscribed in the world economy: as such, they are an inherent part of this drive. Since 2014, non-state conflicts have been on the rise, a trend only matched by that of the early 1990s. For us, war economies transform societies' structures through as well as beyond their destruction, often to the detriment of ordinary civilians, especially women. Given such global economic and conflict trends, this field of inquiry remains more crucial than ever to understand how wartime wealth accumulation shapes and reshapes contemporary societies throughout the world.

Index

Figures and tables are indicated by "f" and "t" following page numbers respectively. Surnames starting with "al-" are alphabetized by the subsequent part of the name.

About the Contributors

Jonathan Benthall is an honorary research Fellow, Department of Anthropology, University College London, and director emeritus, Royal Anthropological Institute. His publications include *Disasters, Relief and the Media* (1993, reprinted 2010), *The Charitable Crescent: Politics of Aid in the Muslim World* (with J. Bellion-Jourdan, 2003, new edition 2009), and *Islamic Charities and Islamic Humanism in Troubled Times* (2016).

Philippe Le Billon is a professor at the University of British Columbia with the Department of Geography and the School of Public Policy and Global Affairs. He works on linkages between environment, development, and security. He is the author of *Oil* (Polity Press, 2017, with Gavin Bridge) and *Wars of Plunder: Conflicts, Profits and the Politics of Resources* (Oxford University Press, 2013).

William Caferro is Gertrude Conaway Vanderbilt professor of History and director of Classical/Mediterranean Studies at Vanderbilt University. He studies the economy of late medieval Italy. His most recent book is *Petrarch's War: Florence and the Black Death in Context* with Cambridge University Press (2018).

Gilles Carbonnier is a professor of development economics at the Graduate Institute of International and Development Studies (Geneva) and vice president of the International Committee of the Red Cross. His research focuses on the political economy of war and humanitarian action, and on natural resource governance. His latest book *Humanitarian Economics. War, Disaster and the Global Aid Market* was published by Hurst and Oxford University Press in 2016.

Nicola Di Cosmo is the Henry Luce Foundation Professor of East Asian Studies at the Institute for Advanced Study. His research interests are in the history of Chinese and Inner Asian frontiers from the ancient to the modern periods, with special reference to Xiongnu, Mongol, and Manchu history. He has written extensively on East Asian military history. His authored and edited books include *Ancient China and Its Enemies: The Rise of Nomadic Power in East Asian History*, *Military Culture in Imperial China*, *Warfare in Inner Asian History*, and *The Diary of a Manchu Soldier in Seventeenth Century China*. He has recently contributed to the *Cambridge World History of Violence, vol. 2 AD 500–AD 1550.* His most recent research focuses on the use of paleoscientific data as historical sources, with special reference to the history of China, Central Asia, and Mongolia.

Christopher Cramer is a professor of the Political Economy of Development at SOAS University of London. He works on the political economy of war and peace in southern Africa and post-conflict reconstruction. He is the author of *Civil War Is Not a Stupid Thing. Accounting for Violence in Developing Countries* (Hurst & Company, 2006) and coauthor of *African Economic Development: Evidence, Theory, Policy* (Oxford University Press, 2020).

Didier Fassin is the James D. Wolfensohn professor at the Institute for Advanced Study, director of Studies at the École des Hautes Études en Sciences Sociales, and annual chair of Public Health at the Collège de France. He studies political and moral issues in contemporary societies, particularly inequality, immigration, punishment, and humanitarianism. He authored fifteen books, among which *Humanitarian Reason. A Moral History of the Present* (University of California Press), *The Will to Punish* (Oxford University Press), and *Life. A Critical User's Manual* (Polity Press). His current research is on solidarity and repression with regard to migrants and refugees at the French-Italian border in the Alps.

Zachariah Mampilly is the Marxe Endowed chair of International Affairs at the City University of New York. He is the author of *Rebel Rulers: Insurgent Governance and Civilian Life during War* (Cornell University Press, 2011) and the coeditor of *Rebel Governance in Civil War* (Cambridge University Press, 2015).

Edward A. McCord is a professor emeritus of History and International Affairs at the George Washington University. His research focuses broadly on the history of Chinese military-civil relations. He is the author of *The Power of the Gun: The Emergence of Modern Chinese Warlordism* (University of

California Press, 1985) and *Military Force and Elite Power in the Formation of Modern China* (Routledge, 2014).

Clémence Pinaud is an assistant professor at the Department of International Studies of Indiana University, Bloomington. She works on the Sudan People's Liberation Army's military history, including its predatory behaviors and marital practices. Her book *War and Genocide in South Sudan* is forthcoming at Cornell University Press.